Collins

easy
Portuguese

HarperCollins Publishers
Westerhill Rd, Bishopbriggs, Glasgow, G64 2QT

www.harpercollins.co.uk

First published 2003
This edition published 2006

Reprint 10 9 8 7 6 5 4 3 2 1 0

ISBN 0 00 720835 9

A catalogue reference for this book is available from
The British Library

Consultants: Edite Vieira and Sue Tyson-Ward

Photography: Blackeye Photography
With additional photography Edite Vieira: pp 78 (3), 80 (2),
81 (1), 97 (1), 99 (2), 100 (1), 101 (2), 104 (1), 106 (1), 108 (1),
109 (2), 110 (1), 112 (1)
and Artville: pp 95 (2), 96 (1), 97 (1), 98 (1), 101 (1), 102 (1),
103 (1), 106 (2), 107 (2), 108 (1), 111 (1), 112 (1), 114 (2)
Additional material from Sue Tyson-Ward
Food Map: Heather Moore
Layout & Origination: The Printer's Devil and
Davidson Pre-Press Graphics Ltd, Glasgow

Other titles in the Collins Easy Photo Phrase Book series:
French (0 00 720840 5)
German (0 00 720839 1)
Greek (0 00 720837 5)
Italian (0 00 720836 7)
Spanish (0 00 720833 2)
These titles are also published in a CD pack containing
a 60-minute CD and Easy Photo Phrase Book.

Printed in China by Imago

Contents

Useful Websites

Currency converters
www.x-rates.com

UK Passport Office
www.passport.gov.uk

Foreign Office travel advice
www.fco.gov.uk

Health advice
www.traveldoctor.co.uk
www.dh.gov.uk/PolicyAndGuidance/
  HealthAdviceForTravellers/fs/en

Pet advice
www.defra.gov.uk/animalh/
  quarantine/index.htm

Facts and figures
www.cia.gov/cia/publications/
  factbook/

Weather
www.bbc.co.uk/weather

Internet cafes
www.cybercafes.com

Hostels
www.hostels.com
europeanhostels.com

Accommodation
www.turihab.pt
  (rural properties to rent)
www.pousadas.com
  (luxury properties to rent,
  often former convents, etc)
www.roteiro-campista.pt
  (guide to campsites of Portugal)

Rail fares and tickets
www.raileurope.co.uk

Transport
www.cp.pt (Portuguese railways)
www.metrolisboa.pt (Lisbon metro)
www.eva-bus.net (Portuguese bus
  company)

Driving abroad
www.drivingabroad.co.uk/driving_
  tips_countries/portugal/driving_in_
  portugal.htm

Food & Wine
www.gastronomias.com
  (in Portuguese only)
www.restaurantes.netopia.pt
  (restaurant guide in Portuguese)
www.ivv.pt (guide to Portuguese
  wine and wine-growing areas)

Facts
www.cia.gov/cia/publications/
  factbook/geos/po.html

Portuguese tourist board
www.portugalinsite.com

Tourism
www.portugal.org
www.portugal-live.net

In the age of the euro, the internet and cash machines that offer a choice of languages, foreign travel might seem less of an adventure than it once was. But English is not the universal language yet, and there is much more to communication than knowing the right words for things. Once out of the airport you will not get far without some idea of the language, and also the way things are done in an unfamiliar culture. Things you might assume are the same everywhere, such as road signs and colour-coding, can turn out not to be. Red for trunk roads and skimmed milk, blue for motorways and full cream? Not everywhere!

You may know the word for 'coffee' but what sort of coffee will you get? Will they understand what you mean when you say you're a vegetarian? What times do the shops open, and which ticket gives you the best deal? *Collins Easy Photo Phrase Books* keep you up to speed with handy tips for each topic, and a wealth of pictures of signs and everyday objects to help you understand what you see around you. Even if your knowledge of the language is excellent, you may still find yourself on the back foot when trying to understand what's on offer in a restaurant, so the food and drink section features a comprehensive menu reader to make sure eating out is a pleasure.

The unique combination of practical information, photos and phrases found in this book provides the key to hassle-free travel. The colour-coding below shows how information is presented and how to access it as quickly as possible.

 General, practical information which will provide useful tips on getting the best out of your trip.

keywords

direita	
dee-**ray**-tuh	
right	
esquerda	
ash-**kehr**-duh	
left	

< keywords

these are words that are useful to know both when you see them written down or when you hear them spoken

key talk >

short, simple phrases that you can change and adapt to suit your own situation

excuse me!	**I'm looking for...**
faz favor!	procuro...
fash fa-**vor**	proh-**koo**-roo...
do you know where...?	
sabe onde è...?	
sab **oñ**-duh e...	

The **food and drink section** allows you to choose more easily from what is on offer, both for snacks and at restaurants.

The practical **Dictionary** means that you will never be stuck for words.

Speaking Portuguese

Portuguese is much easier to read than to speak. However, the pronunciation guide used in this book is as near as possible to the real sound. The syllable to be stressed is marked in **heavy italics**. Note that in conversation, words tend to slide into each other with unstressed syllables being slurred and some sounds being almost swallowed up.

VOWELS (a, e, i, o, u)

open (long) sound
a e.g. **saco** sah-koo
e e.g. **ver** vehr
o e.g. **cobra** koh-bruh

closed (short) sound
e.g. **fama** fam-uh
e.g. **de** duh
e.g. **voltar** vol-tar

NOTE: The article **a** sounds like uh (as in English **the**), unless stressed, e.g. **à**
e can sound like ay, e.g. **fecho fay**-shoo, but tends to be silent at the end of words, e.g. **pode** (pod) unless stressed, e.g. **bebé** (bay-**bay**).
The word **e** (meaning **and**) always sounds like ee (as in **police**)
o can sound like oo, e.g. **vaso vah**-zoo, and the article **o** always sounds like oo
i sounds like ee, e.g. **fica fee**-kuh
u usually sounds like oo, e.g. **luvas loo**-vush

VOWEL COMBINATIONS

ai = y, e.g. **mais** = mysh
ei = ay, e.g. **peixe** = paysh

oi = oy, e.g. **coisa** = **koy**-zuh
ou = oh, e.g. **outro** = **oh**-troo

NASAL VOWELS

Vowels with a tilde ~, or followed by m (**um**) or n (**in**) should be pronounced nasally (let air out through nose as well as mouth), similar to French. We have represented this sound in the pronunciation by ñ, e.g.

tem = tayñ   com = koñ   um = ooñ
pão = powñ   manhã = man-**yañ**   põe = poyñ

OTHER LETTERS

Try to recognize the sounds of the following:

- ç **serviço** ser-**vee**-soo
- nh **tenho ten**-yoo
- ch **chá** sha
- r/rr at the start or middle of word rolled
- g **gelo zhay**-loo (soft like **s** in pleasure)
- s (between vowels) **coisa koy**-zuh
  after vowel and at end of word) **está** shta, **lápis lah**-peesh
- h always silent
- j **loja loh**-zhuh (soft like **s** in pleasure)
- x **caixa ky**-shuh
- lh **mulher** mool-**yehr**
- z (at end of word) **faz** fash

Everyday Talk

> There are three forms of address in Portuguese, formal (**Senhor/a**), semi-formal (**você**) and informal (**tu**). You should always stick to the formal with older people until you are invited to use the informal **tu**.

yes	**no**	**ok/that's fine**
sim	não	está bem
seeñ	*nowñ*	*shta bayñ*

please	**thank you** (said by man)	**thank you** (said by woman)
por favor/faz favor	obrigado	obrigada
poor fa-vor/fash fa-vor	*oh-bree-gah-doo*	*oh-bree-gah-duh*

thanks very much		**don't mention it**
muito obrigado(a)		de nada
mweeñ-too oh-bree-gah-doo(-duh)		*de nah-duh*

hello/hi	**goodbye**	**good morning/day**
olá	adeus	bom dia
oh-la	*a-day-oosh*	*boñ dee-uh*

good afternoon/evening	**good night**	**see you later**
boa tarde	boa noite	até logo
boh-uh tard	*boh-uh noyt*	*a-te log-oo*

excuse me!	**sorry!**	**I am sorry**
por favor/faz favor!	desculpe!	lamento
poor fa-vor/fash fa-vor	*dush-koolp*	*la-meñ-too*

I don't understand	**I don't know**	**it doesn't matter**
não compreendo	nao sei	nao faz mal
nowñ kom-pree-en-doo	*nowñ say*	*nowñ fash mahl*

Addressing people

If you have been introduced to someone, you would greet them with **bom dia, Senhor Lopes** or **bom dia, minha Senhora**. In a shop a simple **olá** and **adeus** is fine. You may hear the expression **não faça cerimónia** (*nowñ fah-suh suh-ree-mon-yuh*). It means 'please don't stand on ceremony' i.e. if you are offered a second helping of food, don't refuse it out of politeness!

how are you?	**fine thanks**	**and you?**
como está?	bem, obrigado(a)	e você?
koh-moo shta	*bayñ oh-bree-gah-doo(-duh)*	*ee voh-suh*

hi, Paula!	**bye, Carlos!**	**see you tomorrow**
olá, Paula!	adeus, Carlos!	até amanhã
oh-la paoo-luh	*a-day-oosh car-loosh*	*a-te a-man-yañ*

*Asking for something in a shop or bar, you would ask for what you want, adding **por favor**.*

keywords keywords keywords

1	**um**
	ooñ
2	**dois**
	doysh
3	**três**
	tresh
4	**quatro**
	kwa-troo
5	**cinco**
	seeñ-koo
6	**seis**
	saysh
7	**sete**
	set
8	**oito**
	oy-too
9	**nove**
	nov
10	**dez**
	desh

a ... please
um/uma ... por favor
*ooñ/**oo**-muh ... poor fa-**vor***

a milky coffee
um galão
*ooñ ga-**lowñ***

a beer
uma cerveja
***oo**-muh suhr-**vay**-zhuh*

a tea and 2 beers, please
um chá e duas cervejas, por favor
*ooñ sha ee **doo**-ush suhr-**vay**-zhush poor fa-**vor***

the ... please
o/a ... por favor
*oo/uh ... poor fa-**vor***

the menu, please
a ementa, por favor
*uh ee-**men**-tuh poor fa-**vor***

the bill, please
a conta, por favor
*uh **koñ**-tuh poor fa-**vor***

my...
o meu/a minha...
*oo **may**-oo/uh **meen**-yuh...*

my passport
o meu passaporte
*oo **may**-oo pas-sa-**por**-tuh*

my room
o meu quarto
*oo **may**-oo **kwar**-too*

my case
a minha mala
*uh **meen**-yuh **mah**-luh*

my key
a minha chave
*uh **meen**-yuh **sha**-vuh*

another...
outro/outra...
***oh**-troo/**oh**-truh...*

is that everything?
é tudo?
*e **too**-doo*

To catch someone's attention

The easiest way to catch someone's attention is with *faz favor* or *desculpe*. Many Portuguese do speak English. If you are trying to get past someone, perhaps in a busy market or street, you can say *com licença* (*koñ lee-**sen**-suh*). You would also use this phrase when entering someone's home.

excuse me!
desculpe!
*deesh-**koolp***

can you help me?
pode-me ajudar?
pod**-muh a-zhoo-**dar

do you know where ... is?
sabe onde é...?
*sab **oñ**-duh e...*

how do I get to...?
como se vai a...?
***koh**-moo suh vy uh...*

By combining key words and phrases you can build up your language and adapt the phrases to suit your own situation.

tem...? **do you have...?**	**do you have a map?** tem um mapa? *tayñ ooñ **ma**-puh*	**do you have a room?** tem um quarto? *tayñ ooñ **kwar**-too*
quanto é? **how much is it?**	**how much is the cheese?** quanto é o queijo? ***kwañ**-too e oo **kay**-zhoo*	**how much is the ticket?** quanto é o bilhete? ***kwañ**-too e oo beel-**yet***
queria... **I'd like...**	**I'd like a cake** queria um bolo ***kree**-uh ooñ **bol**-oo*	**I'd like an ice-cream** queria um gelado ***kree**-uh ooñ zhuh-**lah**-doo*
preciso de... **I need...**	**I need a taxi** preciso dum táxi *pruh-**see**-zoo dooñ **tak**-see*	**I need a receipt** preciso dum recibo *pruh-**see**-zoo dooñ ruh-**see**-boo*
quando? **when?**	**when does it open?** quando abre? ***kwañ**-doo **a**-bruh*	**when does it close?** a que horas fecha? *uh kee **o**-rush **fay**-shuh*
a que horas? **when?**	**when does it leave?** quando parte? ***kwañ**-doo part*	**when does it arrive?** a que horas chega? *uh kee **o**-rush **sheh**-guh*
onde? **where?**	**where is the bank?** onde é o banco? ***oñ**-duh e oo **bañ**-koo*	**where is the hotel?** onde é o hotel? ***oñ**-duh e oo oh-**tel***
há...? **is there...?**	**is there a market?** há um mercado? *a ooñ mer-**kah**-doo*	**where is there a market?** onde á um mercado? ***oñ**-duh ooñ mer-**kah**-doo*
não há... **there is no...**	**there is no bread** não há pão *nowñ a powñ*	**is there no train?** não há comboio? *nowñ a koñ-**boy**-yoo*
posso...? **can I...?**	**can I smoke?** posso fumar? ***pos**-soo foo-**mar***	**can I hire a car?** posso alugar um carro? ***pos**-soo a-loo-**gar** ooñ **kar**-roo*
	where can I buy milk? onde posso comprar leite? ***oñ**-duh **pos**-soo koñ-**prar** layt*	
está...? **is it...?**	**is it open?** está aberto? *shta a-**ber**-too*	**is it closed?** está fechado? *shta fuh-**sha**-doo*
gosto de... **I like...**	**I like dancing** gosto de dançar ***gosh**-too duh dan-**sar***	**I don't like coffee** não gosto de café *nowñ **gosh**-too duh kuh-**fe***

These are a selection of small but very useful words to know.

grande
grañd
large

pequeno
puh-kay-noo
small

um pouco
ooñ poh-koo
a little

chega
sheh-guh
that's enough

mais perto
mysh pehr-too
nearest

quente/frio
kent/free-oo
hot/cold

caro demais
kah-roo duh-mysh
too expensive

e
ee
and

com/sem
koñ/sayñ
with/without

para
pa-ruh
for

o meu/a minha
oo may-oo/uh meen-yuh
my

este/esse
esht/esh
this one/that one

imediatamente
ee-med-yat-a ment
straightaway

mais tarde
mysh tard
later

a large car
um carro grande
ooñ kar-roo grañd

a small car
um carro pequeno
ooñ kar-roo puh-kay-noo

a little, please
um pouco, por favor
ooñ poh-koo poor fa-vor

that's enough
chega
sheh-guh

where is the nearest bank?
onde é o banco mais perto?
oñ-duh e oo bañ-koo mysh pehr-too

it is too expensive
é caro demais
e kah-roo duh-mysh

it is too big
é grande demais
e grañd duh-mysh

is it full?
está cheio?
shtuh shay-oo

is it free?
está livre?
shtuh leev-ruh

a hot chocolate and a cake
um chocolate quente e um bolo
ooñ shoo-koo-laht kayñt ee ooñ boh-loo

with cold milk
com leite frio
koñ layt free-oo

with lemon
com limão
koñ lee-mowñ

without ice
sem gelo
sayñ zhay-loo

without sugar
sem açúcar
sayñ a-zoo-kar

for me
para mim
pa-ruh meeñ

for her/him
para ele/ela
pa-ruh el/el-uh

my passport
o meu passaporte
oo may-oo pas-suh-port

my keys
as minhas chaves
ush meen-yush sha-vush

I'd like this one
queria este
kree-uh esht

I'd like that
queria esse
kree-uh esh

I need a taxi straightaway
preciso dum táxi imediatamente
pruh-see-zoo dooñ tak-see ee-med-yat-a ment

is it far?
é longe?
e lonzh

I'll call back later
chamo mais tarde
sha-moo mysh tard

Outside of the big cities Portuguese people are very relaxed and laid back, enjoying life and not getting stressed. Take the opportunity to chill out and meet people.

my name is...
chamo-me...
sha-moo-muh...

I am from...
sou de...
soh duh...

I am on holiday
estou de férias
shtoh duh fehr-yush

I am here on business
estou aqui a negócios
shtoh a-kee uh nuh-gos-yoosh

I am single
sou solteiro(a)
soh sol-tay-roo(-ruh)

I am married
sou casado(a)
soh ka-zah-doo(-duh)

I have a boyfriend
tenho namorado
teñ-yoo na-moo-rah-doo

I have a girlfriend
tenho namorada
teñ-yoo na-moo-rah-duh

I am a widow
sou viúva
soh vee-oo-vuh

I am a widower
sou viúvo
soh vee-oo-voo

I am divorced
sou divorciado(a)
soh dee-voors-yah-doo(-duh)

I am separated
sou separado(a)
soh suh-pa-rah-doo(-duh)

I have a son/a daughter
tenho um filho/uma filha
ten-yoo ooñ feel-yoo/oo-muh feel-yuh

I have three children
tenho três filhos
ten-yoo tresh feel-yoosh

I work
trabalho
tra-bal-yoo

I am retired
sou reformado(a)
soh ruh-foor-mah-doo(-duh)

I am a student
sou estudante
soh shtoo-dant

the meal was delicious
a refeição estava deliciosa
uh ruh-fay-sowñ shta-vuh duh-lees-yoh-zuh

you have a beautiful home
tem uma linda casa
tayñ oo-muh leeñ-duh kah-zuh

thanks for your hospitality
gratos pelo convite
grah-toosh peh-loo koñ-veet

I've enjoyed myself very much
diverti-me muito
dee-ver-tee-muh mweeñ-too

we'd like to come back
gostaríamos de voltar
goosh-tuh-ree-a-moosh duh vol-tar

we must stay in touch
devemos ficar em contacto
duh-veh-moosh fee-kar ayñ koñ-tak-too

what is your address?
qual é a sua morada?
kwal e uh soo-uh moo-rah-duh

i *Although problems are not something anyone wants, you might come across the odd difficulty, and it is best to be armed with a few phrases to cope with the situation.*

excuse me!
faz favor!
fash fa-vor

can you help me?
pode-me ajudar?
pod-muh a-zhoo-dar

I don't speak Portuguese
não falo português
nown fa-loo poor-too-gezh

do you speak English?
fala inglês?
fa-luh een-glezh

I am lost
estou perdido(a)
shtoh puhr-dee(-duh)

we are lost
estamos perdidos(as)
shta-moosh pur-dee-doosh(-dush)

I have lost...
perdi...
puhr-dee...

my purse
o meu porta-moedas
oo may-oo por-ta-mwed-ush

my passport
o meu passaporte
oo may-oo pa-sa-port

I have left...
deixei...
day-shay...

in the restaurant
no restaurante
noo rush-toh-rant

on the train
no comboio
noo koñ-boy-yoo

I have missed...
perdi...
puhr-dee...

the flight
o voo
voh-oo

my connection
a minha ligação
uh meen-yuh lee-guh-sown

I need to get to...
preciso de ir a...
pruh-see-zoo duh eer a...

how can I get there today?
como posso ir para lá hoje?
koh-moo pos-soo eer pa-ruh la ozh

my luggage hasn't arrived
a minha bagagem não chegou
uh meen-yuh ba-gah-zhayñ nown shuh-goh

the case is damaged
a mala está partida
uh mah-luh shta par-tee-duh

I have no money
não tenho dinheiro
nown ten-yoo deen-yay-roo

this is my address
esta é a minha morada
esht e uh meen-yuh moo-rah-duh

someone's stolen my...
roubaram-me...
roh-bah-rown-muh...

handbag
a mala
uh mah-luh

mobile phone
o telemóvel
oo tuh-luh-moh-vel

money
o dinheiro
oo deen-yay-roo

that man is following me
aquele homem está-me a seguir
a-kel o-mayñ shta-muh uh suh-geer

go away!
vá-se embora!
vah-suh ayñ-boh-ruh

leave me alone!
deixe-me em paz!
day-shuh-muh ayñ pash

I am sorry, I did not know
lamento muito, não sabia
la-men-too mweeñ-too nown sa-bee-uh

The Portuguese expect to receive good service and quality. They will complain when things are not to their liking.

there is no...
não há...
nowñ a...

there is no toilet paper
não há papel higiénico
*nowñ a pa-**pel** eezh-**yen**-ee-koo*

it is dirty
está sujo(a)
*shta **soo**-zhoo(-zhuh)*

the bath is dirty
a banheira está suja
*uh ban-**yay**-ruh shta **soo**-zhuh*

it is broken
está partido(a)
*shta par-**tee**-doo(-duh)*

can you mend it?
pode arranjá-lo?
*pod ar-ran-**zha**-loo*

the ... does not work
o/a ... não funciona
*oo/uh ... nowñ foons-**yoh**-nuh*

the ... do not work
os/as ... não funcionam
*oosh/ush ... nowñ foons-**yoh**-nawñ*

it is very noisy
há muito barulho
*a **mweeñ**-too ba-**rool**-oo*

the room is too small
o quarto é muito pequeno
*oo **kwar**-too e **mweeñ**-too puh-**kay**-noo*

it is very hot *(room)*
é muito quente
*e **mween**-too kent*

it is very cold *(room)*
é muito frio
*e **mween**-too **free**-oo*

it is very expensive
é muito caro(a)
*e **mween**-too **kah**-roo(-ruh)*

why are you charging me so much?
porque está a pedir tanto?
***poor**-kuh shta uh puh-**deer** tan-too*

I want to complain
quero apresentar uma queixa
***keh**-roo a-pruh-sen-**tar oo**-muh **kay**-shuh*

where is the manager?
onde está o gerente?
on**-duh shta oo zhuh-**rent

we want to order
queremos pedir
*kuh-**reh**-moosh puh-**deer***

the service is not good
o serviço não é bom
*oo suhr-**vee**-soo nowñ e boñ*

it is cold *(food, drink)*
está frio(a)
*shta **free**-oo(-uh)*

this coffee is cold
o café está frio
*oo kuh-**fe** shta **free**-oo*

this isn't what I ordered
isto não é o que eu pedi
eesh**-too nowñ e oo **kay**-oo puh-**dee

please take this off the bill
por favor, tire isto da conta
*poor fa-**vor** tee-**reesh**-too duh **koñ**-tuh*

there is a mistake
há um engano
*a ooñ ayñ-**ga**-noo*

please check the bill
por favor, verifique a conta
*poor fa-**vor** vuh-**ree**-fee-kee uh **koñ**-tuh*

I want a refund
quero um reembolso
***keh**-roo ooñ ree-ayñ-**bol**-soo*

I want to return this
quero devolver isto
***keh**-roo duh-vol-**vehr eesh**-too*

Everyday Portugal

The following four pages should give you an idea of the type of things you will come across in Portugal.

Aberto

open

Encerrada

closed

Fechado

Horário de Abertura	—— opening hours
das 8,30h às 15,00h	—— from 08.30 to 15.00
de Segunda a Sexta Feira	—— Monday to Friday

Smaller shops open from 8.30/9am to 12.30/1pm, and again from 2/2.30 to 6 or 7pm, Monday–Friday. Most close at 1pm on Saturday and all day Sunday. Large shopping centres stay open late every day.

EMPURRE

push

PUXE

pull

Casa da sorte, or *House of Luck*, sells lottery tickets.

Informações

information

VOLTA JA

back soon

PREPAGAMENTO

Many cafés and bars insist on payment in advance (indicated by this sign).

Lottery tickets are also sold at shops displaying these signs.

Moedas coins

Notas notes

The euro symbol.

Ticket and paying machines are now more widespread.

Normal post boxes are red.

Blue post boxes are for *Correio azul*, priority mail.

cash desk/pay here

Entrada

entrance

Saída

exit

emergency exit

excuse me!
desculpe!
deesh-koolp

what does this mean?
que quer dizer isto?
kuh kayr dee-zehr eesh-too

how does this work?
como funciona?
koh-moo foonss-yoh-nuh

can you explain?
pode-me explicar?
pod-muh eks-plee-kar

talking

Service is usually included in a restaurant bill so tipping is discretionary.

AR CONDICIONADO

air-conditioned

Vende-se

for sale

NÃO FUMAR

no smoking

Smoking is widespread in Portugal, especially in eating and drinking establishments. It is forbidden to smoke on public transport, although not everyone adheres to the rules.

Vendido

sold

Proíbida a passagem

entry prohibited

You can usually also buy stamps and postcards at a **tabacaria**.

Perigo!

danger!

talking

can I smoke?
posso fumar?
pos-soo foo-mar

I don't smoke
não fumo
nowñ foo-moo

an ashtray, please
un cinzeiro, por favor
ooñ seeñ-zay-roo poor fa-vor

do you mind if I smoke?
importa-se que eu fume?
eeñ-por-tuh-suh kuh ay-oo foom

please don't smoke
por favor não fume
poor fa-vor nowñ foom

in a non-smoking area
em zona de não-fumador
ayñ zoh-na duh nowñ foo-ma-dor

Public toilets in Portugal are hard to find. The best option is to use those at public attractions (museums, etc) where there may be an attendant doling out rations of loo paper. You are expected to tip them out of courtesy. Clean toilets are found in larger stores (not commonplace outside Lisbon or Oporto) or in modern hotels. Most people use the toilets in small bars and cafés, where you may have to ask at the bar for a key. Cleanliness can vary greatly.

Serviços
toilets

quente
hot

Occupado
occupied

frio
cold

Livre
free

Sanitários
(*superloos*) are beginning to appear in some towns and cities.

HOMENS
gents

SENHORAS
ladies

Superloos carry easy-to-follow instructions in Portuguese, French and English.

excuse me! where is the toilet?
por favor! onde é a casa de banho?
*poor fa-**vor** oñ-duh e uh **kah**-zuh duh **ban**-yoo*

do you have a key for the toilet?
tem a chave para a casa de banho por favor?
*tayñ uh shav **pa**-ruh uh **kah**-zuh duh **ban**-yoo poor fa-**vor***

is there a disabled toilet?
há casa de banho para deficientes?
*a **kah**-zuh duh **ban**-yoo **pa**-ruh duh-feess-**yentsh***

where can I change the baby?
onde posso mudar o bébé?
*oñ-duh **pos**-soo moo-**dar** oo bay-**bay***

talking

Asking the Way

i Portuguese people are very polite and helpful and many speak English. Unlike some other Mediterranean countries, the Portuguese are quite happy to queue and wait their turn, which adds to the impression that they are very happy to stop and help you.

Most town centres have street maps.

To find where you are, look for this symbol.

PARA SE SITUAR NA PLANTA PROCURE ESTA MARCA

VOCÊ ESTÁ AQUI

Você está aqui
you are here

tourist information office

ask me Lisboa

Ask me Lisboa
is Lisbon's tourist information service.

excuse me!
desculpe!
dush-koolp

do you know where... is?
sabe onde é...?
sab oñ-duh e...

how do I get to...?
como se vai para...?
koh-moo suh vy pa-ruh...

is this the right way to...?
a/o ... é por aqui?
oo/uh ... e poor a-kee

do you have a map of the town?
tem um mapa da cidade?
tayñ ooñ mah-puh duh see-dad

can you show me on the map?
pode-me indicar no mapa?
pod-muh eeñ-dee-kar noo mah-puh

I'm looking for...
procuro...
proh-koo-roo...

where are...?
onde são...?
oñ-duh sowñ...

is it far?
é longe?
e lonzh

is this the right way to the station?
a estação é por aqui?
uh shta-sowñ e poor a-kee

a street directory
um guia da cidade
ooñ gee-uh duh see-dad

pictogram indicating town centre (*centro*)

town hall

fire station

youth hostel

Normal signs are white; hotels are usually blue; places of interest are brown; and sports venues orange.

Chiado museum

football stadium

shopping area (z. = zona)

Church & Convent of St Francis

largo square

travessa side street

rua road/street

< Esquerda

left

Direita >

right

keywords

à direita
a dee-ray-tuh
to/on the right

à esquerda
ash-kehr-duh
to/on the left

sempre em frente
saynpr ayñ freñt
straight ahead

siga
see-guh
keep going

vire
veer
turn

rua
roo-uh
road

largo/praça
lar-goo/prah-suh
square

semáforo
suh-maf-oo-roo
traffic lights

igreja
ee-gray-zhuh
church

primeira
pree-may-ruh
first

segunda
suh-gooñ-duh
second

longe
lonzh
far

perto de
pehr-too duh
near to

ao lado de
ow lah-doo duh
next to

em frente
ayñ freñt
opposite

até
a-te
until

Banks & Money

i Banks are easy to find in Portugal, and many bank staff speak good English. To exchange money you may have to go first to the **Câmbio** counter, then pick up your money at the **Caixa**. In some banks you take a ticket or disc with a number on it to await your turn at the **Caixa**; your number will then be called out. Modern banks have automatic doors allowing access to cash machines after hours. The Multibanco will ask for a 6-figure PIN, but the normal 4-figure PIN is accepted. Just press confirm or **continuar** button after entering the 4-figure PIN. It is cheaper to use the Multibanco to get cash than changing notes in banks.

Banks' names usually include the words **banco** or **caixa**. The main ones are Banco Espírito Santo, BNU and Caixa Geral de Depósitos.

Multibanco is the term for ATM.

opening times 8.30am to 3pm
Monday – Friday

Banks in tourist areas may open later than the normal 3pm closing.

Multibanco machines are common and offer a range of services. Screen instructions are often in English and Portuguese. To withdraw cash you can key in the exact amount or a combination of pre-set amounts using the keys on the left of the panel.

balance
check
transactions
payment
services
other
amounts

anular
cancel

corrigir
correct/
error

continuar
continue

Indoor *Multibancos* often carry a sign like this (*all hours*).

keywords keywords keywords

cartão de crédito
kar-townñ duh kre-dee-too
credit card

caixa automática
kye-shuh on-too-ma-tee-kuh
cash machine

número de PIN
noo-muh-roo duh peen
PIN number

câmbio
kañ-byoo
change

introduza
eeñ-troh-doo-suh
insert

notas
noh-tush
notes

dinheiro
deen-yay-roo
money/cash

moedas
mway-dush
coins

Portugal's currency is the euro, which breaks down into 100 euro cents.
Notes: 5, 10, 20, 50, 100, 200 and 500 euro.
Coins: 2 euro, 1 euro, 50 cent, 20 cent, 10 cent, 5 cent, 2 cent, 1 cent. Euro notes are the same across Europe. The coins are officially cents, but Portuguese people call them **cêntimos** (*sen-tee-moosh*). The reverse of the coins carry different designs in each European member country.

where is there...?
onde há...?
oñ-duh a...

a bank
um banco
ooñ bañ-koo

a bureau de change
uma casa de câmbio
oo-muh kah-zuh duh kañb-yoo

where can I change money?
onde posso trocar dinheiro?
oñ-duh pos-soo troo-kar deen-yay-roo

I want small notes
quero notas pequenas
keh-roo noh-tush puh-kay-nush

where is the nearest cash machine?
onde é a caixa automática mais perto?
oñ-duh e uh ky-shuh ow-too-ma-tee-kuh mysh pehr-too

I want to change these travellers' cheques
quero trocar estes cheques de viagem
keh-roo troo-kar esh-tush sheksh duh vee-ah-jayñ

the cash machine has swallowed my card
a caixa automática engoliu o meu cartão
uh ky-shuh ow-too-ma-tee-kuh ayñ-goo-lee-uh oo may-oo kar-townñ

talking talking talking

When is...?

 Portugal operates on the same time as the UK.

keywords keywords keywords

manhã
man-yañ
morning

tarde
tard-uh
afternoon

esta tarde
esh-tuh tard-uh
this afternoon

esta noite
esh-tuh noyt-uh
this evening

hoje
ohzh
today

amanhã
a-man-yañ
tomorrow

ontem
oñ-tayñ
yesterday

agora
a-goh-ruh
now

mais tarde
mysh tard-uh
later

13:00
14:00
15:00
16:00
17:00
18:00
19:00
20:00
21:00
22:00
23:00
24:00

at...

às treze horas
ash trez o-rush

às catorze horas
ash ka-torz o-rush

às quinze horas
ash keenz o-rush

às dezasseis horas
ash dez-uh-saysh o-rush

às dezassete horas
ash dez-uh-set o-rush

às dezoito horas
ash dez-oy-too o-rush

às dezanove horas
ash dez-uh-nov o-rush

às vinte horas
ash veent o-rush

às vinte e uma horas
ash veent ee oo-muh o-rush

às vinte e duas horas
ash veent ee doo-ush o-rush

às vinte e três horas
ash veent ee tresh o-rush

às vinte e cuatro horas
ash veent ee kwa-troo o-rush

talking

when is the next...?
quando parte o próximo...?
kwañ-doo part oo pross-ee-moo...

bus
autocarro
ow-too-kar-roo

boat
barco
bar-koo

train
comboio
koñ-boy-yoo

when is...?
a que horas é...?
uh kee o-rush e...

breakfast
o pequeno-almoço
oo puh-kay-noo al-moh-soo

dinner
o jantar
oo zhan-tar

when does it open?
quando abre?
kwañ-doo ah-bruh

when does it close?
quando fecha?
kwañ-doo fay-shuh

when does it leave?
quando parte?
kwañ-doo part

when does it arrive?
quando chega?
kwañ-doo sheh-guh

Days of the week are often abbreviated by dropping the **feira** and sometimes as short as **sex** for Friday.

at...
às...
ash...

às doze
ash dohz

às onze
ash oñz

à uma
a **oo**-muh

às dez
ash desh

às duas
ash **doo**-ush

às nove
ash nov

às três
ash tresh

às oito
ash **oy**-too

às quatro
ash **kwa**-troo

às sete
ash set

às seis
ash saysh

às cinco
ash **seeñ**-koo

às dezanove e trinta
ash dezh-uh-**nov** ee **treeñ**-tuh
at 19.30

às vinte para as ...
ash veent **pa**-ruh ush ...
at twenty past ...

às ... menos um quarto
ash ... **may**-noosh ooñ **kwar**-too
at a quarter to ...

à meia-noite
a may-uh-**noyt**
at midnight

às ... e um quarto
ash ... ee ooñ **kwar**-too
at quarter past ...

às ... menos vinte
ash ... **may**-noosh veent
at twenty to ...

às ... e meia
ash ... ee **may**-uh
at half past ...

what time is it, please?
que horas são, por favor?
kee **o**-rush sowñ poor fa-**vor**

it's...
são...
sowñ...

it's 9 o'clock
são nove horas
sowñ nov **o**-rush

what is the date?
qual é a data?
kwal e uh **dah**-tuh

it is the 8th of May
é o (dia) oito de Maio
e oo (**dee**-uh) **oy**-too duh **my**-oo

it is the 16 of July 2006
é o dezasseis de Julho de dois mil e seis
e oo dez-uh-**saysh** du **zhool**-yoo duh doysh meel ee saysh

which day?
que dia?
kuh **dee**-uh

which month?
que mês?
kuh mesh

talking

Timetables

Categoria
type of train (including
boat transfer for Lisbon)

Número
number

Classe
class

Categoria		R	R	R	R	⛴	IR	R	R	⛴	IC
Número		4701	5903	5709	5804	17829	871	5715	5902	17857	561
Classe		2	2	1-2	2	2	1-2	1-2	2	2	1-2
Serviços Disponibilizados						⚲	⚲			⚲	🍴
Observações											
LISBOA (T. DO PAÇO)	Lisboa (T. do Paço)	P				8.10				13.20	
	Barreiro ⛴	C				8.40				13.50	
BARREIRO	Barreiro	P					8.55				14.25
	Barreiro-A										
	Lavradio										
	Baixa da Banheira										
	Alhos Vedros										
	Moita										
	Penteado										
PINHAL NOVO	Pinhal Novo	C					9.06				
	Pinhal Novo	P					9.08				
	Venda do Alcaide										
	Palmela										
SETÚBAL	Setúbal	C					9.23				
	Setúbal	P					9.25				

**Serviços
disponibilizados**
services available

Observações
information

Train timetables like this can be obtained
from regional or national railway stations.

Alfa Pendular tilting train

Key to timetable symbols

Comboio train

	SIMBOLOGIA:
intercity trains	**IC** Comboio Intercidades
inter-regional trains	**IR** Comboio Interregional
regional trains	**R** Comboio Regional
river ferry connection	⛴ Ligação Fluvial
seat reservation obligatory	🎫 Reserva obrigatória de lugar
bar service	⚲ Serviço de Bar
meal service in 1st class	🍴 Serviço de refeição no lugar em 1ª Classe
restaurant and bar service	✕ Serviço de Restaurante e Bar
not a daily service	{ Comboio não diário

talk

do you have a timetable?	**can you explain the timetable, please?**
tem um horário?	pode-me explicar o horário, por favour?
tayñ ooñ oo-**rar**-yoo	**pod**-muh eks-plee-**kar** oo o-**rar**-yoo poor fa-**vor**

SERVIÇO / PISTA SERVICE / TRACK	PROCEDÊNCIA ORIGIN	DESTINO DESTINATION	CHEGADA ARRIVAL	PARTIDA DEPARTURE	ATRASO DELAY
N02				13:00	
N02		ALBUFEIRA		13:00	
N06		OLHÃO		13:10	
N02		LOULE		13:20	
EX	ÉVORA		13:20		
EX	ELVAS		13:20		
N07		V. R. S. ANTÓ		13:25	
N04		S. B. ALPORT		13:35	
N08		QUARTEIRA		13:35	
N08		ALBUFEIRA		13:35	

Timetables, especially in tourist areas, will often have English translations alongside the Portuguese.

Yellow line bus timetable

Paragem
stop number

Designação
name of stop

Nota: As linhas funcionam de 2ª a 6ª feira de hora a hora, entre as 08H (inclusive) e as 20H (exclusive), aos minutos indicados
Note: the routes operate from Mon to Fri hourly, between 8am (inclusive) and 8pm (exclusive) at the minutes indicated.

partida
par-tee-duh
departure

chegada
sheh-gah-duh
arrival

diário
dee-ar-yoo
daily

dias úteis
dee-ush oo-taysh
weekdays

sábados
sa-ba-doosh
Saturdays

domingos
doo-meeñ-goosh
Sundays

feriados
fuhr-ya-doosh
holidays

só nos...
so noosh...
only on...

Janeiro
(zhuh-nay-roo) Jan

Fevereiro
(fuh-vray-roo) Feb

Março
(mahr-soo) March

Abril
(a-breel) April

Maio
(my-oo) May

Junho
(zhoon-yoo) June

Julho
(zhool-yoo) July

Agosto
(a-gosh-too) Aug

Setembro
(suh-tem-broo) Sep

Outubro
(oh-too-broo) Oct

Novembro
(nov-ayñ-broo) Nov

Dezembro
(duh-zayñ-broo) Dec

2ª-feira
suh-goon-duh-fay-ruh
Monday

3ª-feira
ter-suh-fay-ruh
Tuesday

4ª-feira
kwar-tuh-fay-ruh
Wednesday

5ª-feira
keen-tuh-fay-ruh
Thursday

6ª-feira
saysh-tuh-fay-ruh
Friday

sábado
sa-ba-doo
Saturday

domingo
doo-meen-goo
Sunday

Tickets

*Tickets for transport are **bilhetes**. Tickets for cinema, theatre, museums and other forms of entertainment are also known as **entradas** (admission charges).*

valid only on the day stamped for an unlimited number of journeys

1-day Lisbon travel card for unlimited travel on buses, trams and funiculars. As with all public transport tickets, you must validate it on the first journey you make. Insert the ticket into the validating machine so the blue square at the top right corner is punched.

clipped off

You have to validate any ticket you buy for public transport in a validating machine. These are found at the entrance of buses, train platforms and metro stations. Simply insert your ticket in the slot for punching.

Local train ticket from Lisbon to Cascais.

full return

A 1-trip ticket for one of Lisbon's funicular or lift journeys up the city's steep-sided hills. The top right corner is clipped off by the validating machine.

valid on | *credit card* | *purchase date and time*

| | Cartao de Debito 11 | 158/169878 846 20/07/06 10:44 |

Nº CONTRIBUINTE 500498604

ALBUFEIRA <-> ORIENTE
Ida: 23/07

ALBUFEIRA->ORIENTE
CARR:2   LUG:13   ALFAConf. **180(07:06)**
Volta: 23/07
ORIENTE->ALBUFEIRA
CARR:1   LUG:76   ALFAConf. **183(17:21h)**

● *183 23/7*

| | Pl | **17,30 EUR** Inclui IVA 5% |

outward journey

coach: 1 *seat no: 76* *Alfa train* *(cost) inc 5% VAT*

validate your ticket at the entrance and exit to the metro

10:S00.   0179438
2006/07/23
10:01

Utilizar até:
2006/10/21
simples
1 zone
70 centimos
Metropolitano de Lisboa EP
Cont nº 500 102 855
Preço incluido PA à taxa legal

99
100
101
102

metro M

A single (*simples*) ticket for the Lisbon Underground. There is a range of Metro tickets on offer, including return (*ida e volta*), 10 journey (*10 viagens*), one day (*diário*) and 7-day (*7 dias*).

Bilhete de 1 dia
1 day TravelCard
Lisboa
Train&Bus
Stagecoach PORTUGAL

Saver tickets for unlimited local train and bus travel are available.

advance booking

COMBOIOS DE AMANHÃ E DIAS SEGUINTES   *trains for tomorrow and following days*

um bilhete
ooñ beel-yet
a ticket

uma caderneta de 10 viagens
oo-muh kad-er-nay-tuh duh desh vee-ah-zhayñ
a book of 10 tickets

um passe
ooñ pas
a travel card

simples/de ida
seeñ-pluhsh/ duh ee-duh
single

de ida e volta
duh ee-duh ee vol-tuh
return

hoje/amanhã
ohzh/a-man-yañ
today/tomorrow

adulto
ah-dool-too
adult

criança
kree-añ-suh
child(ren)

estudante
shtoo-dañt
student

de terceira idade
duh ter-say-ruh ee-dad
over-60

deficiente
duh-feess-yent
disabled

i *The bus service is comprehensive throughout Portugal. **EVA** operates services to all parts of Portugal. You can buy single tickets from the driver as you enter, or buy books of multi-tickets (**módulos**) which work out slightly cheaper. As you enter the bus, validate the ticket in the yellow machine behind the driver. On some buses you enter at the front and get off at the middle or back. The tourist card, **Lisboa card**, includes access to public transport.*

bus station
As well as **terminal rodoviário**, you may also see **terminal de camionagem**.

Destination and route numbers are on the front.

stop
platform

start of queue at point marked on pavement

destinations and route numbers

Ticket sales and Information desk for bus carrier Carris.

ticket office/information

A modern ticket office (*bilheteira*)

There are route maps at most bus stops.

The ticket validating machine is behind the driver's seat. You must validate your ticket when you get on board.

Old (above) and new trams (right) in Lisbon.

push the button on the new tram to open the doors

for wheelchair access

---

where do I catch a bus to...?
onde apanho um autocarro para...?
*oñ-**duh** a-**pan**-yoo ooñ ow-too-**kar**-roo **pa**-ruh...*

which bus goes to...?
que autocarro vai para...?
*kuh ow-too-**kar**-roo vy **pa**-ruh...*

is there a bus to...?
há autocarro para...?
*a ow-too-**kar**-roo **pa**-ruh...*

which bus goes to the centre?
que autocarro vai ao centro?
*kuh ow-too-**kar**-roo vy ow **señ**-troo*

is this bus going to...?
este autocarro vai a...?
*esht ow-too-**kar**-roo vy uh...*

can you tell me when to get off?
pode-me dizer quando devo sair?
*pod-**muh** dee-**zehr** kwan-doo **deh**-voo suh-**eer***

excuse me!
com licença!
*koñ lee-**sen**-suh*

this is my stop
esta é a minha paragem
***esh**-tuh e uh **meen**-yuh pa-**rah**-zhayñ*

talking talking

Lisbon has a metro system which was expanded for the Expo 98 exhibition, with modern, tiled stations and new trains. The network is compact, with four different branch lines. You can buy a range of tickets ranging from singles to multi-journey passes. Oporto is gradually constructing and expanding its own system.

Three styles of sign for Lisbon's **Metropolitano** underground system.

Metro maps, with details of stops for transport connections, shopping and parking, are available from Metro stations and Tourist Information Offices.

Colégio Militar

Alameda

Marquês de Pombal

Oriente

blue line   yellow line   green line   red line

Stops on each of the four Metro lines are colour-coded.

key — **Legenda**

you are here — Está aqui

train connections

Interface com caminho de ferro

Interface com autocarros suburbanos — suburban bus connections

Interface com barcos — boat connections

Metro map key

Ticket machines are simple to operate.

Automatic ticket machines are common. Choose your ticket using a touch screen (above) in English, Portuguese, Spanish or French. You can pay by coins (**moedas**), notes (**notas**) or card (shown by the **MB** sign, for **Multibanco**).

ticket barrier

---

a single ticket
um bilhete simples
ooñ beel-yet seeñ-plush

a book of 10 journeys
uma caderneta de dez viagens
oo-muh kad-er-nay-tuh duh desh vee-ah-zhayñ

where is the nearest metro station?
onde é a estação de metro mais próxima?
oñ-duh e uh shta-sowñ duh met-roo mysh pross-ee-muh

have you a map of the metro?
tem um guia do metro?
tayñ ooñ gee-uh doo met-roo

I'm going to...
vou a...
voh uh...

I want to go to...
quero ir para...
kehr-oo eer pa-ruh...

do I have to change?
tenho que mudar?
ten-yoo kuh moo-dar

where?
onde?
oñ-duh

which line is it for...?
qual é a linha para...?
kwal e uh leen-yuh pa-ruh...

in which direction?
em que direcção?
ayñ kuh dee-reh-sowñ

which station is it for...?
qual é a estação de metro para...?
kwal e uh shta-sowñ duh met-roo pa-ruh...

excuse me!
com licença!
koñ lee-señ-suh

I'm getting off here
desço aqui
desh-soo a-kee

talking talking talking

(i) The national rail network is called CP (**Caminhos de Ferro Portugueses**). Tickets can be bought at all stations, and reservations for the **Alfa** and **Rápido** trains may be booked at travel agents. You can also buy train tickets from ATM machines (**multibanco**). High-speed trains link the Algarve with Lisbon, and from there to Oporto and the north. There is also a high-class 'sleeper' from Lisbon to Madrid. Although the total network does not cover all areas, train travel is one of the best ways to see Portugal. Railway timetables are good and there is a 50% discount for young children and pensioners, plus a range of travel cards and passes. It is difficult to transport bicycles on Portuguese trains.

ticket offices

BILHETEIRAS

Logo of Portugal's state railway.

Máquina Automática

automatic machine

where is the station?	**to the station, please**
onde é a estação?	para a estação, por favor
oñ-duh e uh shta-sowñ	*pa-ruh uh shta-sowñ poor fa-vor*
a ticket to...	**a single ticket**
um bilhete para...	um bilhete simples
ooñ beel-yet pa-ruh...	*ooñ beel-yet seeñ-plush*
a return ticket	**2 returns to...**
um bilhete de ida e volta	dois de ida e volta para...
ooñ beel-yet duh ee-duh ee vol-tuh	*doysh duh ee-duh ee vol-tuh pa-ruh...*
a child's ticket to...	
meio bilhete para...	
may-oo beel-yet pa-ruh...	

lst/2nd class	**smoking**	**non smoking**
primeira/segunda classe	fumador	não-fumador
pree-may-ruh/suh-gooñ-duh klas	*foo-ma-dor*	*nowñ foo-ma-dor*
is there a supplement to pay?	**do I need to book?**	
paga-se suplemento?	tenho que reservar?	
pah-ga-suh soo-pluh-meñ-too	*ten-yoo kuh ruh-ser-var*	
I want to book...	**a seat**	**two seats**
queria reservar...	um lugar	dois lugares
kree-uh ruh-ser-var...	*ooñ loo-gar*	*doysh loo-gah-rush*

talking talking talking talking

Destino destination
Hora time
Comboio train type
Linha platform
Partidas departures
Observações information

Hora	Destino	Linha	Comboio	Observações
18:37	LISBOA-S.A.	4	INTERCID	
18:37	AZAMBUJA	5	SUBURB	
18:39	QUELUZ MASSA	7	SUBURB	
18:42	V.FRANC.XIRA	5	SUBURB	
18:42	LISBOA-S.A.	8	SUBURB	
18:54	ALCANT.TERRA	8	SUBURB	
18:57	ALVERCA	5	SUBURB	
19:00	LISBOA-S.A.	4	REGIONAL	

BEM VINDO À ESTAÇÃO DO ORIENTE

welcome (**bem vindo**) to the Eastern Station

Modern ticket validating machine in railway station. As on other forms of public transport, train tickets must be validated before you travel.

Linha and *Gare* both mean 'platform'

simples
seeñ-plush
single

de ida e volta
duh ee-duh ee vol-tuh
return

reserva
ruh-ser-vuh
reservation

suplemento
soop-luh-meñ-too
supplement

ligação
lee-guh-sowñ
connection

lugar
loo-gar
seat

à janela
a zhuh-nel-uh
by the window

voltado
vool-tah-doo
facing

de costas
duh kosh-tush
backwards

fumador
foo-ma-dor
smoking

não-fumador
nowñ-foo-ma-dor
non-smoking

keywords keywords keywords keywords keywords

the train to...
o combio para...
oo koñ-boy-yoo pa-ruh...

is this the train for...?
é este o comboio para...?
e esht oo koñ-boy-yoo pa-ruh...

which platform does it leave from?
de que linha parte?
duh kuh leen-yuh part

this is my seat
este é o meu lugar
esht e oo may-oo loo-gar

talking

Taxi

i Taxis – generally Mercedes – are widely available. You can hire one from a taxi stand or **praça**, hail them in the street or ring for them. They are cheap, but charges rise after 10pm, at weekends and on holidays. Luggage is charged at a flat rate. Meters don't operate outside city limits, so check the fare before you travel.

You cannot hail taxis in the Algarve, you must either go to a taxi rank or order one by phone to a specific point. Most hotels will do this but there is normally a small charge for the call.

If the green lights are on, the taxi is occupied. One light means it's operating at the cheaper rate, 2 lights at the higher rate.

taxi-stand sign
(*2 filas* = 2 queues)

Older taxis are black and green; more modern taxis are beige.

talking talking talking

where can I get a taxi?
onde se pode arranjar um táxi?
oñ-duh suh pod ar-ran-zhar ooñ tak-see

to the airport, please
ao aeroporto, por favor
ow uh-er-roo-por-too poor favor

to this address, please
a esta morada, por favor
uh esh-tuh moo-rah-duh poor favor

please order me a taxi
chame-me um táxi, por favor
shah-muh-muh ooñ tak-see poor fa-vor

for now
para agora
pa-ruh a-goh-ruh

for ... o'clock
para as...
pa-ruh ash...

can I have a receipt
pode-me dar um recibo
pod-muh dar ooñ ruh-see-boo

keep the change
guarde o troco
gward oo troh-koo

how much will it cost?
quanto vai a custar?
kwan-too vy a koosh-tar

how much is it to the centre?
quanto custa ao centro?
kwan-too koosh-tuh ow señ-troo

Car Hire

*Car-hire firms are abundant in the Algarve, and there are desks in the airport and main holiday complexes and hotels. Lisbon and Oporto airports also have car-hire desks. In other areas check in yellow pages (**páginas amarelas**). To hire a car you must be 23 or over and have held a driving licence for a year. Check the policy carefully, what to do in case of problems, and whether you can take the car over the border or on ferries.*

Automóveis Rent a Car

airauto RENT-A-CAR

TARIFA / SPECIAL RATES
Rua dos Bombeiros, Ed. Horizonte, Loja Sul
Tel.: 289 30 02 00 · Fax: 289 30 02 02 · 8125 Quarteira

G R P	MARCA/MODELO	KMS. ILIMITADOS INLIMITED KMS.	KMS. ILIMITADOS INLIMITED KMS.
	TYPE OF CAR	3 · DIAS / 3 · DAYS	7 · DIAS / 7 · DAYS

I'd like to hire a car
queria alugar um carro
*kree-uh a-loo-**gar** ooñ **kar**-roo*

for one day
para um dia
*pa-ruh ooñ **dee**-uh*

for ... days
para ... dias
*pa-ruh ... **dee**-ush*

I'd like...
queria...
kree-uh...

a small car
um carro pequeno
*ooñ **kar**-roo puh-**kay**-noo*

a large car
um carro grande
*ooñ **kar**-roo grañd*

a people carrier
um monovolume
*ooñ moh-noo-voh-**loom***

an automatic
um carro automático
*ooñ **kar**-roo ow-too-**mah**-tee-koo*

how much is it?
quanto é?
kwan-too e

is there a kilometre charge?
paga-se quilometragem?
*pah-guh-suh kee-loh-may-**trah**-zhayñ*

I am ... old
tenho ... anos
*ten-yoo ... **ah**-noosh*

here is my driving licence
aqui está a minha carta de condução
*a-**kee** esh-**tuh** uh **meen**-yuh **kar**-tuh duh koñ-doo-**sowñ***

what is included in the insurance?
que inclui o seguro?
*kuh eeñ-**klwee** oo suh-**goo**-roo*

could you show me how the controls work?
podia mostrar-me os comandos?
*po-**dee**-uh moosh-**trar**-muh oosh koo-**mañ**-doosh*

what do I do if the car breaks down?
que devo fazer se o carro avariar?
*kuh **deh**-voo fa-**zehr** soo **kar**-roo a-va-ree-**ar***

can I hire a child-seat?
posso alugar um assento para crianças?
*pos-soo a-loo-**gar** ooñ uh-**sayñ**-too **pa**-ruh kree-**añ**-sush*

how is it fitted?
como se monta?
*koh-moo suh **moñ**-tuh*

talking talking talking talking talking talking

Boats

In Lisbon there is an extensive system of ferry boats crossing the Tagus, transporting people (and vehicles) to and from the southern banks of the river. Some companies run leisure cruises up and down the river; these are also particularly common and well worth the trip in Oporto, on the river Douro. In the Algarve you will also find day trips exploring the rocky coast, and a good number of fishing trips from resorts such as Portimão and Lagos.

Belém ferry terminal

river quay

River Tagus ferry

timetables

how do I get to the river ferry terminal?
como se vai para a estação fluvial?
koh-moo suh vy pa-ruh uh shta-sowñ floo-vee-al

when is the next...?	**ferry**	**boat**
quando parte o próximo...?	ferry-boat	barco
kwan-doo part oo pros-see-moo...	*ferry-boat*	*bar-koo*

a ticket
um bilhete
ooñ beel-yet

a car and two people
um carro e duas pessoas
ooñ kar-roo ee doo-ush puh-so-ush

where does the boat leave from?
de onde parte o barco?
duh oñ-duh part oo bar-koo

how long is the trip?
quanto dura a viagem?
kwan-too doo-ruh uh vee-ah-jayñ

when do we arrive in...?
a que horas chegamos a...?
uh kee o-rush sheh-gah-moosh uh...

talking talking

Driving

i If you are taking your own car into Portugal you will need your driving licence, registration documents, insurance, breakdown cover and ID (passport). If you don't have the requisite documents in the car, there is a good chance of on-the-spot fines. Driving in Portugal can be a harrowing experience, with overtaking on bends, tailgating and drink-driving all common. As in many southern European countries, impatience is rife, with over-use of the horn. Watch out for older road signs, which still direct you to roads and motorways under old names.

A2	IP4	IC2	N224	M536
12	12	8	15	9

blue **auto-estrada** sign with km markers

red main highway sign

ordinary main-road sign

original main road

urban highway

north **norte**

oeste ⊕ **leste**
west   east

sul south

Speed restrictions

built up area 50km/h
main roads 100km/h
motorway   120km/h

82·87·NU 99 07

P · SUCURSAL CITROËN · FARO

Portuguese number plate
P on the blue panel is for Portugal, and the last 2 letters indicate the district of registration.

we are going to...
vamos a...
vah-moosh uh...

how many kilometres is it?
quantos quilómetros são?
kwan-toosh kee-loh-muh-troosh sown

how do I get to the motorway?
como se vai para a auto-estrada?
koh-moo suh vy pa-ruh uh ow-too-shtrah-duh

which is the best route?
qual é o melhor caminho?
kwa-le oo mel-yor ka-meen-yoo

can you show me on the map?
pode-me indicar no mapa?
pod-muh een-dee-kar noo mah-puh

talking

Cartaxo

Signs you will see on entering (above) and leaving (below) villages.

30km/h limit

end of 30km/h limit

Signs show what vehicles can use each lane on particular days

no parking 9am to 7pm except loading and unloading

SAÍDA

exit

área de serviço Grândola

*services area (**Grândola**)*

toll machine Press the red button and take your ticket.

DEVAGAR

slow down

---

is this the road to ... ?
esta é a estrada para...?
*esht e uh **shtrah**-duh pa-ruh...*

how do I get to... ?
como se vai para...?
koh-moo suh vy pa-ruh...

I am sorry, I did not know that...
desculpe, não sabia que...
*dush-**koolp** nown̄ suh-**bee**-uh kuh...*

it is a one-way street
é sentido único
*e sayn̄-**tee**-doo **oo**-nee-koo*

I could not park here
não é permitido estacionar aqui
*nown̄ e pur-mee-**tee**-doo shtas-yoo-**nar** a-**kee***

there is a ... speed limit
tem um limite de...
*tayn̄ oon̄ **lee**-mee-tay duh...*

talking

*There are a number of motorways (**auto-estradas**) in Portugal. They are toll roads, as are the two bridges into Lisbon from the south. You pay at the toll booth. **Via Verde** is for drivers who subscribe to the automatic express electronic toll service. SOS phones are available for emergency breakdown assistance on motorways.*

Blue motorway signs indicate road numbers and destinations. E indicates this is also a European route.

Motorway sign
auto-estrada

Overhead **Via Verde** indicator. Do not drive in these lanes.

no overtaking

They are very strict about this.

2 marks = safety

1 mark = danger

Chevron-shaped distance warnings are painted on some motorways. Drivers are meant to keep 2 markers behind the car in front.

If you break down on the motorway

If you break down on the motorway put on your hazard warning lights, place your warning triangle about 100m behind the car then make your way to the emergency phone. An arrow on the distance indicator will show you the way to the nearest phone. It is never more than 1km away. The police will arrange for a recovery vehicle to come to you.

my car's broken down
tenho o carro avariado
ten-yoo oo kar-roo a-vuhr-yah-doo

what should I do?
que devo fazer?
kuh dev-oo fa-zehr

I am on my own
estou só
shtoh soh

it is a blue Fiat
é um Fiat azul
e ooñ fee-at a-zool

the registration number is...
a matricula é...
uh mah-tree-koo-luh e...

the car is...
o carro está...
oo kar-roo shta...

after exit...
depois da saída...
duh-poysh duh sah-ee-duh...

before exit...
antes da saída...
an-tesh duh sah-ee-duh...

*Parking can be a real problem in Portuguese towns. You may commonly come across cars parked in strange places, as Portuguese drivers often pull in regardless of conditions. It is safer to look for signs to parking areas and pay a small fee, than end up with a **multa** (fine) or be towed away. Disabled parking spaces are scarce. In busy areas you may see young men and boys finding spaces for drivers. They may look scruffy, but they are also quick to spot gaps and guide you in. Just remember, they expect a tip. Police are very strict with drivers who park in front of garage entrances. There is usually a private sign on the door.*

pay and display sign

get your ticket here

pay here
On-street parking meter sign.

In larger towns, parking may be underground.

payment zone
dias úteis =
weekdays
sábados =
Saturdays

premir para abrir
press to open

Here, the driver presses the red button for a ticket to open the barrier to the car park.

park on pavement

Livre means *spaces*, not that parking is free!

spaces

full

private

towaway zone

tariffs

TARIFAS

car park prices *8am to 8pm*

PARQUE DE ESTACIONAMENTO
PREÇÁRIO

8.00-20.00 horas

end of time (paid)

date

ticket number
amount
date
time
machine

```
Av. Republica, Faro
DATA 2006  FIM DE HORA
27.06 15:59
TALAO NUMERO: 06824
TAXA PAGA: EUR 00.10
DATA: 27.06.06
HORA: 15:39
MAQUINA: 00004
MASITRAVE nif 503496553
Pr. Alex. Herculano,35-2
8000 Faro
```

Place your parking ticket on display in your car.

Introduza e retire bilhete
insert and remove ticket

Introduza cartaõ
insert card

Notas
notes

Informações
assistance

Many automatic machines in Portugal have an English language option.
Most parking meters give change.

talking

where's the best place to park?
onde é o melhor sitio para estacionar?
*oñ-duh e oo mel-**yor** seet-yoo **pa**-ruh shtass-yoo-**nar***

can I park here?
posso estacionar aqui?
*pos-soo shtass-yoo-**nar** a-**kee***

how long for?
por quanto tempo?
*poor **kwan**-too **teñ**-poo*

do I need to pay?
tenho que pagar?
ten**-yoo kuh puh-**gar

the ticket machine doesn't work
o paquímetro não funciona
*oo pa-**kee**-may-troo nowñ foonss-**yoh**-nuh*

Most filling stations operate in the same way as in the UK, with self-service pumps, although in smaller areas you will still find one- or two-pump garages which are attended. Filling stations are scarce in rural areas. Note when you are filling up your car that diesel is **gasóleo** and petrol is **gasolina**.

| **Super** | **Sem Chumbo** | **Gasóleo** |
| LRP | unleaded | diesel |

Pumps are colour coded.

You can pay with major credit cards (listed on the side of the machine) and instructions are in Portuguese and English.

air and water

Larger stations have pre-pay machines. You key in before you begin how much you want to pay.

PRÉ-FIXAÇÃO (em EUROS)

1 NÃO RETIRE A PISTOLA
2 PRESSIONE AS TECLAS AS VEZES NECESSÁRIAS
3 CONFIRME NO MOSTRADOR O VALOR PRETENDIDO
4 RETIRE A PISTOLA, ABASTEÇA E ... ... PAGUE NA CAIXA

pre-fixed amount
1 Don't remove nozzle
2 Press buttons as required
3 Confirm on the keypad the amount required
4 Remove nozzle, fill up, and pay at the cash desk
anular = cancel

switch off engine

---

where is the nearest petrol station?
onde é a estação de serviço mais perto?
oñ-duh e uh shta-sowñ duh sehr-vee-soo mysh pehr-too

... worth of unleaded petrol	**number...**
... euros de gasolina sem chumbo	número...
... eur-oosh duh ga-zoo-lee-nuh sayñ shoom-boo	*noo-muh-roo...*

fill it up, please	**please check the oil**
encha, por favor	pode verificar o óleo, por favor
eñ-shuh poor fa-vor	*pod vuh-ree-fee-kar oo ol-yoo poor fa-vor*

talking

*If you belong to a driving organisation and have European cover, you will be able to use **ACP**, the Portuguese breakdown service. Otherwise, you will have to rely on local garages.*

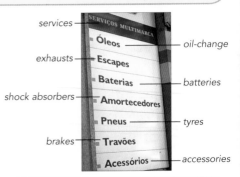

services — SERVIÇOS MULTIMARCA

Óleos — oil-change

exhausts — Escapes

Baterias — batteries

shock absorbers — Amortecedores

Pneus — tyres

brakes — Travões

Acessórios — accessories

my car has broken down
o meu carro está avariado
*oo may-oo **kar**-roo shta a-va-ree-**ah**-doo*

it won't start
não pega
*nowñ **peg**-uh*

the battery is flat
a bateria está descarregada
*uh ba-tuh-**ree**-uh shta dush-kar-ruh-**ga**-duh*

it won't go
não anda
*nowñ **añ**-duh*

I have a flat tyre
tenho um furo
*ten-yoo ooñ **foo**-roo*

I've run out of petrol
não tenho gasolina
*nowñ **ten**-yoo gaz-oo-**lee**-nuh*

where is the nearest garage?
onde é a oficina mais perto?
*oñ-duh e uh o-fee-**see**-nuh mysh **pehr**-too*

the ... is not working
o/a ... não funciona
*oo/uh ... nowñ foons-**yoh**-nuh*

the ... are not working
os/as ... não funcionam
*oosh/ush ... nowñ foons-**yoh**-nowñ*

can you repair it?
pode arranjá-lo?
*pod ar-rañ-**zha**-loo*

how long will it take?
quanto tempo leva?
*kwañ-too **teñ**-poo **leh**-vuh*

when will it be ready?
quando estará pronto?
*kwañ-doo shta-**ra proñ**-too*

how much will it cost?
quanto vai custar?
*kwañ-too vy koosh-**tar***

can you replace the windscreen?
pode substituir o pára-brisas?
*pod sub-shteet-**weer** oo pa-ruh-**bree**-zush*

do you have the parts?
tem as peças?
*tayñ ush **pes**-ush*

is it serious?
é grave?
e grav

talking talking talking talking talking talking

Lisbon District

Green roads are major European routes (E = European, A = Motorway **Auto-estrada**). Red IP routes are main roads. IC signs are white and are for ordinary main roads and yellow M signs indicate urban highways.

Speed limits in Portugal are in km/h.

Pictogram on road signs indicating the town centre.

TODAS AS DIRECÇÕES

all routes

historic centre (old part of town)

Shopping

i *Shopping is an everyday activity in Portugal, with busy town-centre morning markets. Small supermarkets, called **minimercados**, can also be found in many towns. Small shops tend to close for lunch from 1–3pm but are open later in the evening. Normal shops are usually closed on Saturday afternoons and Sundays. Non-EU residents can claim back VAT (**IVA**) on a number of goods – shops display 'Tax Free' signs. Tourists in Lisbon can claim a range of discounts by using the **Lisboa Card**, sold at Tourist Offices.*

keywords keywords keywords

padaria
pa-duh-ree-uh
baker's

talho
tal-yoo
butcher's

charcutaria
shar-koot-uh-ree-uh
delicatessen

mercearia
muhr-see-uh-ree-uh
grocer's

pastelaria
pash-tuh-luh-ree-uh
cake shop

supermercado
soo-per-mer-ka-doo
supermarket

peixaria
pay-shuh-ree-uh
fishmonger's

tabacaria
ta-buh-kuh-ree-uh
tobacconist's

On-street kiosks sell newspapers, magazines, postcards, stamps, cigarettes and novelties.

crafts shop

butcher's

Stationer's with photocopy service.

Older style of tobacconist/newsagent with a small bar.

bookshop

sale

Supermercados and **hipermercados** are usually found on the outskirts of towns. They offer free parking and are open late. Popular chains include **Pão de Açúcar**, **Continente**, **Modelo** and **Pingo Doce**. In the fruit and veg sections you may have to weigh the items on an electronic scale and press a button to print off a price label. All towns and villages have either a small shop **mercado** or a **supermercado**.

Popular supermarket chains.

check the price

Verifique o preço

Signs flag up wall-mounted bar-code scanners.

to take a trolley

Para levar o carrinho

1 - Colocar a moeda de 50 céntimos — 1 insert a 50-céntimos coin

2 - Premir a patilha — 2 remove the key

3 - Levar o carrinho — 3 take the trolley

hypermarket – shops

Hipermercado - Lojas

Este talão é indispensável para efeitos de garantia trocas e devoluções
P.V.P. inclui IVA

*this receipt is needed for guarantee, exchange and refunds (**PVP inclui IVA** = sale price inc. VAT)*

where can I buy...? onde posso comprar...? *oñ-duh pos-soo koñ-prar...*	**matches** fósforos *fosh-foo-roosh*	**a tin-opener** um abre-latas *ooñ a-bruh-la-tush*
do you have...? tem...? *tayñ...*	**how much does it cost?** quanto custa? *kwan-too koosh-tuh*	
I am looking for... estou à procura de... *shtoh a pro-koo-ruh duh...*	**a present** um presente *ooñ pruh-sent*	**a good wine** um bom vinho *ooñ boñ veen-yoo*
where is there a market? onde há um mercado? *oñ-duh a ooñ mer-kah-doo*	**which day?** em que dia? *ayñ kuh dee-uh*	
do you give a discount? nao faz desconto? *nowñ fash dush-kon-too*	**can I pay with this card?** posso pagar com este cartão? *pos-soo pa-gar koñ esht kar-towñ*	

talking talking talking

i Portugal uses all metric weights and measures, so fruit and veg, meat, fish, hams and cheeses are measured in kilos and grams. Some cheeses are also sold in slices (**fatias**) or in small caskets or boxes, such as ricotta-style fresh cheese. Liquids are sold by can, carton, bottle or litre, and wine can be bought in a large demi-john called a **garrafão**.

Fruit and veg are generally sold by the kilo, although larger items, such as cauliflowers, are sold individually.

Pre-packed shellfish, here **mexilhão** (mussels) and **ameîjoa** (clams), are sold by the kilo.

full fat   semi-skimmed (**meio gordo** = half fat)

Milk is sold in colour-coded cartons.

skimmed (**magro** = low-fat)

The general word for bread is **pão**, although there are many variations depending on type, shape and size. This baguette is organically produced (**biológico**).

free-range eggs

6 Ovos Frescos 6

6 fresh eggs

CONSUMIR DE PREFERÊNCIA ANTES DE:

best before:

SEM ADIÇÃO DE AÇÚCAR

without added sugar

-33% Gordura

Graças ao nosso
exclusivo sistema de fabrico,

33% less fat

INGREDIENTES:
Batatas, gordura vegetal e sal.

ingredients:
potatoes, vegetable fat and salt

nutritional information

INFORMAÇÃO NUTRICIONAL		
Conteúdo Médio Por 100g		per 100 g
Valor Energético 470 kcal		calories
	1970 kJ	
Proteínas	8,0 g	protein
Glícidos	58 g	carbohydrate
Lípidos	23 g	fat

a piece of that cheese
um pouco desse queijo
*ooñ **poh**-koo **des**-suh **kay**-zhoo*

a little more
um pouco mais
*ooñ **poh**-koo mysh*

a little less
um pouco menos
*ooñ **poh**-koo **men**-oosh*

that's enough, thanks
chega, obrigado(a)
*sheh-guh oh-bree-**gah**-doo(-duh)*

10 slices of cooked ham
dez fatias de fiambre
*desh fa-**tee**-ush duh fee-**añ**-bruh*

200 grams of cured ham
duzentos gramas de presunto
*doo-**zañ**-toosh **gra**-mush duh pruh-**zoon**-too*

a litre of milk
um litro de leite
*ooñ **lee**-troo duh layt*

a bottle of mineral water
uma garrafa de água mineral
*oo-muh gar-**raf**-uh duh **ag**-wuh mee-nuh-**ral***

still	fizzy
sem gás	com gás
sayñ gazh	*koñ gazh*

a tin of...
uma lata de...
*oo-muh **la**-tuh duh...*

a jar	a packet
um frasco	um pacote
*ooñ **frash**-koo*	*ooñ pa-**kot***

a bottle of wine
uma garrafa de vinho
*oo-muh gar-**raf**-uh duh **veen**-yoo*

that's everything
mais nada
*mysh **nah**-duh*

Everyday Foods

beef	a carne de vaca *karn duh **vah**-kuh*
biscuits	as bolachas *boo-**lah**-shush*
bread	o pão *powñ*
bread (brown)	o pão integral *powñ een-tuh-**gral***
bread roll	o papo-seco ***pah**-poo-**seh**-koo*
butter	a manteiga *man-**tay**-guh*
cakes	os bolos ***boh**-loosh*
cheese	o queijo ***kay**-zhoo*
chicken	o frango ***frañ**-goo*
chocolate	o chocolate *shoo-koo-**laht***
coffee	o café *kuh-**fe***
cream	a nata ***nah**-tuh*
crisps	as batatas fritas *ba-**tah**-tush **free**-tush*
eggs	os ovos ***oh**-voosh*
fish	o peixe *paysh*
flour	a farinha *fa-**reen**-yuh*
ham (cooked)	o fiambre *fee-**am**-bruh*
ham (cured)	o presunto *pruh-**zoon**-too*
herbal tea	a tisana *tee-**za**-nuh*
honey	o mel *mel*
jam	a compota *kom-**pot**-uh*
juice	o sumo ***soo**-moo*
lamb	o borrego *bor-**reg**-oo*
margarine	a margarina *mar-guh-**ree**-nuh*
marmalade	a doce de laranja *dohss duh la-**ran**-zhuh*
milk	o leite *layt*
olives	as azeitonas *a-zay-**ton**-ush*
olive oil	o azeite *a-**zayt***
orange juice	o sumo de laranja ***soo**-moo duh la-**ran**-zhuh*
pasta	as massas ***mas**-sush*
pepper	a pimenta *pee-**men**-tuh*
pork	a carne de porco *karn duh **por**-koo*
quince jam	a marmelada *mar-mel-**ah**-duh*
rice	o arroz *a-**rosh***
salt	o sal *sal*
salt cod	o bacalhau *ba-kal-**yow***
sardines	as sardinhas *sar-**dee**-nush*
stock cube	o cubo concentrado ***koo**-boo kon-sayñ-**trah**-doo*
sugar	o açúcar *a-**soo**-kar*
tea	o chá *sha*
tomatoes (tin)	a lata de tomates ***lah**-tuh duh to-**matsh***
tuna	o atum *a-**tooñ***
vinegar	o vinagre *vee**nah**-gruh*
yoghurt	o iogurte *yoh-**goort***

Fruit

apples	as maçãs *ma-**sañsh***
apricots	os damascos *da-**mash**-koosh*
bananas	as bananas *ba-**nah**-nush*
cherries	as cerejas *suh-**ray**-jush*
grapefruit	a toranja *too-**ran**-juh*
grapes	as uvas *oo-vush*
lemon	o limão *lee-**mowñ***
melon	o melão *me-**lowñ***
nectarines	as nectarinas *nek-tuh-**ree**-nush*
oranges	as laranjas *la-**ran**-zhush*
peaches	os pêssegos *peh-suh-goosh*
pears	as pêras *peh-rush*
pineapple	o ananás *a-nuh-**nash***
plums	as ameixas *a-**may**-shush*
raspberries	as framboesas *frañ-**bway**-zush*
strawberries	os morangos *moo-**rañ**-goosh*
watermelon	a melancia *mel-añ-**see**-uh*

Vegetables

asparagus	os espargos *shpar-goosh*
aubergine	a beringela *ber-een-**zhe**-luh*
broccoli	os brócolos *broh-koo-loosh*
cabbage	a couve *kohv*
carrots	as cenouras *suh-**noh**-rush*
cauliflower	a couve-flor *kohv-**flor***
coriander	os coentros *koo-**eñ**-troosh*
courgettes	as courgettes *koor-**zhetsh***
french beans	o feijão verde *fay-zhowñ-**vehrd***
garlic	o alho *al-yoo*
kale	a couve galega *kohv ga-**leh**-guh*
leeks	os alhos-porros *al-yoosh-**por**-rosh*
lettuce	a alface *al-**fass***
mushrooms	os cogumelos *koo-goo-**mel**oosh*
onions	as cebolas *suh-**bol**ush*
olives	as azeitonas *a-zay-**toh**-nush*
parsley	a salsa *sal-suh*
peas	as ervilhas *ehr-**veel**-yush*
peppers	os pimentos *pee-**men**-toosh*
potatoes	as batatas *ba-**tah**-tush*
pumpkin	a abóbora *a-**bob**-oo-ruh*
spinach	os espinafres *shpee-**na**-frush*
sweet potatoes	as batatas doces *buh-**ta**-tush doh-sush*
tomatoes	os tomates *too-**matsh***
turnip	o nabo *nah-boo*
turnip tops	as nabiças *na-**bee**-sush*

i The cheapest places to buy clothes and shoes are at weekly and monthly markets, or **feiras**, with bargains in jeans, jackets and footwear. In towns, shoe shops are plentiful. Portuguese shoes are elegant and great value for money. The Portuguese are very well-dressed, and Lisbon especially has become a fashion mecca, with names such as Ana Salazar and the popuar Spanish store, **Zara**.

keywords keywords keywords keywords keywords

aberto até às...
a-ber-too a-te ash...
open until...

cave
kav
basement

rés-do-chão
res-doo-shown̄
ground floor

andar/piso
an-dar/pee-soo
floor

caixa
ky-shuh
cash desk

desconto
dush-kon̄-too
discount

saldo
sal-doo
sale

senhoras
sun-yor-suh
ladies'

homem
o-mayn̄
men's

crianças
kree-an̄-sush
children

store guide

R/C
ground floor

Senhora
ladieswear

Comple-mentos
accessories

1º Piso
first floor

Homem
menswear

cash desk

A Lisboa card entitles you to discounts in many shops around the city.

shoe shop

on which floor is/are...?
em que andar está/estão...?
ayn̄ kuh an-dar shta/shtown̄...

toys
os brinquedos
oosh breen̄-kay-doosh

shoes
os sapatos
oosh sa-pah-toosh

household goods
artigos de ménage
ar-tee-goosh duh-may-nazh

Women's clothes sizes

UK/Australia	8	10	12	14	16	18	20	22
Europe	36	38	40	42	44	46	48	50
US/Canada	6	8	10	12	14	16	18	20

Men's clothes sizes (suits)

UK/US/Canada	36	38	40	42	44	46
Europe	46	48	50	52	54	56
Australia	92	97	102	107	112	117

Shoes

UK/Australia	2	3	4	5	6	7	8	9	10	11
Europe	35	36	37	38	39	41	42	43	45	46
US/Canada women	4	5	6	7	8	9	10	11	12	-
US/Canada men	3	4	5	6	7	8	9	10	11	12

Children's Shoes

UK/US/Canada	0	1	2	3	4	5	6	7	8	9	10	11
Europe	15	17	18	19	20	22	23	24	26	27	28	29

can I try this on?
posso provar isto?
pos-soo pro-var eesh-too

I'm just looking
só estou a ver
so shtoh uh vehr

do you have size...?
tem medida...?
tayñ muh-dee-duh...

shoe size 40, please
número quarenta, por favor
noo-muh-roo kwa-reñ-tuh poor favor

do you have this in my size?
tem isto na minha medida?
tayñ eesh-too nuh meen-yuh muh-dee-duh

I take shoe size...
calço número...
kal-soo noo-muh-roo...

it's too big
é muito grande
e mweeñ-too grañd

it's too small
é muito pequeno
e mweeñ-too puh-ke-noo

I need a size...
preciso duma medida...
pruh-see-zoo doo-muh muh-dee-duh...

smaller
mais pequeno
mysh puh-ke-noo

bigger
maior
mah-yor

where are the changing rooms?
onde é o gabinete de provas?
oñ-duh e oo ga-bee-net duh prov-ush

talking talking

i You can buy stamps from tobacconists, kiosks and some hotels, as well as from the post office. Pre-stamped postcards can be purchased from post offices. There are also automatic stamp machines in or near town squares and at airports and railway stations. Phone calls can be made from post offices.

CTT (post office) sign

Next-collection times may be shown by a dial on the post box.

Modern stamp machines have instructions in English.

Blue post boxes are for priority, or first-class post; ordinary post boxes are red.

where is the post office?
onde é o correio?
*oñ-duh e oo koor-**ray**-oo*

do you have stamps?
tem selos?
*tayñ **sel**-oosh*

10 stamps, please
dez selos, por favor
*desh **sel**-oosh poor fa-**vor***

for postcards
para postais
*pa-ruh poosh-**tysh***

for letters
para cartas
*pa-ruh **kar**-tush*

to Britain
para a Grã-Bretanha
*pa-ruh uh grañ-bruh-**tahn**-yuh*

to the US
para os Estados Unidos
*pa-ruh oosh **shtah**-doosh oo-**nee**-doosh*

I'd like to send this...
queria mandar isto...
*kree-uh man-**dar** eesh-too...*

registered
registado
*ruh-zhees-**tah**-doo*

by priority post
por correio azul
*poor koor-**ray**-oo a-**zool***

how much is it to send this parcel?
quanto custa mandar este embrulho?
*kwan-too **koosh**-tuh man-**dar** aysht ayñ-**brool**-yoo*

where can I post these cards?
onde posso pôr estes postais no correio?
*oñ-duh **pos**-soo por **esh**-tesh poosh-**tysh** noo koor-**ray**-oo*

talking talking talking

Photo booths can be found in airports, some railway stations and larger shopping centres.

In the post office, you sometimes take a ticket and wait for your number.

30-minute photo-developing service.

where can I buy film?
onde posso comprar rolos?
oñ-duh pos-soo koñ-prar roh-loosh

a colour film
um rolo a cores
ooñ roh-loo uh koh-rush

can you develop this film?
pode revelar este rolo?
pod ruh-vuh-lar aysht roh-loo

can you take a picture of us, please?
pode-nos tirar uma foto, por favor?
pod-noosh tee-rar oo-muh foh-too poor fa-vor

can I take pictures here?
posso tirar fotos aqui?
pos-soo tee-rar foh-toosh a-kee

tapes for this camcorder
cassettes para este video
ka-setsh pa-ruh esht veed-yoo

24
vinte e quatro
veen-tee-kwa-troo

36
trinta e seis
treen-tuh saysh

when will the photos be ready?
quando estão prontas as fotos?
kwan-doo shtowñ pron-tush ush foh-toosh

talking talking

Phones

i) *Call boxes are easy to find. The older type are silver kiosks with tricky-to-open folding doors; more modern ones are beige or blue, and more open. You can also call internationally from some post offices and telecom shops. Most have instructions in several languages, including English. You can buy phone cards from post offices, telecom shops and newsagents.*

You can usually use coins or a phone card. Older phones take coins only. Emergency numbers are displayed in most phone booths.

talking talking talking talking

do you have phonecards?
tem cartões telefónicos?
tayñ kar-townsh tuh-luh-fo-nee-koosh

a phonecard
um cartão telefónico
ooñ kar-towñ tuh-luh-fo-nee-koo

for 50/100 units
de cinquenta/cem impulsos
duh seeñ-kweñ-tuh/sayñ eeñ-pool-soosh

Mr Lopes, please
o Senhor Lopes, por favor
oo sun-yor lopsh poor fa-vor

Mrs Lopes, please
a Senhora Lopes, por favor
uh sun-yor-uh lopsh poor fa-vor

can I speak to...?
posso falar com...?
pos-soo fa-lar koñ...

this is Caroline
daqui fala Caroline
da-kee fa-luh caroline

can you give me an outside line, please
pode dar-me uma linha, por favor
pod dar-muh oo-muh leen-yuh poor fa-vor

I want to make a reverse charge call
quero fazer uma chamada a cobrar no destinatário
keh-roo fa-zehr oo-muh sha-mah-duh uh koo-brar noo dush-tee-na-tar-yoo

what is you phone number?
qual é o seu número de telefone?
kwal e oo say-oo noo-muh-roo duh tuh-luh-fon

my number is...
o meu número é...
oo may-oo noo-muh-roo e...

Comunicações

Logo of PT, the Portuguese telecoms company.

Phone cards are very popular, with a range from different companies such as **CTT**, **PT**, **Marconi** and **Onicard**.

International dialling codes	
UK 00 44	Australia 00 61
USA 00 1	Portugal 00 351

Páginas Amarelas
paginasamarelas.pt

yellow pages

Portuguese phone numbers are given in single digits			
21	**882**	**03**	**48**
dois, um	oito, oito, dois	zero, três	quatro, oito

cartão telefónico
kar-**towñ** tuh-luh-**fo**-nee-koo
phonecard

telemóvel
tuh-luh-**mo**-vel
mobile

indicativo
een-dee-kuh-**tee**-voo
dialling code

moedas
mwed-ush
coins

marcar
mar-**kar**
to dial

chamada
sha-**mah**-duh
phone call

keywords keywords

telemóvel proibido
mobiles prohibited

I'll call back...
chamarei...
sha-muh-**ray**...

later
mais tarde
mysh tard

tomorrow
amanhã
a-man-**yañ**

have you a mobile?
tem telemóvel?
tayñ tuh-luh-**mo**-vel

what's your mobile number?
qual é o seu número de telemóvel?
kwal e oo **say**-oo **noo**-muh-roo duh tuh-luh-**mo**-vel

my mobile number is...
o meu número de telemóvel é...
oo **may**-oo **noo**-muh-roo duh tuh-luh-**mo**-vel e...

talking

E-mail, Internet, Fax

i As yet there are few internet cafés outside the Algarve, Oporto and Lisbon. Likewise, there are few places you can fax, but hotels, telecom offices and tourist offices may be able to send one for you. The suffix for Portuguese websites is **.pt**

The Portuguese word for 'at' is **arroba** (*ar-roh-buh*).

sapo.pt is a popular Portuguese search engine.

Serviços

A PT Internet café
services

- Telefone assistido por operadora — *operator-assisted calls*
- Telefones com moedas e cartão — *coin- and card-operated phones*
- Telecom Card PT — *PT phone cards*
- Internet com www, chat e webmail — *internet, chat and webmail*
- Word, Excel e Powerpoint — *Word, Excel and Powerpoint access*
- Impressões — *prints*
- Fotocopiadora — *photocopies*
- Fax — *fax*
- Informações — *information*
- Listas Telefónicas — *phone books*

do you have e-mail?
tem e-mail?
tayñ e-mail

my e-mail address is...
o meu endereço de e-mail é...
*oo **may**-oo eñ-duh-ruh-**sowñ** duh e-mail e...*

what is your e-mail address?
qual é o seu endereço de e-mail?
*kwal e oo **say**-oo eñ-duh-ruh-**sowñ** duh e-mail*

caroline.smith@anycompany.co.uk
caroline ponto smith@collins ponto co ponto uk
*caroline **pon**-too smith ar-**roh**-buh **pon**-too co **pon**-too uk*

can I send an e-mail?
posso mandar um e-mail?
*pos-soo man-**dar** ooñ e-mail*

did you get my e-mail?
recebeu o meu e-mail?
*ruh-suh-**bay**-oo oo **may**-oo e-mail*

can you send it by e-mail?
pode mandá-lo por e-mail?
*pod man-**da**-loo poor e-mail*

can I book by e-mail?
posso fazer a reserva por e-mail?
*pos-soo fa-**zehr** uh ruh-**zer**-vuh poor e-mail*

talking talking talking

A public internet phone, usually found at airports. Choose from several options along the top of the touch screen (below).

ajuda
azh-oo-duh
help

notícias
noh-teess-yush
news

pesquisa
pesh-kee-zuh
search

caixa de correio
ky-shuh duh koo-ray-oo
mailbox

procurar
proh-koo-rar
find

corpo/título
kor-poo/tee-too-lo
text/title

ambos
am-boosh
both

telefone   e-mail   **internet**   informações
phone   *188 net*   information
          (national info)

números uteis
useful numbers

I want to send a fax
quero mandar um fax
keh-roo man-dar ooñ faks

do you have a fax?
tem fax?
tayñ faks

can I send a fax from here?
posso mandar um fax daqui?
pos-soo man-dar ooñ faks da-kee

can I receive a fax here?
posso recebir um fax aqui?
pos-soo ruh-suh-beer ooñ faks a-kee

how much is it to send a fax?
quanto custa mandar um fax?
kwan-too kush-tuh man-dar ooñ faks

it has ... pages
tem ... páginas
tayñ ... pah-zhee-nush

what is your fax number?
qual é o seu número de fax?
kwal e oo say-oo noo-muh-roo duh faks

can you confirm the number?
pode confirmar o número?
pod koñ-feer-mar oo noo-muh-roo

my fax number is...
o meu número de fax é...
oo may-oo noo-muh-roo duh faks e...

did you get my fax?
recebeu o meu fax?
ruh-suh-bay-oo oo may-oo faks

Out & About

*It is advisable to visit **Turismo** (tourist information office) to find out about local sites of interest. Most museums are closed on Mondays. For the most part, museums, castles and art galleries charge small admission fees, although younger people and pensioners can usually get in at a discount or for free. Carnival time in Portugal is February; most towns hold parades and many social events.*

Museum street sign. Street signs to places of interest are normally brown.

historic town centre

tourist information office

Blue **rua** (street/road) plaque. This one commemorates a Portuguese governor of India.

Ticket for the football museum in Lisbon.

non-member

Lisbon's 'artshuttle' bus ferries visitors around the city to places of cultural interest. The Lisboa Card, available from tourist offices, lets you travel on the bus for free.

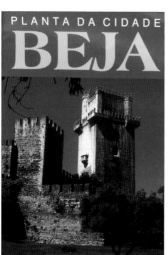

Town maps and what's on guides are available free from all tourist offices.

keywords keywords keywords

espectáculo
shpek-ta-koo-loo
show

exposição
eks-pos-ee-sowñ
exhibition

visitas guiadas
vee-zee-tush
gee-a-dush
guided tours

jardim botânico
zhar-deeñ
boot-a-nee-koo
botanic gardens

diário
dee-a-ree-oo
daily

igreja
ee-gray-zhuh
church

jovens
zho-vayñ
young people (5–15)

crianças
kree-an-sush
children

Museum ticket showing payment details.

talking talking talking

excuse me, where is the tourist office?
desculpe, onde é o turismo?
dush-koolp oñ-duh e oo too-reezh-moo

do you have...?
tem...?
tayñ...

a map of the town
um mapa da cidade
ooñ ma-puh duh see-dad

leaflets
folhetos
fool-yet-oosh

we'd like to visit...
queríamos visitar...
kree-a-moosh vee-zee-tar...

how do we get there?
come se vai para lá?
koh-moo suh vy pa-ruh la

when can we visit...?
quando podemos visitar...?
kwañ-doo poo-de-moosh vee-zee-tar...

when does it close?
a que horas fecha?
uh kee o-rush fay-shuh

are there any excursions?
há algumas excursões?
a al-goo-mush shkoor-soyñsh

where does it leave from?
de onde parte?
duh oñ-duh part

i Most sports are based on outdoor activities: e.g. surfing, fishing and golf, with many world-class courses. In national parks and reserves you can walk, ride and cycle. Football is the most popular spectator sport. Large hotels in tourist areas often have a swimming pool, tennis court and/or gym. Many towns have a public indoor pool where you are expected to wear a swimming cap (**touca**).

sports centre

Portugal's beautiful National Stadium still hosts the cup final every year.

Horse-riding is popular in Portugal. The lovely Lusitano breed is seen at its best at the colourful annual *Golegã (Ribatejo)* Horse Fair in November.

beaches

where can we...?	**play tennis**	**play golf**
onde podemos...?	jogar ténis	jogar golfe
oñ-duh poo-de-moosh...	*zhoo-gar tennis*	*zhoo-gar golf*

where can we go horse-riding?
onde podemos andar a cavalo?
oñ-duh poo-de-moosh an-dar uh ka-va-loo

how much is it...?	**per hour**	**per day**
quanto é...?	por hora	por dia
kwañ-too e...	*poor o-ruh*	*poor dee-uh*

is there a swimming pool?	**is it dangerous?**	**are there currents?**
há piscina?	é perigoso?	há correntes?
a peesh-zee-nuh	*e pree-goh-zoh*	*a koor-reñ-tush*

where can one...?	**go windsurfing**	**go waterskiing**
onde se pode...?	fazer windsurf	fazer esqui aquático
oñ-duh suh pod...	*fa-zer windsurf*	*fa-zer shkee ak-wa-tee-koo*

can I hire a beach umbrella?
posso alugar uma sombrinha?
pos-soo a-loo-gar oo-muh som-breen-yuh

Signs explain beach flag colour-codings.
Red: danger;
Green: clear;
Yellow: caution;
Blue check: safe.

Some beaches are arranged by activity zone.

flyer for a club

Fado poster – traditional Portuguese folk music.

jantar e espectáculo = 20 euros por pessoa (vinho incluído) dinner & show = 20 euros per person (wine included)
só espectáculo = 10 euros por pessoa (2 bebidas incluídas) show only = 10 euros per person (2 drinks included)

---

we'd like to go to a football match
queríamos assistir a um jogo de futebol
kree-uh-moosh a-sees-teer uh ooñ zhoh-goo duh foot-bol

where can we get tickets?
onde podemos comprar bilhetes?
oñ-duh poo-de-moosh koñ-prar beel-yetsh

how do we get to the stadium?
como se vai para o estádio?
koh-moo suh vy pa-ruh oo shtad-yoo

what time is the match?
quando começa o jogo?
kwañ-doo koo-mes-suh oo zhoh-goo

talking

Accommodation

> *There are many types of accommodation: **hotel**, **pensão** or **residência/residencial** (guest houses, offering breakfast only), **albergaria** or **estalagem** (inns), or **pousadas** (state-run luxury hotels, often in sites of historical interest). You can also stay on farms, booked through **Turismo Rural and Agroturismo**, or in private homes, with **Turismo de Habitação**, as well as the normal range of tourist options. Most can be arranged with the help of Tourist Offices.*

Larger hotels are signposted in blue.

Hotels and guest houses are starred 1–5. R means **Residencial**, so this is a guest house.

Residencials are reasonably cheap guest houses. They offer no meals apart from breakfast.

Booking in advance

The Portuguese tourist office (**www.portugalinsite.com**) can help with booking rooms and often get better rates than you could yourself.

I'd like to book a room...
queria reservar um quarto...
kree-uh ruh-zer-var ooñ kwar-too...

single
individual
eeñ-dee-veed-wal

double
de casal
duh ka-zal

we'd like to stay ... nights
queríamos ficar ... noites
kree-uh-moosh fee-kar ... noytsh

from ... till...
do dia ... ao dia...
doo dee-uh ... ow dee-uh...

I will confirm...
confirmarei...
koñ-feer-ma-ray...

by e-mail
por e-mail
poor e-mail

by fax
por fax
poor fax

my name is...
o meu nome é...
oo may-oo nom e...

my credit card number is...
o número de meu cartão de crédito é...
oo noo-muh-roo duh may-oo kar-towñ duh kre-dee-too e...

valid until
válido até...
val-ee-doo a-tay...

reception

Logo of the state-run Pousadas chain.

Room slip. Keep it to get
your key and, in larger
hotels, to get your meals.

Hotels have to post information about rooms
and meals on the back of bedroom doors.

do you have a room for tonight?
tem um quarto para esta noite?
tayñ ooñ kwar-too pa-ruh esh-tuh noyt

a single room um quarto individual *ooñ kwar-too een-dee-veed-wal*	**a double room** um quarto de casal *ooñ kwar-too duh ka-zal*
with twin beds com duas camas *koñ doo-ush ka-mush*	**with a double bed** com cama de casal *koñ ka-muh duh ka-zal*
with bath com casa de banho *koñ ka-zuh duh bahn-yoo*	**with shower** com chuveiro *koñ shoo-vay-roo*

for para *pa-ruh*	**one night** uma noite *oo-muh noyt*	**3 nights** três noites *tresh noyt-ush*
how much is it...? qual é o preço...? *kwal e oo pray-soo...*	**per night** por noite *poor noyt*	**per week** por semana *poor suh-mah-nuh*

can you suggest somewhere else?
pode aconselhar outro sítio?
pod a-kon-sel-yuhr oh-troo seet-yoo

talking talking talking talking

i If you are staying in self-catering accommodation, your gas supply for cooking and water-heating may be bottled. Check you understand how the bottle connects and what you need to do if it runs out (there may be extra bottles supplied). Plugs are 2-pin (20 v), so you will need an adapter for your UK appliances. You can buy these at airports or in travel shops.

apartments for rent

Recycling bins are becoming fairly common; even litter bins in the street are often divided according to the type of rubbish you are throwing away.

paper / cardboard

glass

QUARTOS LIVRES

rooms available
You may also see *vagas*, vacancies.

Esgotado

full
You may also see *lotado*.

packaging

youth hostel
Youth hostels vary in the range of facilities they offer; some of them cater for the disabled.

Logo of Portugal's youth hostel association.

keywords keywords keywords

detergente para a louça
duh-ter-zheñt pa-ruh uh loh-suh
washing-up liquid

detergente para a roupa
duh-ter-zheñt pa-ruh uh roh-puh
washing powder

sabão
suh-bowñ
soap

abre-latas
a-bruh-la-tush
tin-opener

velas
veh-lush
candles

fósforos
fosh-foo-roosh
matches

os sacos do lixo
oosh sa-koosh doo lee-shoo
bin liners

there is no...
não há...
nowñ a...

how does this work?
como é que isto funciona?
koh-moo e kuh eesh-too fooñss-yoh-nuh

how does ... work?
como funciona...?
koh-moo fooñss-yoh-nuh

the cooker
o fogão
oo foh-gowñ

the washing machine
a máquina de lavar roupa
uh mah-kee-nuh duh la-var roh-puh

is there always hot water?
há sempre água quente?
a sem-pruh ahg-wuh kent

what are the neighbours called?
qual é o nome dos vizinhos?
kwal e oo nom doosh vee-zeen-yoosh

whom do I contact if there are problems?
quem posso contactar em caso de problemas?
kayñ pos-soo koñ-tak-tar ayñ kah-zoo duh proo-bleh-moosh

when is the rubbish collected?
quando levam o lixo?
kwañ-doo leh-vowñ oo lee-shoo

where do we leave the rubbish?
onde pomos o lixo?
oñ-duh poh-moosh oo lee-shoo

can you give us an extra set of keys?
pode-nos dar um duplicado das chaves?
pod-noosh dar ooñ doo-plee-kah-doo dush sha-vush

talking talking talking

Camping

i To camp on sites, get an International Card from the UK Camping
and Caravanning club. Overnight stops at non-designated sites
are possible in restricted areas, but not the Algarve. Prices are very
reasonable, but some sites can be pretty basic. The definitive
campsite guide is the **Roteiro Campista**, available from bookshops.
Tourist Offices also have lists of sites.

Road sign for a campsite.

Drivers are warned not to camp on
the beach. Offsite camping is not
allowed in the Algarve.

no places

we're looking for a campsite
procuramos um parque de campismo
*pro-koo-**ra**-moosh ooñ park duh kam-**peezh**-moo*

have you any places?
tem lugares?
*tayñ loo-**ga**-rush*

we'd like to stay for ... nights
queríamos ficar ... noites
*kree-**a**-moosh fee-**kar** ... noytsh*

how much is it a night?
quanto é por noite?
kwañ-too e poor noyt

per tent
por tenda
*poor **teñ**-duh*

per caravan
por caravana
*poor ka-ruh-**va**-nuh*

can we park the caravan here for tonight?
podemos estacionar a caravana aqui para esta noite?
*poo-**deh**-moosh shtas-yoo-**nar** uh ka-ruh-**va**-nuh a-**kee** pa-ruh esht noyt*

is there a restaurant on the campsite?
há um restaurante no parque?
*a ooñ rush-toh-**rant** noo park*

do you have a more sheltered site?
tem um lugar mais abrigado?
*tayñ ooñ loo-**gar** mysh a-bree-**gah**-doo*

can we camp here for tonight?
podemos acampar aqui para esta noite?
*poo-**deh**-moosh a-kam-**par** a-kee **pa**-ruh esht noyt*

WC DEFICIENTES — *disabled WCs*
TÉNIS · PISCINA — *tennis – pool*
MÁQUINAS LAVAR — *washing machines*
POLIVALENTE — *communal area*
CAFÉ RESTAURANTE — *café, restaurant*
PARQUES INFANTIS — *playpark*
SALA CONVÍVIO — *lounge*
GELADARIA — *ice-cream shop*
LAVAGEM CARROS — *car wash*

drinking fountain

RECEPÇÃO
reception

TANQUES
sinks for hand-washing

LAVA LOUÇAS
dishwashers

LAVABOS
toilets

Typical campsite tariff
Preços, por dia
prices per day

PARQUE DE CAMPISMO E CARAVANISMO
do Sindicato dos Bancários do Sul e Ilhas
PINHEIROS DE MARIM
APARTADO 300
8700-912 OLHÃO
ALGARVE · PORTUGAL
TELEF. 289 700 300 · FAX 289 700 300/1
INTERNET: http://www.sbsi.pt/camping
E.MAIL: sbsicamping@mail.telepac.pt

TABELA PARA 2006 (Preços, por dia, com IVA incluído)

QUADRO I		Cr1 a 30/6	1 a 30/9	1/7 a 31/8
adults	ADULTOS	1,70	2,60	3,30
children (5-12)	CRIANÇAS dos 5 e menos de12 anos	0,00	1,50	1,75
small tent	TENDA PEQUENA	1,30	2,05	2,35
large tent	TENDA GRANDE	1,70	2,80	3,20
	TENDA GRANDE (+ 6 m²)	2,50	4,50	5,50
caravan	CARAVANA	2,25	3,70	4,40
	CARAVANA (+ 6 m²)	3,30	5,50	6,60
car	AUTOMÓVEL	1,40	2,30	2,75
bus	AUTOCARRO	4,75	7,15	8,50
motorhome	CARRO-CAMA	2,25	3,70	4,40
	CARRO-CAMA (+ 6 m²)	3,30	5,50	6,60
use of kitchen	COZINHA	0,90	1,45	1,70
extra awning	TOLDO SUPLEMENTAR	0,93	1,45	1,70
motorbikes	MOTORIZADAS	1,00	1,43	1,65
trailers	TENDA REBOQUE	1,70	2,60	3,30
boats/trailer	BARCO E/OU ATRELADO	1,70	2,80	3,30
hot baths	BANHOS QUENTES	0,00	0,90	0,90

t a l k i n g

is there a launderette near here?
há uma lavandaria automática perto daqui?
*a **oo**-muh la-van-duh-**ree**-uh ow-too-**ma**-tee-kuh **pehr**-too da-**kee***

where can I wash some clothes?
onde posso lavar a roupa?
*o**ñ**-duh **pos**-soo la-**var** uh **roh**-puh*

do you have a laundry service?
tem serviço de lavandaria?
*tay**ñ** suhr-**vee**-soo duh la-van-duh-**ree**-uh*

when will my clothes be ready?
quando está pronta a minha roupa?
***kwañ**-doo shta **proñ**-tuh uh **meen**-yuh **roh**-puh*

is there an iron?
há um ferro de engomar?
*a oo**ñ fer**-roo duh ay**ñ**-goo-**mar***

where is the dry-cleaner's?
onde é a tinturaria?
*o**ñ**-duh e uh teen-too-ruh-**ree**-uh*

Special Needs

Access and facilities for the disabled are quite scant, with few toilets, buses with access or buildings with ramps. Lisbon and Oporto have a special dial-a-ride bus for the disabled, and a limited taxi service operates in some larger cities. The organisation **Secretariado Nacional de Reabilitação** *publishes a guide to disabled facilities throughout Portugal.*

disabled parking   **disabled access**   *priority checkout for pregnant and disabled people*

Priority is also given on seats by the door on public transport.

Para aceder ao Piso -1, dirija-se por favor, ao Balcão de Informações
To get to the first floor, please go to the information desk.

are there any disabled toilets?
há casas de banho para deficientes?
a *kah*-zuh duh *ban*-yoo pa-ruh duh-fees-**yeñtsh**

is there a wheelchair accessible entrance?
há uma entrada para cadeiras de rodas?
a *oo*-muh en-**tra**-duh pa-ruh ka-**day**-rush duh **roh**-dush

is it possible to visit ... in a wheelchair?
pode-se visitar ... numa cadeira de rodas?
pod-suh vee-zee-**tar** ... *noo*-muh ka-**day**-ruh duh **roh**-dush

is there a reduction for the disabled?
há desconto para deficientes?
a dush-**koñ**-too pa-ruh duh-fees-**yeñtsh**

I need a bedroom on the ground floor
preciso dum quarto no rés-do-chão
pruh-**see**-zoo dooñ **kwar**-too noo rezh-doo-**showñ**

I use a wheelchair
uso cadeira de rodas
oo-soo ka-**day**-ruh duh **roh**-dush

where is the lift?
onde é o elevador?
oñ-duh e oo ee-luh-va-**dor**

Portugal is a very family-orientated country and children are a focal point of activities. It is not unusual to see children out until quite late in town squares, at café-bars and in restaurants with their families, and they are very well behaved. There are child discounts for train travel, at many attractions and at most hotels.

priority for:
disabled
pregnant
those carrying babies

children's playground

Piso rebaixado *Floor lowers (to help those with prams)*

keywords

criança
kree-an-suh
child

rapaz
ruh-pazh
boy

rapariga
ruh-pa-ree-guh
girl

grávida
gra-vee-duh
pregnant

doces
doh-sush
sweets

gelado
zhuh-lah-doo
ice cream

---

talking talking

a child ticket, please
um bilhete de criança, por favor
ooñ beel-yet duh kree-an-suh poor fa-vor

he/she is ... years old
ele/ela tem ... anos
el/el-uh tayñ ... a-noosh

is there a reduction for children?
fazem descontos para crianças?
fa-zayñ dush-kon-toosh pa-ruh kree-an-sush

do you have ...?
tem...?
tayñ...

a high chair
uma cadeira alta
oo-muh ka-day-ruh

a cot
um berço
ooñ behr-soo

do you sell...?
vende...?
vend...

nappies
fraldas
fral-dush

baby wipes
toalhitas
twal-yee-tush

dummies
chupetas
shoo-pet-ush

is it ok to give to children?
pode-se dar às crianças?
pod-suh dar ash kree-añ-sush

a small portion
uma porção pequena
oo-muh por-sowñ puh-kay-nuh

is there a play park near here?
há um parque infantil perto daqui?
a ooñ park een-fan-teel pehr-too dah-kee

Health

*The E111 (health insurance) form has been replaced by the new European Health Insurance card. Apply at the post office or online at **www.dh.gov.uk** to make sure you are covered. (See p. 74 for more information on hospitals.) For minor ailments, try the **Farmácia** (Pharmacy) in the first instance. They usually have the green cross sign.*

An alternative to hospital for emergencies is a health centre, **centro saúde**.

Duty chemist rotas are available from Tourist offices and in free English-language newspapers in tourist areas.

Duty chemist notices for Saturday (**sábado**) and Sunday (**domingo**)

green cross pharmacy sign

<table>
<tr><th colspan="6">FARMÁCIAS DE SERVIÇO</th></tr>
<tr><th>FARO</th><th>FARO MONTENEGRO</th><th>ALBUFEIRA</th><th>LOULÉ</th><th>OUTRAS LOCALIDADES</th><th>OLHÃO</th></tr>
</table>

(See p. 74 for more information on hospitals.)

talking

where is the nearest chemist?
onde é a farmácia mais perto?
*oñ-duh e uh far-**ma**-see-uh mysh **pehr**-too*

have you something for...?
tem alguma coisa para...?
*tayñ al-**goo**-muh **koy**-zuh **pa**-ruh...*

heartburn
a azia
*uh a-**zee**-uh*

mosquito bites
picadas de mosquitos
*pee-**ka**-dush duh moosh-**kee**-toosh*

diarrhoea
a diarreia
*uh dee-uh-**ray**-uh*

I need...
preciso de...
*pruh-**see**-zoo duh...*

antihistamine
antihistamínico
*an-tee-ees-ta-**mee**-nee-koo*

antibiotics
antibióticos
*an-tee-bee-**ot**-ee-koosh*

dental clinic

CLÍNICA DENTÁRIA BENTO FERREIRA

BOCA e DENTES — *mouth & teeth*

You can call an ambulance using the emergency number 112.

I don't feel well
não me sinto bem
nowñ muh seeñ-too bayñ

he/she is ill
ele/ela está doente
el/el-uh shta doo-ent

I need a doctor
preciso dum médico
pruh-see-zoo dooñ med-ee-koo

can the doctor come here?
o médico pode vir aqui?
oo med-ee-koo pod veer a-kee

my son/my daughter has a very high temperature
o meu filho/a minha filha tem febre muito alta
oo may-oo feel-yoo/uh meen-yuh feel-yuh tayñ feb-ruh al-tuh

he/she has a rash
ele/ela tem uma irritação de pele
el/el-uh tayñ oo-muh ee-ree-tuh-sowñ duh pel

he/she has been sick
ele/ela vomitou
el/el-uh voh-mee-toh

I have a pain here
doi-me aqui
doy-muh a-kee

I am on this medication
estou a tomar este remédio
shtoh a too-mar esht ruh-med-yoo

I'm pregnant
estou grávida
shtoh gra-vee-duh

I am on the pill
tomo a pílula
toh-moo uh pee-loo-luh

I'm breastfeeding
estou a amamentar
shtoh uh a-ma-men-tar

I have cystitis
tenho cistite
ten-yoo seesh-teet

I'm diabetic
sou diabético(a)
soh dee-uh-bet-ee-koo(-kuh)

I am allergic to...
sou alérgico(a) a...
soh a-ler-zhee-koo(-kuh) a...

I have high blood pressure
tenho a tensão alta
ten-yoo uh ten-sowñ al-tuh

are there any contra-indications?
tem contra-indicações?
tayñ koñ-truh-een-dee-kuh-soyñsh

I need a receipt for my insurance
preciso dum recibo para o seguro
pruh-see-zoo dooñ ruh-see-boo pa-ruh oo suh-goo-roo

I need a dentist
preciso dum dentista
pruh-see-zoo dooñ den-tees-tuh

I have toothache
tenho uma dor de dentes
ten-yoo oo-muh dor duh dentsh

my filling has come out
caiu-me o chumbo
ka-yoo-muh oo shooñ-boo

can your repair the dentures?
pode reparar a dentadura?
pod ruh-pa-rar uh den-tuh-doo-ruh

talking talking talking talking talking talking talking

i The Accident and Emergency department (**Serviço de Urgência**) in Portugal works in a similar way to the UK. Be prepared to complete a number of forms in reception – take your passport and other documents, and your Health Insurance card with you.

visitors —
blood unit —
chapel —

Hospital departments directory board.

accident and emergency

red cross ambulance

If you need to go to hospital

will he/she have to go to hospital?
deve andare all'ospedale?
day-vay an-da-ray al-los-ped-a-lay

where is the hospital?
dov'è l'ospedale?
do-ve los-ped-a-lay

where is the nearest A & E department?
dov'è il pronto soccorso più vicino?
do-ve eel pron-to sok-kor-so pyoo vee-chee-no

please take me to the hospital
per favore mi porti all'ospedale
payr fa-vo-ray mee por-tee al-los-ped-a-lay

I need to go to casualty
devo andare al pronto soccorso
day-vo an-da-ray al pron-to sok-kor-so

when are visiting hours?
quando sono le ore di visite?
kwan-do so-no lay o-ray dee vee-zee-tay

which ward?
quale reparto?
kwa-lay ray-par-to

can you explain what is the matter?
può spiegare cos'è il problema?
pwo spyay-ga-ray ko-ze eel prob-lay-ma

The emergency number 112 connects you to any of the emergency services (**Polícia, Bombeiros, Ambulância**). It is operated in Portuguese, French and English. There are several branches of the police: **GNR** (National Guard, military); **PSP** (Public Security Police), **Brigâda de Trânsito** (Traffic Police), the **PJ** (Crimefighters) and **Guarda Fiscal** (Customs & Excise).

PSP and (far left) GNR stations

Bombeiros fire brigade

help!	can you help me?	
socorro!	pode-me ajudar?	
*soo-**kor**-roo*	*pod-muh a-joo-**dar***	

call...	the police	an ambulance
chame...	a polícia	uma ambulância
shahm...	*uh poo-**lees**-yuh*	*oo-muh am-boo-**lans**-yuh*

there's a fire!	call the fire brigade!	
há fogo!	chame os bombeiros!	
*a **foh**-goo*	*sham oosh bom-**bay**-roosh*	

someone has stolen my...	my money	my passport
roubaram-me...	o dinheiro	o passaporte
*roh-**ba**-rown-muh...*	*oo deen-**yay**-roo*	*oo pas-sa-**port***

here are my insurance details	how much is the fine?
aqui está o meu seguro	quanto é a multa?
*a-**kee** shta oo **may**-oo suh-**goo**-roo*	*kwañ-too e uh **mool**-tuh*

I'm lost	I've been raped
estou perdido(a)	fui violado(a)
*shtoh puhr-**dee**-doo(-duh)*	*fwee vee-oh-**lah**-doo(-duh)*

where is the police station?	I want to report a theft
onde é a esquadra?	quero participar um roubo
*oñ-duh e uh **shkwa**-druh*	*keh-roo par-tee-see-**par** ooñ **roh**-boo*

my car has been broken into
assaltaram-me o carro
*sa-sal-**ta**-rown-muh oo **kar**-roo*

I need a report for my insurance
preciso dum relatório para o meu seguro
*pruh-**see**-zoo dooñ ruh-la-**tor**-yoo **pa**-ruh oo **may**-oo suh-**goo**-roo*

talking talking talking talking talking

Food
&
Drink

Portuguese Food

i In Portugal you can expect to find excellent meals at reasonable prices. The Portuguese are very fond of their food, and good places to eat, whether at the higher or lower end of the price range, will always be well patronised by locals – a good indication for visitors. Look out for Lisboa restaurant cards for one or two people or a family of 2 adults and 2 children. It gives 10% discounts.

Breakfast (**pequeno-almoço**) is mostly milky coffee, a roll with butter and perhaps some ham or cheese. It may be taken at a cafeteria on the way to work, to save time.

A mid-morning break might call for another coffee with a cake.

Lunch (**almoço**) is served from 1pm and may be simply bean or vegetable soup with a roll, eaten standing in a café, cafeteria or patisserie (**pastelaria**) if time is short. Many people prefer a proper lunch, usually of soup, a meat or fish dish with vegetables and salad, and dessert (fruit, ice-cream or pudding), with wine, beer or fruit juice and followed by strong coffee.

Dinner (**jantar**), served after 7 or 7.30pm, follows the same pattern as lunch. Portions are large, so don't order too much to begin with. Some restaurants will serve half-portions or allow two people to share.

Salt cod is found everywhere in Portugal. It needs soaking before cooking, when it can be served in innumerable ways. If you are uncertain of the taste, try the dishes below.

Bacalhau com natas salt-cod with cream

Pastéis de bacalhau salt-cod cakes

Sapateira dressed crab

Bacalhau com batatas
salt-cod with potatoes

Portuguese food is generally uncomplicated yet very flavoursome and distinctive. Fish dominates some menus (grilled, fried, poached and sometimes baked) but there is also ample choice of meat dishes, including steak, lamb or kid (stewed and roasted), pork (a favourite meat), game and poultry. Freshly mixed salad laced with the local olive oil is a favourite accompaniment to almost anything in addition to the potatoes, rice or vegetables that may form part of the dish. Every dish (fish, meat or eggs) will always be served with some kind of accompaniment.

Porco Assado *roast pork*

Bread is served at every meal in Portugal, along with butter and other spreads. You will generally be charged for these items only if you eat them, so if you don't want to pay for them send them back. There are many kinds of bread and larger loaves; look out also for maize (polenta) loaves, called **broa**.

where can I/we have a snack?
onde se pode comer alguma coisa?
on-duh suh pod koo-mehr al-goo-muh koy-zuh

can you recommend a good local restaurant?
pode recomendar um bom restaurante local?
pod ruh-koo-men-dar ooñ boñ rush-toh-rant loo-kal

how do we get to the restaurant?
como se vai para o restaurante?
koh-moo suh vy pa-ruh oo rush-toh-rant

are there any vegetarian restaurants here?
há algum restaurante vegetariano aqui?
a al-gooñ rush-toh-rant vuh-zhuh-tuhr-yah-noo a-kee

do I need to book?
preciso de reservar?
pruh-see-zoo duh ruh-ser-var

what do you recommend?
o que recomenda?
oo kuh ruh-koo-men-duh

talking talking talking

i It is common to be served small cheeses (fresh or dried) as a starter to go with the wonderful Portuguese bread and rolls. Cheeses are made from ewes' milk, goats' milk or a mixture of the two. Desserts can be either fresh fruit in season, ice cream or pudding – usually sweet and rich, made with lots of eggs.

keywords

pudim flan
poo-*deeñ* flan
crème
caramel

queijo fresco
kay-zhoo
fresh-koo
fresh cheese

fruta
froo-tuh
fruit

bolo
boh-loo
cake

mais nada
mysh *nah*-duh
nothing else

Torta de laranja
orange roll (left)
Pastéis or
bolos de nata
custard cakes
are a speciality

Bolo de arroz rice cake

Bolos de amêndoa
almond cakes

talking talking

I'd like a drink
queria uma bebida
kree-uh *oo*-muh buh-*bee*-duh

I'd like a ... please
queria um/uma ... por favor
kree-uh ooñ/*oo*-muh ... poor fa-*vor*

what would you like?
que quer tomar?
kuh kehr too-*mar*

a white coffee
um café com leite
ooñ kuh-*fe* koñ layt

an espresso
um café
ooñ kuh-*fe*

a decaff coffee
um café descafeinado
ooñ kuh-*fe* dush-ka-fay-*nah*-doo

a hot chocolate
um chocolate quente
ooñ shoo-koo-*laht* keñt

a tea with milk
um chá com leite
ooñ sha koñ layt

with toast
com torradas
koñ toor-*rah*-dush

an orange juice
um sumo de laranja
ooñ *soo*-moo duh luh-*rañ*-zhuh

a strawberry milkshake
um batido de morangos
ooñ ba-*tee*-doo duh moo-*rañ*-goosh

a half bottle of white wine
meia garrafa de vinho branco
may-uh gar-*rah*-fuh duh *veen*-yoo *brañ*-koo

a lager
uma cerveja
oo-muh suhr-*vay*-zhuh

a bottle of mineral water
uma garrafa de água mineral
oo-muh gar-*rah*-fuh *dahg*-wuh mee-nuh-*ral*

sparkling
com gás
koñ gas

still
sem gás
sayñ gas

Popular **bolo podre** (rotten cake – the name coming from the cake's dark colour) is made with honey, olive oil and aniseed. It comes from the Ribatejo and Alentejo provinces where olive oil is produced.

keywords keywords keywords

hortelã
or-tel-añ
mint

morango
moo-rañ-goo
strawberry

limão
lee-mowñ
lemon

ananás
an-uh-nash
pineapple

pêssego
peh-suh-goo
peach

avelã
uh-vel-añ
hazelnut

chocolate
shoo-koo-laht
chocolate

baunilha
baoo-neel-yuh
vanilla

casquinha
kash-keen-yuh
cone

Sandes e sumo
sandwiches and juice
Served at cafés and snack bars.

In the tourist towns of the Algarve it can be difficult to find a great variety in ice-creams (**gelados**).

talking

can we eat?
podemos comer?
poo-day-mosh koo-mehr

a table for two
uma mesa para dois
oo-muh may-zuh pa-ruh doysh

do you have a dish of the day?
tem prato do dia?
tayñ prah-too doo dee-uh

what is the dish of the day?
qual é o prato do dia?
kwal e oo prah-too doo dee-uh

what sandwiches do you have?
que sandes tem?
kuh santsh tayñ

what cakes do you have?
que bolos tem?
kuh boh-loosh tayñ

I'd like an ice cream
queria um gelado
kree-yuh ooñ zhuh-lah-doo

what flavours do you have?
que sabores tem?
kuh suh-boh-rush tayñ

i In Portugal, many restaurants close on Sunday or Monday, so check beforehand if there is a place you particularly want to eat. All establishments have to display their prices outside, so you will be prepared for the cost before going in. Brasiliero restaurants serving meat dishes are becoming more popular.

1a on the sign outside denotes a first-class restaurant.

There are specialist shellfish restaurants (*marisqueira*) in both seaside and inland towns, but ordinary restaurants will also have a range of shellfish dishes.

open-air

A *casa de pasto* is a modest restaurant serving homely food.

Booking a table

I'd like to book a table
queria reservar uma mesa
kree-uh ruh-zer-**var** **oo**-muh **may**-zuh

for ... people
para ... pessoas
pa-ruh ... puh-**so**-ush

for tonight
para esta noite
pa-ruh **esh**-tuh noyt

for tomorrow night
para amanhã à noite
pa-ruh a-man-**yañ** a noyt

for lunch
para o almoço
pa-ruh oo al-**moh**-soo

at mid-day
ao meio-dia
ow may-oo-**dee**-uh

for dinner
para o jantar
pa-ruh oo zhun-**tar**

at 8 o'clock
às oito
ash **oy**-too

in a non-smoking area
em zona de não-fumador
ayñ **zoh**-nuh duh nowñ-foo-muh-**dor**

in the name of Smith
em nome de Smith
ayñ nom duh smith

Especialidades tostas mistas
Cheese and ham toasted sandwiches are a speciality!

A **casa das tostas** is a snack-bar selling toasted sandwiches, a very popular snack.

Churrascarias (also spelt **churrasqueira**) are popular take-away establishments which sell **frango à piri-piri**, or **frango de churrasco** (barbecued chicken with chilli sauce), a legacy from the ex-colony of Mozambique and now adapted to European tastes.

where should we sit?
onde podemos sentar-nos?
*oñ-duh poo-**day**-moosh señ-**tar**-noosh*

the menu, please
a ementa, por favor
*uh ee-**men**-tuh poor fa-**vor***

the wine list, please
a lista de vinhos, por favor
*uh **leesh**-tuh duh **veen**-yoosh poor fa-**vor***

can you recommend a local dish?
pode recomendar uma especialidade local?
*pod ruh-koo-men-**dar oo**-muh shpuss-yalee-**dahd** loo-**kal***

what is this?
o que é isto?
*oo kuh e **eesh**-too*

I'll have this
quero isto
***keh**-roo **eesh**-too*

is it good?
é bom?
e boñ

do you have any vegetarian dishes?
tem algum prato vegetariano?
*tayñ al-**gooñ prah**-too vay-zhuh-tuhr-**yah**-noo*

more bread, please
mais pão, por favor
*mysh powñ poor fa-**vor***

more butter, please
mais manteiga, por favor
*mysh muhn-**tay**-guh poor fa-**vor***

the bill, please
a conta, por favor
*uh **koñ**-tuh poor fa**vor***

we would like to pay separately
queremos pagar separadamente
*kuh-**reh**-moosh puh-**gar** suh-pa-rah-duh-**ment***

talking talking talking talking talking

i Many restaurants offer an **Ementa Turística**, a set menu with a few choices, usually including traditional cuisine, offering an excellent way of eating well and cheaply. Check if wine is included. **Pratos do Dia**, or Dish of the Day, is another menu heading to look out for. If you don't want to be charged for bread, butter and other spreads, send them back.

Dishes of the Day

Conquilhas/Amêijoas *cockles/clams*
Dobrada feijão branco
tripe with beans (stew)
Massinha corvina *sea bream pasta*
Iscas à Portuguesa
liver Portuguese style
Bifes Atum Cebolada
tuna steaks in onion and tomato sauce
Pescada c/ (= com) feijão verde
poached hake with green beans
Sardinhas p/ (= para) assar
grilled sardines
Carapau p/ assar
grilled horse mackerel
Sargo p/ grelhar *grilled sea bream*
Eirós p/ grelhar *grilled large eel*
Bacalhau p/ assar *baked salt-cod*
Carapau (arr.) conquilhas (arroz de)
horse mackerel with cockles risotto
Eirós c/ arroz de conquilhas
large eel with cockles risotto

You will often be given fairly substantial appetisers before the meal you have ordered arrives.

Look out for **açordas** in Portuguese restaurants. These are homely dishes which are very popular in family-run restaurants. They consist of bread cooked with herbs (such as coriander and garlic), sometimes served with fried or grilled fish. They can also be main dishes in their own right. It is worth trying these local specialities as they are extremely tasty, although not necessarily elegant to look at. This is comfort food at its best.

Açorda de gambas
large prawns in thick bread soup
Atum cebolada
tuna in onion and tomato sauce
Picanha fatiada
sliced beef

Bifes do lombo fillet steak
A Porto fino with fine Port sauce
Tropical with a spicy sauce
Ao pimenta with a pepper sauce
Cogumelos e natas with a mushroom and cream sauce

A traditional set menu
As it does not mention bread, butter, wine or water, these items may be charged for separately, along with taxes.

menu

ementa

traditional kale, potato and **chouriço** soup — caldo verde

*

baked salt-cod with potatoes — bacalhau assado no forno com batatas
and e
special dish for children — prato especial p/a criança

*

fruit salad — salada de fruta

*

coffee — café

i Coffee in Portugal is generally good, although the quality can be mixed in hotels. If you want a small, strong, espresso-like coffee, ask for **um café** or **uma bica**. A small, white coffee, is called **um garoto** (or **um pingo**, in the Oporto area). A regular-size milky cup will be **um café com leite**. That same size cup of black coffee will be **um duplo** – a double. A large white coffee is called **um galão**, and is served in a tall glass. Tea is, of course, available as well but will be on the weak side and without milk or lemon. If wanting it strong, ask for **chá forte** (strong tea). For milk, ask for **leite frio** to avoid being served hot milk. Lemon is **limão**. Herb tea is **tisana**. A very pleasant, fragrant caffeine-free beverage is **chá de limão** (lemon tea), consisting of boiling water poured over lemon rind. Drinking chocolate, hot or cold (**chocolate quente/frio**) is another option. In Lisbon, the chocolate at Nicola's, the famous tea/coffee house, is a must.

Specialist tea and coffee shops stock a great variety of those products, but especially coffee – Portugal's preferred drink. Most cafés serve decaffeinated coffee.

People go to cafés all day long, for their caffeine fix and for socialising. Cafés also serve snacks and simple meals.

*Despite the high consumption of wine, beer is a common drink, the most popular being **Sagres** and **Super Bock**. Portuguese beer is served chilled, often with a savoury snack. In Portugal beer is lager. There is no such distinction as lager, ale, bitter, etc. Draught beer is stronger (over 4%) and is sold at beer houses, **cervejarias**, where you can also find food, as a rule. A small glass of draught beer is **um fino** or **uma imperial**. A tankard (approx. 1 pint) is **uma caneca** and a litre tankard is **uma girafa**. You can also find dark ale (**cerveja preta**), bottled. All eating places sell beer, even chains such as KFC and McDonalds.*

popular beer varieties
You can also find all the big names from Britain, Germany and elsewhere, usually produced under licence in Portugal. Sometimes there are special offers from the beer companies –
cerveza plus sandes
(beer and sandwich).

Cervejaria
Beer houses normally serve food, which is often excellent. Some are particularly well-known for their steak, normally served with a fried egg on top, and plenty of gravy-like sauce, with very good chips.

talking

can you recommend a good beer house?
pode recomendar uma boa cervejaria?
pod ruh-koo-men-dar ooñ boh-uh suhr-vay-zhar-ee-uh

I'd like a beer
queria uma cerveja
kree-uh oo-muh suhr-vay-zhuh

what beers do you have?
que cervejas tem?
kuh suhr-vay-zhush tayñ

a small draught beer
uma imperial
oo-muh eeñ-pehr-yal

a large beer (pint)
uma caneca
oo-muh kuh-nay-kuh

a litre of beer
uma girafa
oo-muh zhee-rah-fuh

Wine

_i_ A great effort on the part of winemakers and producers over the last 15 years or so has placed Portuguese wines on a par with some of the best that Europe has to offer. Instead of concentrating mainly on the large internal market, they are now successfully producing a great variety of wines taking into account foreign trends as well. This, together with the natural flair of very competent winemakers and the quality of a vast number of interesting native grapes (with a small percentage of international varieties, such as Cabernet Sauvignon, Merlot, Pinot Noir and Chardonnay) translates into intriguing wines, generally very fruity and easy on the palate. In fact, one of the joys in Portugal is discovering its delicious wines, ideal partners to the country's flavoursome food. Restaurants will have a comprehensive wine list (**lista dos vinhos**) but normally their housewine (**vinho da casa**) is trustworthy, despite its low price. This may be served in a jug, but is often bottled privately for that establishment, perhaps from vineyards belonging to the owner's family.

Red wine is the best, although there are many worthwhile exceptions, such as the lemony and zesty Vinho Verde (e.g. Aveleda), from the Minho region, highly suitable for seafood and for drinking on its own, well chilled. In other regions, some splendid whites are made from Bical grape, Arinto and Fernão Pires (known also as Maria Gomes). As a rule, whites are better drunk young.

D'ouro table wines are normally red, made from the same grapes as port and by the same producers. They are rich and elegant, smooth and fruity, with excellent body and good tannins. They include varieties such as Quinta

do Crasto, Poças, Cockburns and many others. D'ouro is a DOC region (**denominação de origem controlada**), meaning that it must follow very stringent controls and use only native grapes.

Dão, an old classic region, is improving, with more modern, interesting wines than in previous years.

Regional wines are also subject to tight controls but allow some use of grapes other than native ones, which adds extra interest. However, some are single-grape varieties, such as Bairrada's Baga, perfect for drinking with the local dish of suckling pig. Bairrada belongs to the large Beiras region, three provinces which offer, between them, exciting, complex wines.

The region also produces a number of reasonably good champagne-type wines (**espumantes**), from very dry to sweet, such as Raposeira.

Luis Pato

Vinha Pan

2000

VINHO REGIONAL BEIRAS

Criado e engarrafado por
Luis Pato, Anadia, Portugal

PRODUCE OF PORTUGAL

keywords keywords keywords

vinho branco
veen-yoo brañ-koo
white wine

vinho tinto
veen-yoo teeñ-too
red wine

velho
vel-yoo
mature

seco
seh-koo
dry

doce
dohs
sweet

encorpado
en-kor-pah-doo
full-bodied

natural
nah-too-ral
at room temperature

fresco
fresh-koo
chilled

---

talking talking

the wine list, please
a lista de vinhos, por favor
uh leesh-tuh duh veen-yoosh poor fa-vor

what wines do you have?
que vinhos tem?
kuh veen-yoosh tayñ

what are the local wines?
quais são os vinhos da região?
kwysh sowñ oosh veen-yoosh duh ruh-zhowñ

can you recommend a good wine?
pode recomendar um bom vinho?
pod ruh-koo-meñ-dar ooñ boñ veen-yoo

a glass of red wine
um copo de vinho tinto
ooñ ko-poo duh veen-yoo teeñ-too

a glass of white wine
um copo de vinho branco
ooñ ko-poo duh veen-yoo brañ-koo

a bottle of...
uma garrafa de...
oo-muh guh-rra-fuh duh...

red wine
vinho tinto
veen-yoo teeñ-too

white wine
vinho branco
veen-yoo brañ-koo

another bottle
outra garrafa
oh-truh guh-rra-fuh

another glass
outro copo
oh-troo koh-poo

a glass of port
um cálice de Porto
ooñ kah-lee-suh duh por-too

The Ribatejo region, in the centre of Portugal, has a long-standing wine-making tradition. Favoured grapes include Trincadeira Preta and Castelão, also known as Periquita, which practically guarantee excellent wines, such as those by Casa Cadaval, Falua, DFJ and many other producers.

Estremadura, North of Lisbon, and the vast Alentejo region, are home to outstanding, plummy wines, with a judicious amount of oak. In Estremadura look out for wines from Alenquer, Torres Vedras, Colares and Bucelas. Reguengos, Borba and Vidigueira are some of the areas of the Alentejo where modern winemakers have been producing remarkable wines. Esporão, Cartuxa, Quinta do Carmo and Chaminé are among the region's prestigious names. South of Lisbon, the Setúbal peninsula is flanked by Terras do Sado and Palmela, with spicy, very drinkable red wines, and the excellent João Pires white. Setúbal itself is famous for its Moscatel fortified wine, made from locally grown Muscat grapes. The Alambre range is particularly good.

is this wine produced here?
este vinho é produzido aqui?
esht **veen**-yoo e proh-doo-**zee**-doo a-**kee**

is it possible to visit any vineyards?
é possível visitar uma vinha?
e poos-**see**-vel vee-zee-**tar** oo-muh **veen**-yuh

Within the fortified category, Madeira and Port wines are specific to Portugal and have a long tradition associated with the UK. These wines are ideal for many occasions, from aperitif to cheese and dessert, and also with some foods, such as pâté, game, cured meats, roasts and smoked fish, as well as dried fruits, nuts and chocolate. Madeira wines comprise four styles (Sercial, Verdelho, Boal and Malvasia, or Malmsey), from dry to sweet. Their extraordinary bouquet and length makes them very special and their unique maturation system gives them exceptional keeping qualities.

Port wines can be white (dry to sweet) – these should be chilled – or red (Ruby, Tawny and Vintage). Other categories are LBV (late bottled vintage), Vintage Character, and so on. Read the label or ask for guidance. Tawnys (semi-sweet to sweet) are perhaps the most popular. The best indicate their age (10, 20, 30 years), reflected in price and quality. Grapes for Port (many exclusive to the region) are grown along the spectacular, forbidding slopes of the D'ouro river, in the north of Portugal. This was the very first demarcated wine region in the world, back in 1756, and is also the most difficult to cultivate.

Flavours of Portugal

Caldo verde
*soup made with kale, potato,
olive oil and chouriço*
Pastéis de bacalhau *salt cod cakes*
Arroz de pato *(Braga) duck with rice*
Rojões
cubes of marinated pork spiced with cumin
Broa *maize bread*
Pudim Abade de Priscos
egg pudding flavoured with port
Sopa dourada
*dessert of sponge cake, ground
almonds and egg yolks*
Wines *vinho verde Alvarinho, Aveleda*

Rancho
*thick soup made with assorted
meats, vegetables and pasta*
**Bacalhau à lagareiro com
batatas à murro**
*baked salt cod and baked potatoes,
soaked in olive oil*
Açordas
*bread dishes generally with
cured meats, salt cod or shellfish*
Caldeirada de enguias
eel stew
Leitão assado à Bairrada
roast suckling pig from Bairrada region
Chanfana
rich lamb stew
Queijo da Serra
*buttery ewes' cheese from
Estrela Mountain*
Arroz doce
rice pudding
Ovos moles
soft egg sweet (yolks and sugar)
Pastéis de Tentúgal
egg-filled pastries
Wines
Bical, Baga (Bairrada), Dão

Sopa de pedra
stone soup: meat, bean and vegetable soup
Favas à moda do Ribatejo
*broad beans with pork, cured meats,
garlic and coriander*
Cabrito assado *Roast kid*
Fatias de Tomar
sponge slices in syrup
Tigeladas de Abrantes
baked egg custard
Wines
*Reds: Segada, Senda do Vale,
Quinta de Lagoalva*

Açorda de marisco
shellfish bread dish
Rissóis de camarão
creamy prawn rissoles
Sardinhas assadas
*char-grilled sardines served with
boiled potatoes and a tomato,
onion and roast pepper salad*
Salmonetes grelhados
*grilled mullet with a butter
and lemon sauce*
Amêijoas à Bulhão Pato
clams with garlic and fresh coriander

Bacalhau à Brás
*salt cod with onion and potatoes,
bound with eggs*
Bife à café
*steak in creamy sauce topped
with a fried egg*
Pastéis de nata *Rich custard tarts*
Queijadas de Sintra
cheese and cinnamon cakes
Wines
*Periquita, Torres Vedras, J.M. Fonsec
and Moscatel (Muscat) from Setúbal*

Bragança

TRÁS-OS-MONTES

Braga

MINHO

Vila Real

Porto

Aveiro

BEIRAS

Guarda

Coimbra

Castelo
Branco

Leiria

ESTREMADURA

RIBATEJO

Santarém

Lisboa

Setúbal

Évora

TERRAS
DO SADO

ALENTEJO

Beja

ALGARVE

Faro

Sopa de castanhas
chestnut soup with beans and rice
Feijoada
bean stew with pork
Cozido à Portuguesa
*assorted fresh and cured meats
cooked with vegetables*
Presunto de Chaves
smoked cured ham from Chaves
Queijo do Monte
rich ewes' cheese
Nozes *Walnuts*
Azeite *Olive oil*

Sopa de moganga
pumpkin soup
Atum salpresado
*salted tuna steak with red beans,
sweet potatoes, corn and salad*
Cavalas com molho de vilão
marinated, fried mackerel in vinegar sauce
Cozido à madeirense
*boiled assorted fresh and cured
meats and vegetables*
Espetada
*large kebab shared among
the people at the table*
Milho frito *Fried polenta*
Bolo de mel da Madeira
*dark and spicy cake with
molasses and nuts*
Wine *Madeira
(Sercial, Verdelho, Bual, Malmsey)*

Sopa azeda
sour soup with a dash of vinegar
Arroz de lapas *limpet rice*
Garoupa recheada *stuffed grouper*
Polvo guisado *stewed octopus*
Alcatra
beef braised slowly in wine
Inhame *yam*
Pudim de coalhada
rich cheesecake
Covilhetes de leite
custard tarts from Terceira Island
Wine
Verdelho (Pico and Biscoitos)

Sopa à alentejana
*bread soup with garlic, coriander
and poached egg*
Migas
*omelette-like bread dish generally
with cured meats*
Empadas de galinha
chicken pies (Évora)
Ensopado de borrego
rich lamb stew on bread slices
Carne de porco na cataplana
*marinated pork cooked with
clams in a cataplana*
Bolos podres
*cakes made with honey,
olive oil and spices*
Queijadas *cheese tartlets*
Queijo de Nisa
strong ewes' milk cheeses
Queijinhos de Évora
*small and delicious ewes' milk
cheeses from Évora*
Wines *Cartuxa, Esporão,
Cortes de Cima*

Sardinhas *sardines*
Choquinhos com tinta
squid in its own ink
Amêijoas na cataplana
*clams cooked with chouriço
in a cataplana*
Lulas recheadas
small stuffed squid
Arjamolho *gaspacho soup*
Bolos de Dom Rodrigo
egg cakes in syrup
Bolinhos de amêndoa
*almond cakes in fruit shapes,
with egg filling*
Morgado de figo
pressed dried spicy figs
Figos cheios
dried figs stuffed with almonds

There are times when you cannot eat some things. It is as well to warn the waiter before making your choice.

I'm vegetarian
sou vegetariano(a)
*soh vuh-zhay-tuhr-**yah**-noo(-nuh)*

I don't eat meat/pork
não como carne/porco
*nowñ **koh**-moo karn/**por**-koo*

I don't eat fish/shellfish
não como peixe/marisco
*nowñ **koh**-moo paysh/muh-**reesh**-koo*

I'm allergic to shellfish
sou alérgico(a) a marisco
*soh a-**lehr**-zhee-koo(-kuh) uh muh-**reesh**-koo*

I can't eat raw eggs
não posso comer ovos crus
*nowñ **pos**-soo koo-**mehr oh**-voosh kroosh*

I am on a diet
estou de dieta
*shtoh duh dee-**yeh**-tuh*

I am allergic to peanuts
sou alérgico(a) a amendoins
*soh a-**lehr**-zhee-koo(-kuh) uh a-mayñ-doh-**eeñsh***

I can't eat liver
não posso comer fígado
*nowñ **pos**-soo koo-**mehr fee**-guh-doo*

I don't drink alcohol
não tomo bebidas alcoólicas
*nowñ **toh**-moo buh-**bee**-dush al-koo-**ol**-ee-kush*

what is this made with?
de que é feito?
*duh kuh e **fay**-too*

is it raw?
está cru?
shta kroo

is it made with unpasteurised milk?
é feito com leite não-pasteurizado?
*e **fay**-too koñ layt nowñ-push-tay-oo-ree-**zah**-doo*

is it made with vegetable stock?
é feito com caldo vegetal?
*e **fay**-too koñ **kal**-doo vay-zhuh-**tahl***

frito
free-too
fried

cozido
*ko-**zee**-doo*
boiled

a vapor
*uh va-**por***
steamed

assado
*as-**sah**-doo*
roast

molho
mol-yoo
sauce

recheado
*ruh-chay-**ah**-doo*
stuffed

grelhado
*gruhl-**yah**-doo*
grilled

fumado
*foo-**mah**-doo*
smoked

guisado
*gee-**sah**-doo*
stewed

escalfado
*shkul-**fah**-doo*
poached

estufado
*shtoo-**fah**-doo*
braised

no forno
*noo **for**-noo*
cooked in oven

doce
doss
sweet

salgado
*sal-**gah**-doo*
salty

Menu Reader

...à caçadora *hunter-style (poultry or game marinated in wine and garlic)*

...à jardineira *garden-style with vegetables like green beans and carrots*

...à lagareiro *baked dish made with lots of olive oil*

...à marinheira *with white wine, onions and parsley*

...à portuguesa *Portuguese fashion, i.e. with tomato sauce*

abacate *avocado*

abacaxi *pineapple*

abóbora *pumpkin*
  sopa de abóbora *pumpkin soup*

açafrão *saffron*

acelga *swiss chard*

acepipes *appetisers*

acompanhamentos *side dishes*

açorda *typical Portuguese dish with bread*
  açorda com peixe frito *thick bread soup accompanying fried fish*
  açorda de alho *thick bread soup with garlic and beaten egg (generally served with fried fish in traditional restaurants)*

açorda de marisco *thick bread soup with shellfish and a beaten egg, typical of the Lisbon area*

açorda de sável *thick bread soup with shad*

açorda de Sesimbra *thick bread soup with fish, garlic and coriander*

açúcar *sugar*

adocicado *slightly sweet*

agrião *watercress*

água *water*
  água mineral com gás *sparkling mineral water*
  água mineral sem gás *still mineral water*
  água tónica *tonic water*

aguardente *brandy*
  velha *old* or **velhíssima** *very old*

aipo *celery*

albardado *in batter*

alcachofra *artichoke*

fundo de alcachofra *artichoke heart*

alcaparra *caper*

alcatra *braised beef, typical of the Azores*

alecrim *rosemary*

aletria *fine noodles*

alface *lettuce*

alfenim *moulded sugar, a speciality of the Azores*

alheiras *chicken and garlic sausage from Trás-os-Montes*

alho *garlic*
  alho francês *leek*

almoço *lunch*

almôndegas *meatballs*

alperces *apricots*

amargo *bitter*

amarguinha *bitter-almond liqueur made in the Algarve region*

amêijoas *clams*
  amêijoas à Bulhão Pato *clams with garlic and coriander*
  amêijoas ao natural *steamed clams with herbs and lemon butter*
  amêijoas na cataplana *clams cooked in a 'cataplan' pot, with **chouriço** and herbs*

ameixa *plum*
  ameixas de Elvas *preserved greengages from Elvas (Alentejo)*
  ameixa seca *prune*

amêndoas *almonds*
  amêndoas doces *sugared almonds*

amendoim *peanut*

amora *blackberry*

ananás *pineapple*

anchovas *anchovies*

aniz *aniseed liqueur*

ao *in the style of*

aperitivo *aperitif*

areias de Cascais *small cookies from Cascais*

arenque *herring*

arjamolho *kind of gazpacho soup, typical of the Algarve*

arroz branco *plain rice*

arroz de Cabidela *chicken or rabbit highly seasoned risotto*

arroz de ervilhas *pea rice*

arroz de frango *chicken with rice*

arroz de lampreia *lamprey with rice*

arroz de lapas *limpets with rice (typical of the Azores)*

arroz de manteiga *rice with butter*

arroz de marisco *shellfish with rice*

arroz de pato *rice with duck*

arroz de polvo *octopus with rice*

arroz de tomate *tomato rice*

arroz doce *rice pudding Portuguese-style made on top of the stove with lemon rind, vanilla and topped with cinnamon*

arroz no forno *rice cooked in the oven*

arrufadas de Coimbra *sweet buns from Coimbra*

assado *roasted*
  assado no forno *oven-roasted*
  assado no espeto *spit roasted*

atum *tuna fish*
  atum assado *braised tuna with onions and tomatoes*
  atum de cebolada *tuna steak with onions and tomato sauce*
  atum de conserva *canned tuna*
  atum salpresado *salted tuna dish often eaten during festivities in Madeira*

bolos de amêndoas

azeite

bacalhau com natas

aveia *oats*

avelã *hazelnut*

aves *fowl*

azeda *sorrel*
  azedas *sharp Azorean soups, containing a little vinegar*

azedo *sour*

azeite *olive oil*

azeitonas *olives*
  preta *black*
  verde *green*

azevias *half-moon shaped cakes*

bacalhau *salt cod*
  bacalhau à Brás *traditional dish with salt cod, onion and potatoes all bound with scrambled eggs*
  bacalhau à Gomes de Sá *good salt cod dish with layers of potatoes, onions and boiled eggs, laced with olive oil and baked*
  bacalhau à lagareiro *salt cod baked with lots of olive oil*
  bacalhau com natas *salt cod in cream sauce au gratin*
  bacalhau com todos *salt cod poached with potatoes and vegetables*
  bacalhau assado *charcoal-grilled cod*
  bacalhau na brasa *salt cod grilled on charcoal, served with olive oil*

bagaceira *brandy similar to eau-de-vie*

banana *banana*

banha *lard*

barriga de freira *a sweet made with yolks and sugar, slightly caramelised*

batata *potato*
  batata doce *sweet potato*
  batata doce assada *baked sweet potato*
  batatas a murro *potatoes baked in their own skins then soaked in olive oil*
  batatas assadas *baked potatoes*
  batatas fritas *chips*
  batatas cozidas *boiled potatoes*

bacalhau com batatas a murro

batido de fruta *fruit milkshake*
batido de morango *strawberry milkshake*
baunilha *vanilla*
bebida *drink*
bebida sem álcool/não alcoólica *non-alcoholic drink*
bem passado *well done*
berbigão *cockle*
beringela *aubergine*
besugo *sea bream*
beterraba *beetroot*
bica *strong small black coffee*
bifana *hot meat, normally pork tenderloin in a roll*
bife *steak (and chips and perhaps fried egg)*
...bem passado *well done*
...mal passado *medium*
...muito mal passado *rare*
bife à café *steak in cream sauce topped with a fried egg (with chips)*
bife à Portuguesa *steak in mustard sauce topped with a fried egg (with chips)*
bife do lombo *sirloin steak*
bifes de atum *tuna steaks*
bifes de peru *turkey steaks*
bifinhos de vitela *veal fillet served with Madeira sauce*
biscoitos *cookies*

bolo podre

biscoitos de azeite *olive oil biscuits*
bitoque *small steak with fried egg and chips*
bola *layered bread and cured meat pie*
bola de Berlim *doughnut*
bolachas *biscuits*
bolachas de água e sal *water biscuits (crackers)*
boleimas *cakes with a bread dough base with olive oil, sugar, eggs and spices*
bolinhos de bacalhau *cod croquettes*
bolo caseiro *homemade cake*
bolo de chocolate *chocolate cake*
bolo de mel *honey cake*
bolo de mel da Madeira *Madeira molasses cake made with lots of spices and eaten traditionally at Christmas*
bolo de Natal *Christmas fruitcake*
bolo podre *delicious dark cake made with honey, olive oil and spices*
bolo rei *a cake-ring made with a sweet dough with dried and crystallised fruits, eaten at Epiphany*

bolo de arroz

bolos *cakes*
  bolos de Dom Rodrigo *cakes
  made with egg yolks, sugar,
  almonds and cinnamon, and
  sold in little pointed foil parcels
  to keep the syrup inside*
  bolos de ovos *egg cakes*

borracho *young pigeon*

borrego *lamb*

branco *white*
  cerveja branca *white beer*
  vinho branco *white wine*

broa *a crusty rustic maize bread*
  broas de mel *small honey cakes
  eaten at Christmas*
  broas podres de Natal *small
  spicy cakes eaten at Christmas*

brócolos *broccoli*

Bucelas *a type of wine from
  the Estremadura region*

bucho *pork haggis*

cabrito *kid*
  cabrito assado *roast kid with
  a spiced marinade*
  cabrito frito *fried kid*
  cabrito montês *roebuck*
  cabrito à ribatejana *marinated
  roast kid with paprika typical
  of Ribatejo*

caça *game*

cacau *cocoa*

cachorro *hotdog*

cachucho *small sea bream*

café *coffee*
  bica *small, strong black coffee
  (espresso)*
  carioca *small but slightly weaker
  black coffee*
  com leite *white coffee*
  duplo *large cup of black coffee*
  frio *iced coffee*
  galão *large white coffee served
  in a tall glass*
  garoto *small white coffee*
  meia de leite *ordinary size cup
  of half coffee, half milk*
  sem cafeína *decaffeinated*

caipirinha *rum and lemon*

caju *cashew nut*

caldo verde

caldeirada *fish stew*
  caldeirada à fragateira *seafood
  stew, as prepared by fishermen*
  caldeirada de enguias *eel stew*
  caldeirada de peixe *fish stew*

caldo *broth*
  caldo de carne *beef broth*
  caldo de galinha *chicken broth*
  caldo verde *green broth, made
  with shredded kale and potatoes
  with a little **chouriço** and olive oil*

camarões *shrimps*

caneca *medium-sized beer glass*

canela *cinnamon*

canja *chicken soup, thickened
  with rice or small pasta and
  chicken pieces*

capão *capon*

capilé *drink made with iced
  coffee, lemon rind and sugar*

caracóis *snails (small, cooked in
  a tasty broth and served with a
  toothpick)*

caranguejo *crab*

carapau *horse mackerel, served
  whole, fried or grilled*

caril *curry*

carioca *small weak coffee*

carioca de limão *lemon infusion*

carne *meat*
  carne assada *roast meat
  (generally beef, sometimes pork)*

carapau

carne de porco à alentejana
highly seasoned pork dish with clams, typical of the Alentejo
carne de vaca *beef*
carne de vaca assada *roast beef*
carne de vaca à antiga
marinated roast beef, served with new potatoes (speciality from the Azores)
carne de vinha d'alhos *popular festive Madeiran dish, with marinated pork, bread, sweet and new potatoes*
carneiro *mutton*
carnes frias *cold meats*
carta dos vinhos *winelist*
casa de chá *tea-house*
casa de pasto *restaurant serving cheap, homely meals*
castanha *chestnut*
castanhas assadas *roasted chestnuts*
castanhas cozidas *boiled chestnuts with aniseed*
cataplana *meat, fish or shellfish dish cooked with potatoes and a tomato sauce in a cataplana pot in the oven*
cavala *mackerel*
cavalas com molho de vilão
marinated and fried mackerel, served with a reduced marinade (Madeiran speciality)
cebola *onion*

cebolada *fried onion garnish*
cenoura *carrot*
sopa de puré de cenoura *carrot purée soup*
cereja *cherry*
cerveja *beer/lager*
cerveja à pressão *draught beer*
cerveja em garrafa *bottled beer*
cerveja preta *dark ale*
cervejaria *beer house, serving food*
chá *tea*
chá com leite *tea with milk*
chá com limão *tea with lemon*
chá forte *strong tea*
chá de ervas/tisana *herb tea*
chanfana *rich lamb/kid stew*
chanfana da Bairrada *kid stew*
cherne *species of grouper with dark skin, a very prized fish normally served grilled*
chicória *endive*
chila or **gila** *type of pumpkin (spaghetti squash) made into jam, used as a filling for many cakes and desserts all over Portugal*
chispalhada *pig's trotters stew*
chispe com feijão *trotters with beans, cured meats and vegetables*

chouriço assado

chocolate *chocolate*
  chocolate frio *cold chocolate*
  chocolate quente *hot chocolate*
chocos com tinta *cuttlefish in its own ink*
choquinhos *squid*
  choquinhos com tinta *squid in its ink*
chouriço *spicy smoked sausage*
chuchu *marrow*
churrasco *barbecued/cooked on charcoal*
churrasqueira *restaurant specialising in* **frango à piri-piri** *(chicken with piri-piri)*
clarete *light red wine*
coco *coconut*
codorniz *quail*
coelho *rabbit*
  coelho à caçadora *hunter's rabbit or hare, cooked in wine and herbs*
coentrada *with fresh coriander*
coentros *fresh coriander*
cogumelos *mushrooms*
colares *a type of wine from the Estremadura region*
colorau *sweet paprika*
comidas *meals*
cominho *cumin seed*
compota *jam or compote*
congro *conger eel*
conhaque *cognac*
conta *bill*
copo *glass*
coração *heart*
cordeiro *lamb*
costeletas de porco *pork chops*
  costeletas de porco grelhadas *grilled pork chops*

coentros

couve *cabbage*
  couve-de-bruxelas *brussels sprouts*
  couve-flor *cauliflower*
  couve-lombarda *savoy cabbage*
  couve portuguesa *Portuguese cabbage (a large and very tender cabbage), commonly used to accompany poached fish, when in season*
  couve-roxa *red cabbage*
covilhetes de leite *custard tarts from the Azores*
cozido *boiled or poached*
  cozido à Madeirense *boiled Madeira-style pork and vegetables, with pumpkin and couscous*
  cozido à portuguesa *boiled assorted meats, vegetables and rice, served in a large platter*
cravinhos *cloves*
creme *custard*
  creme de leite *milk custard*

costeletas de porco

criação *fowl*

croissants com fiambre *ham-filled croissants*

croissants recheados *filled croissants*

croquetes de carne *meat croquettes*

cru *raw*

cuba livre *rum and coke*

damasco *apricot*

digestivo *digestive e.g. brandy*

dobrada *tripe*
  dobrada à moda do Porto *tripe Oporto fashion in a bean stew*

DOC *(denominação de origem controlada) denotes a very good wine*

doce *sweet*
  doces de amêndoa *marzipan sweets*
  doce de fruta *jam*
  doce de laranja *marmalade*

dourada *sea bream*

eirós *large eel generally fried and served with an* **escabeche** *sauce*

ementa *menu*

empadão de batata *shepherd's pie*

empadas *small chicken or veal pies*

endívia *endive*

enguias de caldeirada *eel stew, typical of Aveiro*

figos

enguias fritas *fried eels*

ensopado *fish or meat stew served on bread slices*

ensopado de borrego *rich lamb stew served on bread slices*

entradas *starters*

entrecosto *entrecôte steak*

erva-doce *aniseed*

ervilhas *peas*
  ervilhas com paio e ovos *peas with garlic sausage and poached eggs*

escabeche *a special sauce containing vinegar, normally served with cold fried fish*

escalfado *poached*
  ovo escalfado *poached egg*

espada *the name given in Madeira to* **peixe espada** *(scabbard fish)*

espadarte *swordfish*
  espadarte fumado *smoked swordfish*

esparguete *spaghetti*

espargos *asparagus*

esparregado *spinach purée with garlic*

especiarias *spices*

esperanças *delicate cakes from the Azores, filled with almonds*

espetada *kebab*

esplanada *open-air restaurant/café*

damascos

espinafre spinach
espumante sparkling wine (champagne type)
estragão tarragon

estufado braised
carne estufada braised meat
esturjão sturgeon
extra-seco extra-dry
farinha flour
farinheira sausage made with flour and pork fat
farófias 'floating islands' made with egg whites and custard sauce
fartes de batata square cakes of sweet potato purée with spices and almonds
fataça grey mullet
fatias de Tomar sponge slices served in a light syrup
fatias douradas slices of bread dipped in egg, fried and covered with sugar and cinnamon
favada à portuguesa broad beans cooked with smoked meats, onions and coriander
favas broad beans
febras thin slices of roast pork
febras de porco à alentejana pork fillet with onions, chouriço and bacon

feijão beans
feijão encarnado red beans
feijão frade black-eyed beans
feijão guisado beans stewed with bacon in a tomato sauce
feijão preto black beans
feijão verde cozido boiled French beans
feijoada bean stew with pork meat and **chouriço**
fiambre ham
fígado liver
fígado de coentrada pork liver with coriander
fígado de galinha chicken liver
fígado de porco de cebolada pork liver with onions
figos figs
figos cheios dried figs stuffed with almonds
figos secos dried figs
filetes de pescada hake fillet in batter
filhós fritters eaten at Christmas
filhós de abóbora pumpkin purée fritters eaten at Christmas
filhoses festive fried cakes sprinkled with sugar and cinnamon or dipped into honey or syrup
fofas do Faial choux-type pastry filled with cream or custard, typical of the Azores

favada à portuguesa

garoupa

folar *a sweet loaf with spices, topped with boiled eggs and eaten at Easter*

folhados de carne *meat puff-pastries*

framboesa *raspberry*

frango *young chicken*
  frango à piri-piri *barbecued tender chicken with chilli*
  frango assado *roast tender chicken*
  frango no churrasco *barbecued tender chicken in a hot sauce (piri-piri)*

fresco/a *cold or fresh*
  uma cerveja muito fresca *a very cool beer*

fressura de porco guisada *pork offal casserole*

fricassé *meat or fish (generally chicken) served with an egg and lemon sauce*

frio *cold*

fritada de peixe *deep-fried mixed fish*

frito *fried*

fruta *fruit*
  fruta cristalizada *candied fruit*
  fruta da época *fruit in season*
  fruta em calda *fruit in syrup*

fumado *smoked*
  salmão fumado *smoked salmon*

fundo de alcachofra *artichoke heart*

galheteiro *cruet stand*

galinha *chicken*

galinhola *woodcock*
  galinhola à Alentejana *Alentejo woodcock, cooked with wine, garlic and seasonings, with a tasty filling*

galão *milky coffee served in a large glass*

gambas *large prawns*
  gambas na chapa *large prawns cooked on the hot plate*

ganso *goose*

garoto *small white coffee*

garoupa *grouper*
  garoupa recheada *stuffed and baked grouper, a typical dish from the Azores*

garrafa *bottle*

gasosa *soft drink with gas*

gaspacho *cold soup with finely cut vegetables*

gelado *ice-cream*

geleia *jelly*

gelo *ice*

gengibre *ginger*

gim *gin*

ginjinha *morello-cherry liqueur typical of Portugal*

girafa *beer glass (equivalent to a pint)*

goiaba *guava*

granizado de café *iced coffee*

grão *chickpeas*
 bacalhau com grão *poached salt cod with boiled chickpeas, seasonings, olive oil and boiled egg*

gratinado *au gratin*

grelhado *grilled*
 grelhado misto *mixed grill*

groselha *red currant*

guisado *stewed*

hortaliça *generic name given to vegetables*
 sopa de hortaliça *vegetable soup*

hortelã *mint*
 chá de hortelã *mint tea*

hortelã-pimenta *peppermint*

imperial *small beer glass*

incluído *included*

inhame *yam, very popular on some of the Azores islands*

iscas *traditional pork liver dish made with wine and garlic*
 iscas com elas *well-seasoned liver dish served with boiled potatoes, a Lisbon speciality*

jantar *dinner*

jardineira *mixed vegetables*

jarro *carafe*

javali *wild boar*

jeropiga *fortified dessert wine*

Joaquinzinhos *small horse-mackerel fried whole (like white-bait), very popular in some restaurants*

lagosta *lobster*

lagostim-do-rio *freshwater crayfish*

lagostins *king prawns*

lampreia *lamprey (an eel-like fish)*
 lampreia de ovos *egg lamprey, a rich dessert*

lanche *afternoon snack consisting of tea and cakes or buttered toast*

lagostins

lapas limpets, popular in Madeira and the Azores
  lapas Afonso limpets served with a tasty onion sauce
laranja orange
  laranja descascada peeled orange, normally served with a sprinkle of sugar
laranjada engarrafada bottled orange juice
laranjada fizzy orange
lavagante species of lobster
lebre hare
legumes vegetables
leitão assado à moda da Bairrada crisply roasted suckling pig from the Bairrada region
leite milk
  leite-creme crème brûlée
  leite frio/quente cold/hot milk
lentilha lentil
licor de leite milk liqueur
  licor de tangerina mandarin liqueur
lima lime
limão lemon
limonada lemonade
língua tongue
  língua estufada braised tongue
linguado sole
  linguado frito fried sole
  linguado grelhado grilled sole
linguiça pork sausage with paprika
lista dos vinhos wine list
lombinho de porco pork loin
lombo de porco pork fillet
louro bay leaf
lulas squid
  lulas à Algarvia squid in garlic, Algarve style
  lulas cheias local name in the Algarve for **lulas recheadas** (stuffed squid)
  lulas guisadas stewed squid
  lulas recheadas small squid stuffed with rice and seasonings
maçã apple
  maçã assada large baked russet apple

maçapão marzipan
macarrão macaroni

macedónia de frutas mixed fruit salad
madeira wine from Madeira
maduro mature
maionese mayonnaise
malagueta hot pepper

maçãs assadas

mal passado *rare*

mandioca *cassava root*

manga *mango*

manjar celeste *sweet made with eggs, bread crumbs, almonds and sugar*

manjericão *basil*

manteiga *butter*

mãozinhas de vitela guisadas *stewed calves' trotters*

maracujá *passion fruit*

marinado/a *marinated*

marisco *shellfish*

marisqueira *a restaurant or bar specialising solely in shellfish*

marmelada *quince jam – excellent with cheese*

marmelo *quince, a popular fruit, often baked*

massa *pasta*

medalhão *medallion*

medronheira *strawberry-tree fruit liqueur*

meia-dose *half-portion*

meia garrafa *half bottle*

meio-doce *medium-sweet*

meio-seco *medium-dry*

mel *honey*

mel de cana *molasses*

melancia *watermelon*

melão *melon*

melão com presunto *melon with cured ham slices, a starter*

menu turístico *budget tourists' menu, good value menu based on local dishes*

merenda *afternoon snack consisting of tea and cakes or buttered toast*

merendinha *pastry filled with* **chouriço** *or* **presunto** *(ham)*

merengue *meringue*

mero *red grouper fish*

mexilhões *mussels*

migas *bread cooked with well-seasoned ingredients to form a kind of omelette*

migas à alentejana *thick bread soup with pork meat and garlic*

migas à lagareiro *bread cooked with cabbage, salt cod and olive oil*

migas de pão de milho *thick maize bread soup with olive oil and garlic*

mil-folhas *millefeuille (custard pastry)*

milho *corn (maize)*

milho doce *sweetcorn*

milho frito *polenta fried in cubes, popular in Madeira*

miolos *brains*

misto *mixed*

molho *sauce*

molho béchamel *béchamel sauce*

molho de caril *curry sauce*

molho de escabeche *a special sauce containing vinegar, normally served with cold fried fish*

molho de tomate *tomato sauce*

molho tártaro *piquant mayonnaise with capers, gherkins and olives*

morangos *strawberries*

morcela *spicy black pudding*

morgado de figo *dried pressed figs with spices*

moscatel de Setúbal *medium-sweet muscat wine*

mostarda mustard

mousse de chocolate
chocolate mousse

nabiça turnip greens

nabo turnip

...na brasa char-grilled

...na cataplana stewed in cataplana vessel (typical double-wok pot used in the Alentejo and Algarve)

...na frigideira sautéed or fried

natas cream

nata batida whipped cream

natural plain, without dressing or served at room temperature (usually wine or water)

...no espeto kebab/on the spit

...no forno roasted or cooked in the oven

nozes walnuts

nozes de Cascais caramelised walnuts, from Cascais

óleo vegetable oil

omeleta de cogumelos mushroom omelette

omeleta de fiambre ham omelette

omeleta de queijo cheese omelette

omeleta simples plain omelette

ostras oysters

ouriço-do-mar sea-urchin

ovas fish roe

ovos eggs

ovos cozidos boiled eggs

ovos escalfados poached eggs

ovos estrelados fried eggs

ovos mexidos scrambled eggs

ovos moles soft egg sweet

ovos quentes soft-boiled eggs

paio thick smoked sausage made with lean meat

palha de Abrantes sweet made with eggs, looking like straw

nozes

pão

panados *slices of meat coated in egg and breadcrumbs and fried*

pão *bread*
  pão de centeio *rye bread*
  pão de forma *sliced bread for toast*
  pão-de-ló *light sponge cake*
  pão de milho *maize bread*
  pão saloio *country-style bread*
  pãozinho *roll*

papaia *papaya*

papas *polenta soup*
  papas de milho doces *sweet polenta*

papo seco *bread roll*

papos de anjo *small egg cakes with syrup*

pargo *red bream*

parrilhada *grilled fish*

passas de uva *raisins*

pastéis *tarts, cakes, pasties*
  pastéis de arroz *rice tarts from the Azores*
  pastéis de bacalhau *salt cod cakes*
  pastéis de carne *meat pasties*
  pastéis de feijão *tarts made with beans, eggs and almonds*
  pastéis de nata/de Belém *egg custard tarts from Belém (Lisbon)*
  pastéis de Santa Clara *pastries with a filling of almonds, egg yolk and sugar*

pastéis

  pastéis de Tentugal *small pastries with an egg filling*

pastelaria *pâtisserie/pastry shop*

pastel de massa tenra *meat pasty*

pataniscas (de bacalhau) *salt cod fritters*

paté de fígado *liver pâté*

pato *duck*
  pato assado com arroz *roast duck with rice*

pé de porco com feijão *pigs' trotters with beans*

peito *breast*

peixe *fish*
  peixe assado/cozido/ frito/grelhado *baked/poached/ fried/grilled fish*
  peixe e marisco *fish and shellfish*
  peixe espada *scabbard fish*

pastéis de bacalhau

peixe espada

peixe espada frito fried scabbard fish
peixe espada grelhado grilled scabbard fish
peixe-galo John Dory
peixinhos da horta French beans fried in batter
pepino cucumber
pequeno almoço breakfast
pêra pear
percebes barnacles, highly prized shellfish
perdiz partridge
perdiz à Montemor Montemor-style partridge, cooked with wine and spices
perdiz com couve lombarda partridge with cabbage
perna leg
perna de porco au forno roast pork

pernil ham
peru turkey
pescada hake
pescada com todos hake poached with potatoes and vegetables
pescadinhas de rabo na boca whole rolled-up small fried hake
pêssego peach
pêssego careca nectarine
petisco savoury or snack
pezinhos de porco de coentrada pork trotters with coriander and garlic
picante spicy
pimenta pepper (spice)
pimentos peppers
pimentos assados grilled peppers
pinhão pine kernel
pinhoada pinenut brittle
pinhões peanuts
piri-piri chilli sauce
polvo octopus
polvo grelhado grilled octopus
polvo guisado stewed octopus
pombo pigeon
porco pork
porco à alentejana traditional dish with pork, clams and herbs

pescadinha

pescada frita

pêssego

porco assado roast pork
  porco preta black pork, only
  available at certain times of the
  year and has a completely
  different taste to ordinary **leitao**,
  roast suckling pig
  porco assado roast pork
posta à mirandesa spit-roasted
  veal, Miranda-style
pouco picante mild
prato dish
  prato do dia dish of the day
  prato principal main dish
  pratos de carne meat dishes
preço price
pregado turbot
prego steak in a roll
  prego com fiambre steak with
  sliced ham
  prego no pão steak roll
  prego no prato steak with fried
  egg and chips served on a plate
presunto cured ham
preta dark
  cerveja preta dark beer
pudim Abade de Priscos rich
  egg pudding flavoured with port
  and lemon
pudim de bacalhau salt cod loaf
  served with tomato sauce
pudim da casa restaurant's own
  dessert (often crème caramel)
pudim de coalhada popular
  Azorean rich, fresh cheese
  pudding

pudim de pão bread pudding
pudim de queijo cheese pudding
pudim de requeijão ricotta-type
  cheese pudding
pudim flan crème caramel
pudim Molotov egg-white
  pudding with egg sauce or
  caramel
puré de batata mashed potato
queijadas de Évora cheese tarts
  made with cheese from ewes' milk
queijadas da Madeira small
  Madeiran cheese cakes
queijadas de requeijão ricotta-
  type cheese tarts
queijadas de Sintra little cheese
  cakes with cinnamon made in
  Sintra
queijinhos de amêndoa little
  almond cheeses
queijinhos do céu egg yolk and
  sugar sweets
queijinhos frescos small fresh
  cheeses (cows', ewes' or goats'
  milk)
queijinhos secos small dried
  cheeses
queijo cheese
  queijo de Alverca small cheese
  from Alverca, near Lisbon

porco assado

queijo

queijo cabreiro *goats' cheese*
queijo cardiga *cheese made from ewes' and goats' milk*
queijo da Ilha *cheddar-type cheese from the Azores, also known as* **queijo de São Jorge**
queijo de Évora *small ewes' cheese from Évora*
queijo da Serra *buttery cheese from Estrela Mountain, a soft, runny cheese made with ewes' milk*
queijo de Azeitão *hard or soft cheese made with ewes' milk*
queijo de cabra *goats' cheese*
queijo de Nisa *a rich ewe's cheese from Nisa (Alentejo)*
queijo de ovelha *small, dried ewes' milk cheeses*
queijo fresco *fresh cheese*
queijo saloio *small cheese made with ewes' milk or a mixture of goats' and ewes' milk*
quente *hot*
quiabo *okra*
rabaçal *mild cheese from the Coimbra region*

rabanada *french toast*
rabanete *radish*
raia *skate*
rancho *a substantial soup*
recheado com... *stuffed/ filled with…*
recheio *stuffing*
regiões demarcadas *demarcated wine regions*
repolho *cabbage*
requeijão *fresh curd cheese resembling ricotta*
rim (rins) *kidney*
rins à Madeira *kidneys served in Madeira wine sauce*
rins com vinho do Porto *kidneys in port wine sauce*
rissóis de camarão/peixe *shrimp or fish rissoles*
robalo *sea bass*
rojões *crisp pieces of marinated pork*
romas *pomegranate*

sal *salt*

salada *salad*
  salada de feijão frade *black-eyed bean salad, with boiled egg, olive oil and seasonings*
  salada de fruta *fruit salad*
  salada de polvo *a starter with cold octopus, seasoned with olive oil, coriander, onion and vinegar*
  salada mista *mixed salad (tomato, lettuce, cucumber, onion)*
  salada russa *Russian salad*

salgados *savouries (snacks)*

salmão *salmon*
  salmão fumado *smoked salmon*
  salmonetes grelhados *grilled red mullet in a butter and lemon sauce*

saloio *small cheese made from ewes' or goats' milk, often served as a pre-starter to a meal in the Lisbon region*

salpicão *slices of large* **chouriço**

salsa *parsley*

salsichas *sausages*

salteado *sautéed*

salva *sage*

sandes *sandwich*
  sandes de fiambre *cooked ham sandwich*
  sandes de lombo *steak sandwich*

sandes e sumo

sandes de presunto *cured ham sandwich*

sandes de queijo *cheese sandwich*

sandes mista *ham and cheese sandwich*

santola *spider crab*

sapateira *crab (generally dressed)*

sarapatel *a highly seasoned Madeiran dish made with pork blood and liver*

sarda *mackerel*

sardinhas assadas *char-grilled sardines*

sapateira

sardinhas

sardinhas na telha *oven-baked sardines cooked on a roof tile with olive oil and seasoning*

sável *shad*

seco *dry*

sericaia *baked custard with cinnamon*

serpa *a type of ewes' milk cheese from the Alentejo region*

serra *a creamy cheese made from ewes' milk, from the Serra da Estrela region*

serviço incluído *service included*

sidra *cider*

simples *neat (as in 'neat whisky')*

sobremesas *desserts*

solha *plaice*

sonho *doughnut-type small fried cake, dipped in sugar and cinnamon*

sopa *soup*

  sopa à alentejana *soup Alentejo-style, made with chunks of bread, olive oil, fresh coriander and garlic, topped with poached egg*

  sopa azeda de feijão *bean soup with vegetables and bread, sweet potatoes, cinnamon and a spoonful of vinegar (Azores)*

sopa de cabeça de peixe *fish head soup, using the head of a large fish, tomatoes, potatoes, stale bread and seasonings (Algarve)*

sopa de camarão *prawn soup*

sopa de castanhas piladas *hearty soup made with dried chestnuts, beans and rice*

sopa de ervilhas *pea soup*

sopa de espinafres *spinach soup*

sopa de feijão *bean soup with vegetables*

sopa de feijão frade *black-eyed bean soup*

sopa de feijão verde *green bean soup*

sopa de funcho *fennel soup with beans and bacon fat (Azores)*

sopa de grão *chickpea soup*

sopa de legumes *vegetable soup*

sopa de marisco *shellfish soup*

sopa de moganga *Madeiran pumpkin soup*

sopa de pedra *a rich soup with lots of meat, beans and vegetables*

sopa de peixe *fish soup*

sopa de poejos *pennyroyal soup with eggs (Alentejo)*

sopa de rabo de boi *oxtail soup*

sopa de tomate *tomato soup*

sopa do dia *soup of the day*

sopa do Espírito Santo *'Holy Spirit' soup made with meats, vegetables, bread, herbs and spices (Azores)*

sopa dos campinos *salt cod and tomato soup*

sopa dourada *dessert made with egg yolks*

sopa e um papo-seco *soup and roll*

sopa seca *thick bread soup with meats*

sorvete *sorbet*

sumo de fruta *fruit juice*

  ananás *pineapple*

  laranja *orange*

  maçã *apple*

  pêra *pear*

  pêssego *peach*

  tomate *tomato*

  uva *grape*

suspiros *meringues*

tainha *grey mullet*

tâmara *date*

tamboril *monkfish*

tangerina *mandarin*

tarte de amêndoa *almond tart*

tarte de limão *lemon tart*

tarte de maçã *apple tart*

tasca *small taverna serving cheap food and drink*

tasquinha *small taverna serving cheap food and drink*

tempero *seasoning*

tenro *tender*

tibornas *slices of freshly baked bread sprinkled with coarse sea salt and olive oil*

tigeladas de Abrantes *individually baked custards in special cups*

tinto *red wine*

tisana *herbal tea*

tisana de camomila *camomile tea*

tisana de Lúcia-Lima *vervaine tea*

tomate *tomato*

toranja *grapefruit*

tornedó *prime cut of beef*

torradas *toast*

uvas

Torres Vedras *red wine from the Estremadura region*

torta *swiss roll*

torta de laranja *orange sponge roll*

torta de Viana *a sponge roll filled with a rich egg sweet*

tosta *toasted sandwich*

  tosta mista *ham and cheese toasted sandwich*

toucinho *bacon*

toucinho do céu *'bacon from heaven', an egg and almond pudding*

tremoços *lupin seeds, commonly consumed with beer*

tripas à moda do Porto *tripe stew with beans and various meats, Oporto-style*

trufa *truffle*

truta *trout*

  trutas à moda do Minho *trout cooked in wine and rich seasonings*

  truta de Barroso *traditional northern dish of fried trout stuffed with ham*

tutano *marrow*

uísque *whisky*

uvas *grapes*

vaca *beef*

vagens *runner beans*

variado *assorted*

verdelho *local Azorean wine*

vermute *vermouth*

vieira *scallop*

vinagre *vinegar*

vinha d'alhos *marinated in wine and garlic*

vinho abafado *locally made fortified wine*

vinho adamado *sweet wine*

vinho branco *white wine*

vinho branco seco *dry white wine*

vinho branco meio-seco *medium-dry white wine*

vinho da casa *house wine*

vinho espumante *sparkling wine*

vinho generoso *fortified wine*

vinho Moscatel *muscat wine*

vinho regional/da região *local wine*

vinho tinto *red wine*

vinho tinto encorpado *full-bodied red wine, ideal with red meats*

vinho tinto meio-encorpado *medium-bodied red wine, ideal with salted fish dishes or light meats*

vinho tinto velho *mature red wine, ideal with red meats*

vinhos do Porto

vinho verde *dry, sparkling 'green' wine made with slightly unripe grapes from the Minho region*

vinhos espumantes *sparkling wines*

vinhos da Madeira *madeira wines*

vinhos do Porto *port wines*

vitela *veal*

vitela no espeto *veal cooked on the spit*

xarope *syrup*

xarope de groselha *blackcurrant syrup*

xarope de morango *strawberry syrup*

xerez *sherry*

A

a um (uma)
abbey a abadia
able: to be able (to) poder
abortion o aborto
about (roughly) mais ou menos
  a book about... um livro sobre...
  about ten o'clock por volta das dez
above acima de
abroad adv no estrangeiro
  to go abroad ir ao estrangeiro
abscess um abcesso
accelerator o acelerador
accent o acento
  (pronunciation) a pronúncia
to accept aceitar
  (approve of) aprovar
access o acesso
  wheelchair access o acesso para
  cadeiras de rodas
accident o acidente
accommodation o alojamento
to accompany acompanhar
account (bill) a conta
  (in bank) a conta (bancária)
account number o número da conta
accountant o/a contabilista
to ache doer
  my head aches dói-me a cabeça
  it aches dói-me
acid o ácido
actor/actress o actor/a actriz
to adapt adaptar
adaptor (electrical) o adaptador
adder a cobra
address a morada
  what is your address? qual é a sua
  morada?
address book a agenda
admission charge/fee o preço de
  entrada
admit: to admit to hospital ingresar
  no hospital
adult o/a adulto(a)
  for adults para adultos
advance: in advance antecipadamente
advertisement o anúncio
to advise aconselhar
aerial a antena
aeroplane o avião
aerosol o aerossol
afraid: to be afraid of ter medo de
after depois
  after lunch depois do almoço
afternoon a tarde
  this afternoon esta tarde

  in the afternoon à tarde
  tomorrow afternoon amanhã à tarde
aftershave o aftershave
again outra vez
against prep contra
  I am against that sou contra isso
age a idade
  old age a idade avançada
agency a agência
ago: 2 days ago há 2 dias
to agree concordar
agreement o acordo
AIDS a SIDA
air bag o airbag
air bed o colchão de ar
air conditioning o ar condicionado
  is there air conditioning? tem ar
  condicionado?
air freshener o purificador do ambiente
airline a linha aérea
airmail a via aérea
airplane o avião
airport o aeroporto
airport bus o autocarro do aeroporto
air ticket o bilhete de avião
aisle (plane, theatre, etc) a coxia
alarm o alarme
alarm clock o despertador
alcohol o álcool
alcohol-free sem álcool
alcoholic adj alcoólico(a)
all todo(a), todos(as)
allergic alérgico(a)
  I'm allergic to sou alérgico(a) a
allergy a alergia
alley a travessa
to allow permitir
  to be allowed estar permitido
all right está bem
  are you all right? você está bem?
almond a amêndoa
almost quase
alone sozinho(a)
alphabet o alfabeto
already já
also também
altar o altar
aluminium foil a folha de alumínio
always sempre
a.m. da manhã
amber (light) amarelo(a)
ambulance a ambulância
America os Estados Unidos
American (norte-) americano/a
amount: total amount o total

anaesthetic a anestesia
  general anaesthetic a anestesia geral
  local anaesthetic a anestesia local
anchor a âncora
anchovy a anchova
ancient antigo(a)
and e
angel o anjo
angina a angina de peito
angry zangado(a)
animal um animal
aniseed a erva-doce
ankle o tornozelo
anniversary o aniversário
to announce anunciar
announcement o anúncio
annual anual
another um(a) outro(a)
  another beer? mais uma cerveja?
answer *n* a resposta
to answer responder
answerphone o gravador de chamadas
ant a formiga
antacid o antiácido
antibiotic o antibiótico
antifreeze o anticongelante
antihistamine o anti-histamínico
anti-inflammatory o anti-inflamatório
antiques as antiguidades
antique shop a loja de antiguidades
antiseptic o antiséptico
any *(some)* algum(a)
  (negative) nenhum(a)
  I haven't any money não tenho
  dinheiro
  have you any apples? tem maçãs?
anyone *(in questions)* alguém
  (negative) ninguém
anything *(in questions)* alguma coisa
  (negative) nada
  I haven't got anything não tenho
  nada
anywhere *(in any place at all)* em qualquer
  parte
  (negative) em nenhuma parte
  I haven't seen him anywhere não o
  vi em nenhuma parte
apartment o apartamento
aperitif o aperitivo
appendicitis a apendicite
apple a maçã
application form o formulário de
  requerimento
appointment *(meeting)* o encontro
  (doctor) a consulta
  (hairdresser) a hora marcada
  I have an appointment tenho un
  encontro marcado

approximately aproximadamente
apricot o damasco
April Abril
architect o/a arquitecto(a)
architecture a arquitectura
arm o braço
armbands *(to swim)* as braçadeiras
armchair a poltrona
aromatherapy a aromaterapia
to arrange organizar
to arrest prender
arrival a chegada
to arrive chegar
art a arte
art gallery a galeria de arte
arthritis a artrite
artichoke a alcachofra
artificial artificial
artist o/a artista
ashtray o cinzeiro
to ask *(question)* perguntar
  (to ask for something) pedir
asparagus o espargo
asleep: he/she is asleep está
  adormecido(a)
aspirin a aspirina
  soluble aspirin aspirina efervescente
asthma a asma
  I have asthma tenho asma
at em ; a
  at home em casa
  at 8 o'clock às oito
  at once imediatamente
  at night à noite
Atlantic Ocean o oceano Atlântico
ATM Multibanco®
to attack atacar
attractive *(person)* atraente
aubergine a beringela
auction o leilão
audience a platéia
August Agosto
aunt a tia
au pair o/a au pair
Australia a Austrália
Australian australiano(a)
author o/a autor(a)
automatic automático(a)
automatic car o carro automático
autumn o outono
available disponível
avalanche a avalancha
avenue a avenida
average a média
  (adj) médio(a)
avocado o abacate
to avoid evitar

awake: to be awake estar acordado(a)
awful terrível
axle o eixo

B

baby o bebé
baby food a comida de bebé
baby milk o leite infantil
baby's bottle o biberão
baby seat (in car) o assento do bebé
baby-sitter o/a babysitter
baby-sitting service serviço de
  baby-sitting
baby wipes as toalhitas
bachelor o solteiro
back (of body) as costas
backache a dor de costas
backpack a mochila
back seat o assento traseiro
bacon o toucinho
bad (weather, news) má (mau)
  (fruit, vegetables) podre
badminton o badminton
bag o saco
  (handbag) o saco de mão
  (case) a mala
baggage a bagagem
baggage allowance o peso limite
  da bagagem
baggage reclaim a recolha
  de bagagem
bait (for fishing) a isca
baked assado
baker's a padaria
balcony a varanda
bald (person) calvo(a) ; careca
  (tyre) careca
ball a bola
ballet o ballet
balloon o balão
banana a banana
band (music) a banda musical
bandage a ligadura
bank o banco
  (river) a margem
bank account a conta bancária
banknote a nota (bancária)
bankrupt falido(a)
bar o bar
bar of chocolate a barra de chocolate
barbecue o churrasco
  to have a barbecue fazer um
  churrasco
barber o barbeiro
to bark ladrar
barn o celeiro

barrel o barril
basement a cave
basil o manjericão
basket o cesto
basketball o basquete(bol)
basketwork os artigos de vime
bat (animal) o morcego
  (for table tennis) a raqueta
bath o banho
  to have a bath tomar banho
bathing cap a touca de banho
bathroom a casa de banho
  with bathroom com casa de banho
battery (for car) a bateria
  (for torch, radio, etc) a pilha
bay a baía
bayleaf a folha de louro
B&B o quarto com pequeno-almoço
  (place) a pensão
to be ser ; estar
beach a praia
  private beach a praia particular
  sandy beach a praia arenosa
  nudist beach a praia naturista
beach hut a barraca
bean o feijão
  broad bean a fava
  French/green bean o feijão verde
  kidney bean o feijão encarnado
  soya bean o feijão de soja
bear (animal) o urso
beard a barba
beautiful belo(a) ; lindo(a)
beauty salon o salão de beleza
because porque
to become tornar-se
bed a cama
  double bed a cama de casal
  single bed a cama de solteiro
  sofa bed o sofá-cama
  twin beds as camas separadas
bedding a roupa de cama
bedclothes a roupa de cama
bedroom o quarto
bee a abelha
beef a carne de vaca ; a vitela
beer a cerveja
beetroot a beterraba
before antes (de)
  before breakfast antes do pequeno-
  almoço
beggar o/a mendigo(a)
to begin começar
behind atrás (de)
  behind the bank atrás do banco
beige bege
to believe acreditar

bell *(door)* a campainha
(church) o sino
to belong to pertencer a
below debaixo (de)
(less than) abaixo (de)
belt o cinto
bend *(in road)* a curva
berth *(in ship)* o beliche
beside *(next to)* ao lado (de)
beside the bank ao lado do banco
best: the best o/a melhor
to bet on apostar em
better (than) melhor (do que)
between entre
bib o babador
bicycle a bicicleta
by bicycle de bicicleta
bicycle lock o cadeado da bicicleta
bicycle repair kit o estojo de
ferramentas
bidet o bidé
big grande
bigger (than) maior que
bike *(motorbike)* a moto
(pushbike) a bicicleta
mountain bike a bicicleta de
montanha
bikini o bikini
bill *(in hotel, restaurant)* a conta
(for work done) a factura
(gas, telephone) a conta
bin o caixote do lixo
bin liner o saco do lixo
binoculars os binóculos
bird o pássaro
biro a esferográfica
birth o nascimento
birth certificate a certidão de
nascimento
birthday o aniversário
happy birthday parabéns
my birthday is on... faço anos no...
birthday card o cartão de aniversário
birthday present a prenda de anos
biscuits as bolachas
bit: a bit (of) um bocado (de)
bite *(snack)* a merenda; o lanche
(of animal) a mordedura
(of insect) a picada
let's have a bite to eat vamos comer
algo
to bite *(animal)* morder
(insect) picar
bitten *(by animal)* mordido(a)
(by insect) picado(a)

bitter amargo(a)
black preto(a)
blackberry a amora silvestre
blackcurrant a groselha
blank o espaço em branco
blanket o cobertor
bleach a lixívia
to bleed sangrar
blender *(for food)* o liquidificador
blind *(person)* cego(a)
blind *(for window)* a persiana
blister a bolha
block of flats o prédio de
apartamentos
blocked *(pipe, sink)* entupido(a)
(road) cortada ao trânsito
blond *(person)* louro(a)
blood o sangue
blood group o grupo sanguíneo
blood pressure a tensão arterial
blood test a análise ao sangue
blouse a blusa
blow-dry o brushing
to blow-dry fazer um brushing
blue azul
dark blue azul escuro
light blue azul claro
blunt *(knife, etc)* embotado(a)
boar o javali
boarding card o cartão de embarque
boarding house a pensão
boat o barco
boat trip a viagem de barco
body o corpo
to boil ferver
boiler a caldeira
boiled cozido(a)
bomb a bomba
bone o osso
fish bone a espinha
bonfire a fogueira
bonnet *(of car)* a capota
book o livro
book of tickets a caderneta
de bilhetes
to book reservar
booking a reserva
booking office a bilheteira
bookshop a livraria
boot *(of car)* o porta-bagagem
boots as botas
border a fronteira
boring aborrecido(a)
boss o/a chefe
(employer) o patrão/a patroa

both ambos(as)
bottle a garrafa
  a bottle of wine uma garrafa de vinho
  a half bottle uma meia-garrafa
bottle opener o abre-garrafas
bowl *(for washing)* a bacia
  (for food) a tigela
bow tie o laço
box a caixa
box office a bilheteira
boxer shorts os boxers
boy o rapaz
boyfriend o namorado
bra o soutien
bracelet a pulseira
brain o cérebro
to brake travar
brake fluid o óleo dos travões
brake light a luz de travagem
brake shoes as sapatas
brakes os travões
branch *(of tree)* o ramo
  (of business, etc) a sucursal
brand *(make)* a marca
brandy o conhaque
brass o latão
bread o pão
  French bread o cacete
  sliced bread o pão de forma
  wholemeal bread o pão integral
breadcrumbs o pão ralado
bread roll o papo-seco ; pãozinho
to break quebrar
breakable frágil
breakdown *(car)* a avaria
  (nervous) o colapso nervoso
breakdown service o pronto-socorro
breakdown van o pronto-socorro
breakfast o pequeno-almoço
breast *(chicken)* o peito
to breastfeed amamentar
to breathe respirar
brick o tijolo
bride a noiva
bridegroom o noivo
bridge a ponte
  (game) o bridge
briefcase a pasta
bright brilhante
Brillo pad® a esponja de aço
brine a salmoura
to bring trazer
Britain a Grã-Bretanha
British britânico(a)
broad largo(a)
broccoli os brócolos

brochure a brochura
broken partido(a)
broken down *(car, etc)* avariado(a)
bronchitis a bronquite
bronze o bronze
brooch o broche
broom a vassoura
brother o irmão
brother-in-law o cunhado
brown castanho(a)
bruise a nódoa negra
brush a escova
Brussels sprouts as couves-de-Bruxelas
bubble bath a espuma para o banho
bucket o balde
buffet car o vagão restaurante
to build construir
building o edifício
building site o terreno de construção
bulb *(light)* a lâmpada
bull o touro
bullfight a tourada
bullfighter o toureiro
bullring a praça de touros
bumbag a carteira de cintura
bumper *(on car)* o pára-choques
bunch *(of flowers)* o ramo
  (of grapes) o cacho
bungee jumping o bungee jumping
bureau de change a casa de câmbio
burger um hambúrguer
burglar o ladrão/a ladra
burglar alarm o alarme de roubo
burglary o roubo
to burn queimar
burnt *(food)* queimado(a)
burst rebentado(a)
bus o autocarro
bus pass o passe de autocarro
bus station a estação de autocarros
bus stop a paragem de autocarros
bus ticket o bilhete de autocarro
bus tour a excursão de autocarro
business os negócios
  on business de negócios
business card o cartão-de-visita
business class a classe executiva
businessman/woman o homem/
  a mulher de negócios
business trip a viagem de negócios
busy ocupado(a)
but mas
butcher's o talho
butter a manteiga
button o botão
to buy comprar

by por
  (near) perto (de)
  (next to) ao lado (de)
  by bus de autocarro
  by car de carro
  by ship de barco
  by train de comboio
bypass *(road)* o desvio

C

cab *(taxi)* o táxi
cabaret o cabaré
cabbage a couve
cabin *(on boat)* o camarote
cabin crew os tripulantes de cabine
cable car o teleférico
cable TV a televisão por cabo
café o café
  internet café o cibercafé
cafetière a cafeteira
cake o bolo
cake shop a pastelaria
calamine lotion a loção de calamina
calculator a calculadora
calendar o calendário
calf *(young cow)* o vitelo
to call chamar
call *(telephone)* uma chamada
  a long-distance call uma chamada
  interurbana
calm calmo(a); tranquilo(a)
camcorder a camcorder
camera a máquina fotográfica
camera case o estojo da máquina
  fotográfica
to camp acampar
camping gas o gás para campismo
camping stove o fogão portátil; o
  fogão de campismo
campsite o parque de campismo
can *(verb – to be able)* poder
  I/we can posso/podemos
  I/we cannot nao posso
  can I...? posso ...?
  can we...? podemos ...?
can a lata
canned goods as conservas
can opener o abre-latas
Canada o Canadá
Canadian canadiano(a)
canal o canal
to cancel cancelar
cancellation o cancelamento
cancer o cancro
candle a vela
canoe a canoa

to go canoeing fazer canoagem
cap *(hat)* o boné
  (diaphragm) o diafragma
capital *(city)* a capital
cappuccino o cappuccino
car o carro
  car alarm o alarme do carro
  car ferry o barco de passagem
  car hire o aluguer de automóveis
  car insurance o seguro de automóveis
  car keys as chaves do carro
  car park o parque de estacionamento
  car parts as peças sobressalentes
  car radio o rádio do carro
  car seat *(for children)* o banco para
  crianças
  car wash a lavagem automática
carafe a garrafa
caravan a caravana
carburettor o carburador
card *(business)* o cartão (de visita)
  (greetings) o cartão
  (playing) a carta de jogar
cardboard o cartão
cardigan o casaco de lã
careful cuidadoso(a)
  to be careful ter cuidado
  be careful! cuidado!
carnation o cravo
carpet a carpete ; alcatifa
  (rug) o tapete
carriage a carruagem
carrot a cenoura
to carry transportar
carton o pacote
case *(suitcase)* a mala
cash o dinheiro
to cash *(cheque)* levantar
cash desk a caixa
cashier o/a caixa
cash machine a caixa automática
casino o casino
casserole *(dish)* o tacho
  (meal) o guisado (no forno)
cassette a cassete
cassette player o toca-fitas
castle o castelo
casualty department o Serviço
  de Urgências
cat o gato
cat food a comida para gatos
catacombs as catacumbas
catalogue o catálogo
to catch *(bus, train, etc)* apanhar
cathedral a catedral
Catholic católico(a)

cauliflower a couve-flor
cave a caverna
cavity *(in tooth)* a cárie dentária
CD o disco compacto
CD player o leitor de discos compactos
ceiling o tecto
celery o aipo
cellar a cave
cellphone o telefone celular
cemetery o cemitério
centimetre o centímetro
central central
central heating o aquecimento central
central locking o fecho centralizado
cent o cêntimo *(i.e. 1/100th of a euro)*
centre o centro
century o século
   19th century o século dezanove
   21st century o século vinte e um
ceramics a cerâmica
cereal *(for breakfast)* os cereais
certain certo(a)
certificate o certificado
chain a corrente
chair a cadeira
chairlift o teleférico
chalet o chalé
challenge o desafio
chambermaid a empregada de quarto
Champagne o champanhe
change *(loose coins)* o dinheiro trocado
   (money returned) o troco
to change trocar ; mudar
   to change money trocar dinheiro
   to change (clothes) mudar de roupa
   to change (train, etc) mudar
changing room o gabinete de provas
Channel: the English Channel o Canal
   da Mancha
chapel a capela
charcoal o carvão
charge o custo
   cover charge o couvert
   please charge it to my account por
   favor ponha na minha conta
charger *(for battery)* o carregador
charter flight o voo charter
cheap barato(a)
cheaper mais barato(a)
to check verificar
to check in *(at airport)* fazer o check-in
   (at hotel) apresentar-se
check-in desk o balcão do check-in
cheek a bochecha
cheerful alegre
cheers saúde!
cheese o queijo

cheeseburger um hambúrguer com
   queijo
chef o cozinheiro-chefe/a cozinheira-
   chefe
chemist's a farmácia
cheque o cheque
chequebook o livro de cheques
cheque card o cartão de cheques
cherry a cereja
chess o xadrez
chest *(of body)* o peito
chestnut a castanha
chewing gum a pastilha elástica
chicken a galinha ; o frango
chicken breast o peito de galinha
chickenpox a varicela
child a criança
child safety seat *(car)* o banco de
   segurança para crianças
children as crianças
chilli a malagueta
chimney a chaminé
chin o queixo
china a porcelana
chips as batatas fritas
chocolate o chocolate
chocolates os chocolates
choice a escolha
choir o coro
to choose escolher
chop *(meat)* a costeleta
chopping board a tábua da cozinha
christening o baptizado
Christian name o nome próprio
Christmas o Natal
   merry Christmas! feliz Natal!
Christmas card o cartão de Boas Festas
Christmas Eve a véspera de Natal
Christmas present a prenda de Natal
church a igreja
cider a sidra
cigar o charuto
cigarette o cigarro
cigarette lighter o isqueiro
cigarette papers as mortalhas
cinema o cinema
circle *(theatre)* o balcão
circuit breaker o disjuntor
circus o circo
cistern a cisterna
citizen o cidadão/a cidadã
city a cidade
city centre o centro (da cidade)
claim a reclamação
to clap bater palmas
class: *first class* primeira classe
   second class segunda classe

clean limpo(a)
to clean limpar
cleaner *(person)* o/a empregado(a) de limpeza
  (product) produto de limpeza
cleanser o leite de limpeza
clear claro(a)
client o/a cliente
cliff o rochedo
to climb subir
climbing o alpinismo
climbing boots as botas de alpinismo
clingfilm® a película aderente
clinic a clínica
cloakroom o vestiário
clock o relógio
to close fechar
closed fechado(a)
cloth *(fabric)* o tecido
  (rag) o trapo
clothes as roupas
clothes line o estendal
clothes peg a mola da roupa
clothes shop a loja de roupa
cloudy nublado(a)
clove *(spice)* o cravinho
club o clube
clutch a embraiagem
coach a camioneta
coach station a rodoviária
coach trip a viagem de camioneta
coal o carvão
coast a costa
coastguard a polícia marítima
coat o casaco
coat hanger o cabide
Coca Cola® a Coca-Cola®
cockroach a barata
cocktail o cocktail
cocoa o cacau
coconut o coco
cod o bacalhau
code o código
coffee o café
  white coffee o café com leite
  large white coffee o galão
  small black coffee a bica
  decaffeinated coffee o café descafeinado
coil *(contraceptive)* o DIU
coin a moeda
Coke® a Coca-Cola®
colander o coador
cold frio(a)
  I'm cold tenho frio
  it's cold está frio
  cold water a água fria

cold *(illness)* a constipação
  I have a cold tenho uma constipação
cold sore a herpes labial
collar *(of dress)* a gola
  (of shirt) o colarinho
collarbone a clavícula
colleague o/a colega
to collect coleccionar
  (to collect someone) ir buscar
collection a colecção
colour a cor
colour-blind daltónico(a)
colour film *(for camera)* o rolo a cores
comb o pente
to come vir
  (arrive) chegar
to come back voltar
to come in entrar
  come in! entre!
comedy a comédia
comfortable confortável
company *(firm)* a companhia
compartment o compartimento
compass a bússola
to complain queixar-se (de)
  I want to complain of... Quero queixar-me de...
complaint uma queixa
  complaints book livro de reclamações
  I wish to make a complaint quero fazer uma reclamação
complete completo(a)
to complete completar
composer o/a compositor(a)
compulsory obrigatório(a)
computer o computador
computer disk *(floppy)* uma disquete
computer game o jogo de computador
computer program o programa de computador
computer software o software
concert o concerto
concert hall a sala de concertos
concession o desconto
concussion o traumatismo craniano
condensed milk o leite condensado
condition *(requirement)* a condição
  (state) o estado
conditioner o amaciador
condom o preservativo
conductor *(of orchestra)* o maestro/a maestrina
cone o cone
conference a conferência
confession a confissão
to confirm confirmar
  please confirm é favor confirmar

confirmation *(of booking)* a confirmação
confused confuso(a)
congratulations! parabéns!
connection *(flight, etc)* a ligação
constipated com prisão de ventre
constipation a prisão de ventre
consulate o consulado
to consult consultar
to contact pôr-se em contacto com
contact lens cleaner o líquido para as lentes de contacto
contact lenses as lentes de contacto
to continue continuar
contraception a anticoncepção
contraceptive o preservativo ; o anticoncepcional
contract o contrato
convenient: is it convenient? é conveniente?
convulsions as convulsões
to cook cozinhar
cooked cozinhado(a)
cooker o fogão
cookies os biscoitos
cool fresco(a)
cool box *(for picnics)* a caixa refrigerada
copper cobre
copy a cópia
to copy copiar
coriander os coentros
cork *(in bottle)* a rolha
corkscrew o saca-rolhas
corner o canto
corridor o corredor
cortisone a cortisona
cost o custo
to cost custar
  how much does it cost? quanto (é que) custa?
costume o traje
  (swimming – men) os calções de banho
  (swimming – women) o fato de banho
cot o berço
cottage a casa de campo
cotton o algodão
cotton buds os cotonetes
cotton wool o algodão *(hidrófilo)*
couchette a couchette
to cough tossir
cough a tosse
cough mixture o xarope para a tosse
cough sweets as pastilhas para a tosse
counter *(shop, bar etc)* o balcão
country o país
countryside o campo
couple *(two people)* o casal
  a couple of... um par de

courgettes as courgettes
courier *(tour guide)* o guia turístico/ a guia turística
courier service o mensageiro
course *(of meal)* o prato
  (of study) o curso
cousin o/a primo(a)
cover charge o couvert
cow a vaca
crab o caranguejo
crafts o artesanato
craftsman/woman o artesão/a artesã
cramps as cãibras
crash *(car)* o choque
to crash colidir
crash helmet o capacete
cream *(for face, etc)* o creme
  (on milk) a nata
  soured cream as natas azedas
  whipped cream o chantilly
creche a creche
credit card o cartão de crédito
crime o crime
crisps as batatinhas fritas
crop a colheita
croissant o croissant
to cross *(road)* cruzar
cross a cruz
crossed lines as linhas cruzadas
crossing *(sea)* a travessia
crossroads o cruzamento
crossword puzzle as palavras cruzadas
crowd a multidão
crowded cheio(a) de gente
crown a coroa
cruise o cruzeiro
crutches as muletas
to cry *(weep)* chorar
crystal o cristal
cucumber o pepino
cufflinks os botões de punho
cul-de-sac o beco sem saída
cumin o cominho
cup a chávena
cupboard o armário
curlers os rolos
currant a passa de corinto
currency a moeda
current a corrente
curtain a cortina
cushion a almofada
custard o leite-creme
custom *(tradition)* o costume
customer o freguês/a freguesa
customs *(at airport etc)* a alfândega
customs declaration a declaração alfandegária

customs officer o/a funcionário(a) aduaneiro(a)
to cut cortar
  we've been cut off foi interrompida a ligação
cut o corte
  cut and blow-dry cortar e secar
cutlery os talheres
to cycle andar de bicicleta
cycle track a pista para ciclistas
cycling o ciclismo
cyst o cisto
cystitis a cistite

D

daily cada dia
dairy produce os lacticínios
daisy a margarida
dam a barragem
damage os danos
damp húmido(a)
dance o baile
to dance dançar
danger o perigo
dangerous perigoso(a)
dark o escuro
  (adj) escuro
  after dark depois do anoitecer
date a data
date of birth a data de nascimento
daughter a filha
daughter-in-law a nora
dawn o amanhecer
day o dia
  every day todos os dias
  per day ao/por dia
dead morto(a)
deaf surdo(a)
dear *(on letter)* querido(a)
  (expensive) caro(a)
death a morte
debt a dívida
decaff o café descafeinado
  have you decaff? tem café descafeinado?
decaffeinated coffee o café descafeinado
December Dezembro
deckchair a cadeira de lona
to declare: *nothing to declare* nada a declarar
deep fundo(a)
deep freeze o congelador
deer o veado
to defrost descongelar

to de-ice descongelar
delay a demora
  how long is the delay? quanto tempo é o atraso?
delayed atrasado(a)
delicatessen a charcutaria
delicious delicioso(a)
demonstration *(political)* a manifestação
dental floss o fio dental
dentist o/a dentista
dentures a dentadura postiça
deodorant o desodorizante
to depart partir
department o departamento
department store o grande armazém
departure lounge a sala de embarque
departures as partidas
deposit o depósito
to describe descrever
description a descrição
desk a secretária
  (in hotel, airport) o balcão
dessert a sobremesa
details os pormenores
detergent o detergente
detour o desvio
to develop desenvolver
diabetes a diabetes
diabetic *(person)* diabético(a)
  (food) comida para diabéticos
  I'm diabetic sou diabético(a)
to dial marcar
dialect o dialecto
dialling code o código
dialling tone o sinal
diamond o diamante
diaper a fralda
diaphragm *(in body)* o diafragma
  (contraceptive) o diafragma
diarrhoea a diarreia
diary o diário ; a agenda
dice os dados
dictionary o dicionário
to die morrer
diesel o gasóleo
diet a dieta
  I'm on a diet estou de dieta
  special diet o regime especial
different diferente
difficult difícil
digital camera a câmara digital
digital radio o rádio digital
to dilute diluir
dinghy o bote
dining room a sala de jantar
dinner o jantar
  to have dinner jantar

D

dinner jacket o smoking
diplomat o/a diplomata
direct directo(a)
directions (instructions) instrucções
  to ask for directions pedir indicações
directory (phone) a lista telefónica
directory enquiries as informações
  telefónicas
dirty sujo(a)
disability a incapacidade
disabled deficiente
  disabled person o/a deficiente
to disagree discordar
to disappear desaparecer
disappointed desiludido(a)
disaster o desastre
disco a discoteca
discount o desconto
to discover descobrir
disease a doença
dish o prato
dishtowel o pano de cozinha
dishwasher a máquina de lavar louça
dishwasher powder o detergente
  em pó
disinfectant o desinfectante
disk (computer) o disco
  floppy disk a disquete
  hard disk o disco duro
to dislocate (joint) deslocar
disposable descartável
distance a distância
distant distante
distilled water a água destilada
district o distrito
to disturb incomodar
to dive mergulhar
diver o/a mergulhador(a)
diversion o desvio
diving mergulhar
divorced divorciado(a)
  I'm divorced sou divorciado(a)
DIY shop a loja de bricolage
dizzy tonto(a)
to do fazer
doctor o/a médico(a)
documents os documentos
dog (male) o cão
  (female) a cadela
dog food a comida para cães
dog lead a correia
doll a boneca
dollar o dólar
domestic doméstico(a)
domestic flight o voo doméstico
dominoes o dominó
donor card o cartão de doador

donkey o burro
door a porta
doorbell a campainha
double o dobro
double bed a cama de casal
double room o quarto de casal
doughnut a bola de Berlim
down: to go down descer
downstairs em baixo
dragonfly a libélula
drain (sewer) o esgoto
draught (of air) a corrente de ar
  there's a draught há uma corrente
  de ar
draught lager a imperial
drawer a gaveta
drawing o desenho
dress o vestido
to dress (oneself) vestir-se
dressing (for food) o tempero ;
  o molho
  (for wound) o penso
dressing gown o roupão
drill (tool) a broca
drink a bebida
to drink beber
drinking chocolate o chocolate
drinking water a água potável
to drive conduzir
driver o/a condutor(a)
driving licence a carta de condução
drizzle o chuvisco
drought a seca
to drown afogar
drug (medicine) o medicamento
  (narcotic) a droga
drunk bêbedo(a)
dry seco(a)
to dry secar
dry-cleaner's a limpeza a seco
dryer o secador
duck o pato
due: when is it due? está previsto
  para quando?
dummy (for baby) a chupeta
during durante
dust o pó
to dust limpar o pó
duster o pano do pó
dustpan and brush pá e vassoura
duty (tax) o imposto
duty-free livre de impostos
duvet o edredão
duvet cover o saco do edredão
dye a tinta
dynamo o dínamo

E

each cada
eagle a águia
ear a orelha
earache a dor de ouvidos
  I have earache doem-me os ouvidos
earlier mais cedo
early cedo
earphones os auscultadores
earplugs as borrachinhas (de ouvido)
earrings os brincos
earth *(planet)* a terra
earthquake o terramoto
east o leste
Easter a Páscoa
  happy Easter! feliz Páscoa!
easy fácil
to eat comer
ebony o ébano
echo o eco
economy a economia
edge a beira ; a borda
eel a enguia
effective eficaz
egg o ovo
  fried egg o ovo estrelado
  hard-boiled egg o ovo cozido
  scrambled eggs os ovos mexidos
  soft-boiled egg o ovo quente
egg white a clara de ovo
egg yolk a gema de ovo
either... or... ou... ou...
elastic band o elástico
Elastoplast® o penso
elbow o cotovelo
electric eléctrico(a)
electric blanket o cobertor eléctrico
electrician o/a electricista
electricity a electricidade
electricity meter o contador de
  electricidade
electric razor a máquina de barbear
electric shock o choque eléctrico
elevator o elevador
elegant elegante
e-mail o correio electrónico ; e-mail
  to e-mail someone mandar um
  e-mail
e-mail address o endereço de e-mail
embarrassing embaraçoso(a)
embassy a embaixada
emergency a emergência
emergency exit a saída de emergência
emery board a lixa de unhas
empty vazio(a)
end o fim

engaged comprometido(a)
  (phone, toilet, etc) ocupado(a)
engine o motor
engineer o/a engenheiro(a)
England a Inglaterra
English inglês (inglesa)
  (language) o inglês
Englishman o inglês
Englishwoman a inglesa
enjoy oneself divertir-se
  I enjoy swimming gosto de nadar
  I enjoy dancing gosto de dançar
  enjoy yourself! diverte-te!
  enjoy your meal! bom apetite!
to enlarge aumentar
enormous enorme
enough bastante
  that's enough chega
enquiries as informações
enquiry desk o balcão de informações
to enter entrar (em)
entertainment a diversão
enthusiastic entusiástico(a)
entrance a entrada
entrance fee o bilhete de entrada
envelope o envelope
epileptic epiléptico(a)
epileptic fit o ataque epiléptico
equipment o equipamento
eraser a borracha
error o erro
eruption a erupção
escalator a escada rolante
to escape escapar
escape ladder a escada de salvação
espadrilles as alpercatas
espresso a bica ; o café
essential essencial
estate agent o/a agente imobiliário(a)
estate agent's a imobiliária
establish estabelecer
euro o euro
euro cent o cêntimo
Europe a Europa
European europeu (européia)
European Union a União Européia
eve a véspera
  Christmas eve a véspera de Natal
  New Year's eve a véspera de Ano
  Novo
even *(number)* par
evening a noite
  in the evening à noite
  this evening esta noite
  tomorrow evening amanhã à noite
evening dress o traje de cerimónia
evening meal o jantar

every cada
everyone toda a gente ; todos
everything todas as coisas, tudo
everywhere por todo o lado
examination o exame
example: for example por exemplo
excellent excelente
except excepto
excess baggage/luggage o excesso de bagagem
to exchange trocar
exchange rate o câmbio
exciting emocionante
excursion a excursão
excuse a desculpa
  excuse me! desculpe!
exercise *(physical)* o exercício
exercise book o caderno
exhaust pipe o tubo de escape
exhibition a exposição
exit a saída
expenses as despesas
expensive caro(a)
expert o/a perito(a)
to expire *(ticket, etc)* caducar
expiry date o vencimento
to explain explicar
explosion a explosão
to export exportar
express *(train)* o expresso
express: to send a letter express mandar uma carta por correio expresso
extension *(electrical)* a extensão
extra extra
  an extra bed uma cama adicional
to extinguish apagar
eye o olho
eyebrows as sobrancelhas
eyedrops as gotas para os olhos
eyelashes as pestanas
eyeliner o lápis para os olhos
eyeshadow a sombra para os olhos

F

fabric o tecido
face a cara ; o rosto
face cloth a toalha de rosto
facial a limpeza facial
facilities as facilidades; instalações
factory a fábrica
to fail fracassar
  (engine, brakes) falhar
to faint desmaiar
fainted desmaiado(a)
fair *(hair)* louro(a)

fair *(just)* justo(a)
fair *(funfair)* o parque de diversões
  (trade) a feira
fairway *(golf)* o fairway
fake falso(a)
fall *(autumn)* o Outono
to fall cair
  he/she has fallen ele/ela caiu
false teeth os dentes postiços
family a família
famous famoso(a)
fan *(hand-held)* o leque
  (electric) a ventoínha
  (football, jazz) o/a fan
fan belt a correia da ventoínha
fancy dress o traje de Carnaval
far longe
  is it far? é longe?
  how far is it to...? a que distância fica…?
fare *(train, bus, etc)* o preço
  (da passagem)
farm a quinta
farmer o/a agricultor(a)
farmhouse a casa da quinta
fashionable de moda
fast rápido(a)
  too fast rápido demais
to fasten *(seatbelt)* apertar
fat gordo(a)
  saturated fats gorduras saturadas
  unsaturated fats gorduras insaturadas
father o pai
father-in-law o sogro
fault *(defect)* o defeito
  it's not my fault a culpa não é minha
favour o favor
favourite favorito(a)
fax o fax
  by fax por fax
to fax mandar por fax
fax number o número de fax
feather a pena
February Fevereiro
to feed alimentar
to feel apalpar ; sentir
  I feel sick tenho náuseas
  I don't feel well sinto-me mal-disposto(a)
feet os pés
fellow o companheiro
felt-tip pen a caneta de feltro
female mulher
ferry o ferry-boat
festival o festival
to fetch *(to bring)* trazer
  (to go and get) ir buscar

fever a febre
few poucos(as)
  a few alguns (algumas)
fiancé(e) o/a noivo(a)
field o campo
fig o figo
fight a briga
to fight brigar
file *(computer)* o ficheiro
  (nail) a lima
  (folder) a pasta
filigree a filigrana
to fill encher
  fill it up! encha o depósito!
  to fill in (form) preencher
fillet o filete
filling *(in tooth)* a obturação
filling station a estação de serviço
film *(at cinema)* o filme
  (for camera) o rolo de filme
  colour film o rolo a cores
  black and white film o rolo a
  preto e branco
Filofax® a agenda
filter o filtro
to find achar
fine *(to be paid)* a multa
fine fino(a)
fine arts as belas-artes
finger o dedo
to finish acabar
finished acabado(a)
fire o fogo
fire alarm o alarme contra incêndios
fire brigade os bombeiros
fire engine o carro dos bombeiros
fire escape a saída de incêndios
fire extinguisher o extintor
fireplace a lareira
fireworks os fogos de artifício
firm *(company)* a firma
first o/a primeiro(a)
first aid os primeiros socorros
first aid kit o estojo de primeiros
  socorros
first class a primeira classe
first-class de primeira classe
first floor o primeiro andar
first name o nome próprio
fish o peixe
to fish pescar
  to go fishing ir pescar
fisherman o pescador
fishing permit a licença de pesca
fishing rod a cana de pesca
fishmonger's a peixaria
to fit: *it doesn't fit me* não me serve

fit o ataque
  he had a fit ele teve um ataque
to fix reparar ; consertar
  can you fix it? pode arranjá-lo?
fizzy gasoso(a)
flag a bandeira
flame a chama
flash *(for camera)* o flash
flashlight a lanterna
flask o termo
flat *(apartment)* o apartamento
flat plano(a)
  (battery) descarregado
  this drink is flat esta bebida
  já perdeu o gás
flat tyre o furo
flavour sabor
  which flavour? de que sabor?
flaw a falha
fleas as pulgas
fleece *(top/jacket)* de fibra polar
flesh a carne
flex o cabo eléctrico
flight o voo
flip flops os chinelos
flippers as barbatanas
flood a inundação
  flash flood a inundação repentina
floor o chão
  (storey) o andar
  which floor? qual é o andar?
  ground floor o rés-do-chão
  first floor o primeiro andar
  second floor o segundo andar
floorcloth o pano do chão
floppy disk a disquete
florist's shop a florista
flour a farinha
flower a flor
flu a gripe
fly a mosca
to fly voar
fly sheet o duplo-tecto
fog o nevoeiro
foggy nevoento
foil *(silver)* o papel de alumínio
to follow seguir
food a comida
food poisoning a intoxicação alimentar
fool tonto(a)
foot o pé
  on foot a pé
football o futebol
football match o jogo de futebol
football pitch o campo de futebol
football player o jogador de futebol
footpath o caminho

for para
  for me para mim
  for you para si
  for him/her/us para ele/ela/nós
  for them para eles (elas)
forbidden proibido(a)
forecast a previsão
  weather forecast a previsão do tempo
forehead a testa
foreign estrangeiro(a)
foreigner o/a estrangeiro(a)
forest a floresta
forever para sempre
to forget esquecer-se de
to forgive perdoar
fork *(for eating)* o garfo
  (in road) a bifurcação
form *(document)* o formulário
formal dress o traje de cerimónia
fortnight a quinzena
fortress a fortaleza
forward(s) para a frente
foul *(in football)* a falta
fountain a fonte
four-wheel drive o quatro-vezes-quatro
fox a raposa
fracture a fractura
fragile frágil
fragrance a fragrância
frame *(picture)* a moldura
France a França
free *(not occupied)* livre
  (costing nothing) grátis
freezer o congelador
French francês (francesa)
  (language) o francês
French beans o feijão-verde
French fries as batatas fritas
frequent frequente
fresh fresco(a)
fresh water a água doce
Friday a sexta-feira
fridge o frigorífico
fried frito(a)
friend o/a amigo(a)
friendly simpático(a)
frog a rã
from de
  from England da Inglaterra
  from Scotland da Escócia
front a frente
  in front of em frente de
front door a porta da frente
frost a geada
frozen congelado(a)
fruit a fruta
  dried fruit os frutos secos

fruit juice o sumo de frutas
fruit salad a salada de frutas
to fry fritar
frying pan a frigideira
fuel *(petrol)* a gasolina
fuel gauge o medidor de gasolina
fuel pump a bomba de gasolina
fuel tank o depósito
full cheio(a)
full board a pensão completa
fumes *(of car)* os fumos de escape
fun a diversão
funeral o funeral
funfair o parque de diversões
funny engraçado(a)
  (strange) estranho(a)
fur a pele
furnished mobilado(a)
furniture a mobília
fuse o fusível
fuse box a caixa de fusíveis
futon o futon
future o futuro

G

gallery *(art)* a galeria de arte
gallon = approx. 4.5 litres
game o jogo
  (animal) a caça
garage *(private)* a garagem
  (for repairs) a oficina (de reparos)
  (for petrol) a estação de serviço
garden o jardim
gardener o/a jardineiro(a)
garlic o alho
to garnish guarnecer
gas o gás
gas cooker o fogão a gás
gas cylinder a botija de gás
gastritis a gastrite
gate *(airport)* a porta
gay *(person)* gay
gear a velocidade
  first gear a primeira velocidade
  second gear a segunda velocidade
  third gear a terceira velocidade
  fourth gear a quarta velocidade
  fifth gear a quinta velocidade
  neutral o ponto morto
  reverse a marcha atrás
gearbox a caixa de velocidades
generous generoso(a)
gents' *(toilet)* Homens
  where is the gents'? onde é o lavabo
  de homens?
genuine *(leather, antique etc)* autêntico(a)

German alemão (alemã)
  (language) o alemão
German measles a rubéola
Germany a Alemanha
to get *(to obtain)* obter
  (to receive) receber
  (to fetch) ir buscar
to get in *(vehicle)* subir em
to get into entrar em
to get off descer de
to get on *(vehicle)* subir para
gift o presente ; a prenda
gift shop a loja de lembranças
gin and tonic um gim tónico
ginger o gengibre
girl a rapariga
girlfriend a namorada
to give dar
to give back devolver
glacier o glaciar
glass *(substance)* o vidro ; o cristal
  (to drink out of) o copo
  a glass of water um copo de água
glasses os óculos
glasses case a caixa dos óculos
gloss o brilho
gloves as luvas
glue a cola
to go ir
  I'm going to... vou para…
  we're going to... vamos para…
to go back voltar
to go down descer
to go in entrar (em)
to go out sair
goat a cabra
God o Deus
godchild o/a afilhado(a)
goggles os óculos protectores
gold o ouro
golf o golfe
golf ball a bola de golfe
golf clubs os tacos de golfe
golf course o campo de golfe
good bom (boa)
  very good muito bom
good afternoon boa tarde
goodbye adeus
good evening boa noite
good morning bom dia
good night boa noite
goose o ganso
gooseberry a groselha branca
Gothic gótico(a)
graduate o/a licenciado(a)
gram o grama
grandchild o/a neto(a)

granddaughter a neta
grandfather o avô
  great grandfather o bisavô
grandmother a avó
  great grandmother a bisavó
grandparents os avós
grandson o neto
grapefruit a toranja
grapefruit juice o sumo de toranja
grapes as uvas
  green grapes as uvas brancas
  black grapes as uvas pretas
grass a erva
grated *(cheese, etc)* ralado(a)
grater *(for cheese, etc)* o ralador
greasy oleoso(a) ; gorduroso(a)
great *(big)* grande
  (wonderful) óptimo(a)
Great Britain a Grã-Bretanha
green verde
green card *(car insurance)* o cartão verde
greengrocer's a frutaria
greetings card o cartão de felicitações
grey cinzento(a)
grill a grelha
to grill grelhar
grilled grelhado(a)
grocer's a mercearia
ground *(earth)* a terra
  (floor) o chão
ground floor o rés-do-chão
  on the ground floor... no rés-do-chão…
groundsheet a cobertura impermeável
group o grupo
to grow crescer
guarantee a garantia
guard o guarda
guest o/a convidado(a)
  (in hotel) o/a hóspede
guesthouse a pensão
guide o/a guia
to guide guiar
guidebook a guia
guided tour a excursão guiada
guitar a guitarra
gun a pistola
gym o ginásio
gym shoes os ténis

H
haberdasher's a retrosaria
haddock o eglefim
haemorrhoids as hemorróidas
hail o granizo
hair o cabelo

hairbrush a escova de cabelo
haircut o corte de cabelo
hairdresser o/a cabeleireiro(a)
hairdryer o secador de cabelo
hair dye a tinta para o cabelo
hair gel o gel para o cabelo
hairgrip o gancho de cabelo
hair mousse a espuma para o cabelo
hairspray a laca
hake a pescada
half a metade
  a half bottle of meia garrafa de
  half an hour meia hora
half board a meia pensão
half fare meio-bilhete
half-price pela metade do preço
ham *(boiled)* fiambre
  (smoked) presunto
hamburger o hambúrguer
hammer o martelo
hand a mão
handbag a bolsa
handicapped *(person)* deficiente
handkerchief o lenço
handle *(of cup)* a asa
  (of door) a maçaneta
handlebars os guiadores
hand luggage a bagagem de mão
hand-made feito(a) à mão
hands-free phone kit de mãos livres
handsome bonito(a), giro(a)
to hang up *(phone)* desligar
hanger o cabide
hang gliding a asa-delta
hangover a ressaca
to happen acontecer
  what happened? o que aconteceu?
happy feliz
  happy birthday! feliz aniversário! ;
  parabéns!
harbour o porto
hard duro(a)
  (difficult) difícil
hard disk o disco duro
hardware shop a loja de ferragens
hare a lebre
harm o mal ; o dano
harvest a colheita
hat o chapéu
to have ter
  I have... eu tenho…
  I don't have... eu não tenho…
  we have... nós temos…
  we don't have... nós não temos…
  do you have...? tem…?
to have to ter que ; ter de
hay fever a febre dos fenos

hazelnut a avelã
he ele
head a cabeça
headache a dor de cabeça
  I have a headache dói-me a cabeça
headlights os faróis
headphones os auscultadores
head waiter o chefe de mesa
health a saúde
health food shop a loja de produtos
  dietéticos
healthy saudável
to hear ouvir
hearing aid o aparelho auditivo
heart o coração
heart attack o ataque de coração
heartburn a azia
heartstroke a insolação
to heat up aquecer
heater o aquecedor
heating o aquecimento
heaven o Céu
heavy pesado(a)
heel *(of foot)* o calcanhar
  (of shoe) o salto
heel bar o sapateiro
height a altura
helicopter o helicóptero
hello olá
  (on phone) está?
helmet o capacete
help a ajuda
  help! socorro!
to help ajudar
  can you help me? pode-me ajudar?
hem a bainha
hen a galinha
hepatitis a hepatite
herb a erva aromática
herbal tea a tisana
here aqui
  here is... aqui está…
  here is my passport aqui está
  o meu passaporte
hernia a hérnia
hi! olá!
to hide *(something)* esconder
  (oneself) esconder-se
high *(price, speed, building)* alto(a)
  (number) grande
high blood pressure a tensão alta
highchair a cadeira de bebé
high tide a maré alta
hill a colina
hill-walking o alpinismo
him *(direct object)* o
  (indirect object) lhe
  (after preposition) ele

hip a anca
hip replacement a prótese de anca
hire o aluguer
  car hire o aluguer de carros
  bike hire o aluguer de bicicletas
  boat hire o aluguer de barcos
  ski hire o aluguer de esquis
to hire alugar
historic histórico(a)
history a história
to hit bater
to hitchhike andar à boleia
HIV o vírus da SIDA
HIV positive seropositivo(a)
hobby o passatempo
to hold *(to contain)* conter
hold-up o engarrafamento
hole o buraco
holiday as férias
  (public holiday) o feriado
  on holiday de férias
holiday rep o/a representante
  da agência de viagens
hollow oco(a)
holy santo(a)
home a casa
  at home em casa
  to go home voltar para casa
homeopath o/a homeopata
homeopathic homeopático(a)
homeopathy a homeopatia
homesick: to be homesick ter
  saudades de casa
  I'm homesick tenho saudades de casa
homosexual homossexual
honest honesto(a)
honey o mel
honeymoon a lua-de-mel
hood *(of jacket)* o capuz
  (of car) a capota
hook *(for fishing)* o anzol
to hope esperar
  I hope so/not espero que sim/não
horn *(of car)* a buzina
hors d'œuvre a entrada
horse o cavalo
horse racing as corridas de cavalo
horse riding: to go horse riding
  montar a cavalo
hosepipe a mangueira
hospital o hospital
hostel a pousada (de juventude)
hot quente
  I'm hot tenho calor
  it's hot está quente
  it's hot (weather) faz/está calor
hot chocolate o chocolate quente

hotel o hotel
hot water a água quente
hot-water bottle o saco de água quente
hour a hora
  half an hour meia hora
  1 hour uma hora
  2 hours duas horas
house a casa
housewife/husband a/o dona(o) de
  casa
house wine o vinho da casa
housework o trabalho doméstico
hovercraft o hovercraft
how como
  how much? quanto(a)?
  how many? quantos(as)?
  how are you? como está?
hundred cem
  five hundred quinhentos
hungry: I am hungry tenho fome
hunt a caça
to hunt caçar
hunting permit a licença de caça
hurry: I'm in a hurry tenho pressa
to hurt doer
  that hurts isso dói
  my back hurts tenho dor de costas
husband o marido
hut a cabana
hydrofoil o hidrofólio
hypodermic needle a agulha
  hipodérmica

I

I eu
ice o gelo
  (cube) o cubo de gelo
  with ice com gelo
  without ice sem gelo
ice box o frigorífico
ice cream o gelado
iced coffee o café gelado
iced tea o chá gelado
ice lolly o gelado ; picolé
ice rink o rinque de patinagem
to ice-skate patinar sobre
  o gelo
ice skates os patins de lâmina
idea a idéia
identity card o bilhete de identidade
if se
ignition a ignição
ignition key a chave de ignição
ill doente
  I'm ill estou doente
illness a doença

immediately imediatamente
immersion heater o esquentador de imersão
immigration a imigração
immunisation a imunização
to import importar
important importante
impossible impossível
to improve melhorar
in em
   (within) dentro de
   in 10 minutes dentro de dez minutes
   in London em Londres
in front of em frente de
inch = approx. 2.5 cm
included incluído(a)
inconvenient inconveniente
to increase aumentar
indicator *(on car)* o pisca-pisca
indigestion a indigestão
indigestion tablets os comprimidos para indigestão
indoors em casa
inefficient ineficiente
infection a infecção
infectious contagioso(a)
informal *(person)* sem formalidades
   (costume) informal
information a informação
information desk o balcão de informações
information office o departamento de informações
ingredient o ingrediente
inhaler *(for medication)* o inalador
injection a injecção
to injure lesionar
injured ferido(a)
injury a lesão
ink a tinta
inn a estalagem
inner tube a câmara-de-ar
inquiries as informações
inquiry desk o balcão de informações
insect o insecto
insect bite a picada de insecto
insect repellent o repelente contra insectos
inside dentro
instalment a prestação
instant coffee o café instantâneo
instead of em vez de
instructor o/a instrutor(a)
insulin a insulina
insurance o seguro
insurance certificate a apólice de seguro

to insure pôr no seguro
insured: *to be insured* estar no seguro
intelligent inteligente
to intend to do tencionar fazer
interesting interessante
internet a internet
internet café o cibercafé
international internacional
interpreter o/a intérprete
interval o intervalo
interview a entrevista
into em ; a ; para
   into the centre ao centro
to introduce someone to someone apresentar alguém a alguém
invitation o convite
to invite convidar
invoice a factura
Ireland a Irlanda
Irish irlandês (irlandesa)
iron *(metal)* o ferro
   (for clothes) o ferro de engomar
to iron passar a ferro
ironing board a tábua de engomar
ironmonger's a loja de ferragens
island a ilha
Italian italiano(a)
   (language) o italiano
Italy a Itália
itch a comichão
to itch fazer comichão
   it itches faz comichão
item o artigo
itemized bill a factura detalhada
ivory o marfim

J

jack *(for car)* o macaco
jacket o casaco
   waterproof jacket o casaco impermeável
jackpot o prémio (de lotaria, rifa)
jacuzzi® o jacuzzi
jam a compota
jammed *(stuck)* bloqueado(a)
January Janeiro
jar o jarro
jaundice a icterícia
jaw o queixo
jazz o jazz
jealous ciumento(a)
jeans as jeans
jelly a geleia
jellyfish a medusa; a alforreca
jet ski a motonáutica
jetty o quebra-mar

jewel a jóia
jewellery a joalharia
Jewish judeu (judia)
job o emprego
to jog ir fazer jogging
to join *(club)* associar-se a
to join in participar
joint *(of body)* a articulação
joke a piada; a anedota
to joke brincar
journalist o/a jornalista
journey a viagem
judge o juiz (a juíza)
jug o jarro
juice o sumo
  apple juice o sumo de maçã
  orange juice o sumo de laranja
  tomato juice o sumo de tomate
  a carton of juice um pacote de sumo
July Julho
to jump saltar
jump leads os cabos para ligar a bateria
junction o cruzamento
June Junho
just: *just two* apenas dois
  I've just arrived acabo de chegar

K

karaoke o karaokê
to keep guardar
  (retain) ficar com
  keep the change! fique com o troco!
kennel a casota
kettle a chaleira
key a chave
  card key a chave-cartão
keyboard o teclado
keyring o porta-chaves
to kick *(person)* dar um pontapé em
  (ball) chutar
kid *(young goat)* o cabrito
  (child) a criança
kidneys os rins
to kill matar
kilo o quilo
  a kilo of apples um quilo de maçãs
  2 kilos dois quilos
kilogram o quilograma
kilometre o quilómetro
kind *(person)* amável
kind *(sort)* a espécie
king o rei
kiosk o quiosque
kiss o beijo
to kiss beijar

kitchen a cozinha
kitchen paper o papel de cozinha
kite o papagaio
kitten o/a gatinho(a)
knee o joelho
knickers as cuecas
knife a faca
to knit fazer malha
to knock *(on door)* bater
to knock down *(with car)* atropelar
to knock over *(vase, glass)* derrubar
knot o nó
to know *(have knowledge of)* saber
  (person, place) conhecer
  I don't know não sei
to know how to do something saber
  fazer alguma coisa
  to know how to swim saber nadar
kosher kosher

L

label a etiqueta
lace a renda
laces *(for shoes)* os atacadores
ladder a escada
ladies' *(toilet)* Senhoras
lady a senhora
lager a cerveja
  bottled lager a cerveja de garrafa
  draught lager a imperial
lake o lago
lamb o cordeiro
lame coxo(a)
lamp a lâmpada
lamppost o poste de iluminação
lampshade o abajur
land a terra
  (country) o país
to land aterrar
landing *(of plane)* a aterragem
landlady a senhoria
landlord o senhorio
landslide o desabamento
lane *(on motorway)* a faixa
language a língua
language school a Escola de Línguas
laptop o computador portátil
large grande
last último(a)
  the last bus o último autocarro
  the last train o último comboio
  last night ontem à noite
  last week a semana passada
  last year o ano passado
  the last time a última vez

late tarde
  the train is late o comboio está atrasado
  sorry we are late desculpe o atraso
later mais tarde
to laugh rir
launderette a lavandaria automática
laundry service o serviço de lavandaria
lavatory o lavabo
lavender a alfazema
law a lei
lawn o relvado
lawyer o/a advogado(a)
laxative o laxante
layby a berma
lazy preguiçoso(a)
lead *(electrical)* o cabo
  (for dog) a correia
lead *(metal)* o chumbo
lead-free sem chumbo
leaf a folha
leak *(of gas, liquid)* o escape; o derrame
to leak: *it's leaking (pipe)* está a verter
  (gas) escape de gás
  (roof) infiltração
to learn aprender
lease o arrendamento
least: *at least* pelo menos
leather o couro
leather goods os cabedais
to leave *(leave behind)* deixar
  (train, bus etc) partir
  when does it leave? a que horas parte?
  when does the bus leave? a que horas parte o autocarro?
  when does the train leave? a que horas parte o comboio?
leek o alho francês
left: *on/to the left* à esquerda
left-handed canhoto(a)
left luggage *(office)* o depósito de bagagens
left luggage locker o cacifo
leg a perna
legal legal
lemon o limão
lemonade a limonada
lemon tea o carioca de limão
to lend emprestar
length o comprimento
lens *(of glasses)* a lente
  (of camera) a objectiva
lenses *(contact lenses)* as lentes de contacto
lesbian a lésbica

less menos
  less than menos do que
lesson a lição
let *(allow)* deixar
  (lease) alugar
letter a carta
  (of alphabet) a letra
letterbox o marco do correio
lettuce a alface
level crossing a passagem de nível
library a biblioteca
licence a licença
  (driving) a carta de condução
lid a tampa
lie *(untruth)* a mentira
to lie down deitar-se
life a vida
lifebelt o cinto salva-vidas
lifeboat o salva-vidas
lifeguard o guarda salva-vidas
life insurance o seguro de vida
life jacket o colete de salvação
life raft a bolsa salva-vidas
lift *(elevator)* o elevador
  (in car) a boleia
light a luz
  have you a light? tem lume?
light *(not heavy)* leve
  (colour) claro(a)
light bulb a lâmpada
lighter o isqueiro
lighthouse o farol
lightning os relâmpagos
lights out luzes apagadas
like como
  it's like this é assim
to like gostar de
  I like coffee gosto de café
  I don't like... não gosto de…
  I'd like to... gostava de…
  we'd like to... gostávamos de…
lilo o colchão de ar
lime a lima
line *(row, queue)* a fila
  (phone) a linha
linen *(cloth)* o linho
  (bed linen) a roupa de cama
lingerie a roupa interior
lion o leão
lip reading a leitura de lábios
lips os lábios
lip salve a manteiga de cacau
lipstick o bâton
liqueur o licor
list a lista
to listen to ouvir

litre o litro
  a litre of milk um litro de leite
litter *(rubbish)* o lixo
little pequeno(a)
  a little... um pouco de...
to live viver ; morar
  I live in Edinburgh moro em
  Edimburgo
  he lives in London ele vive
  em Londres
  he lives in a flat ele vive num
  apartamento; ele mora num
  apartamento
liver o fígado
living room a sala de estar
lizard o lagarto
loaf *(of bread)* o pão
lobster a lagosta
local local
to lock fechar com chave
lock a fechadura
  the lock is broken a fechadura
  está quebrada
  bike lock o cadeado da bicicleta
locker *(luggage)* o depósito de bagagem
locksmith o/a serralheiro(a)
log o tronco
log book *(for car)* a documentação
  do carro
lollipop o chupa-chupa
London Londres
  in London em Londres
  to London a Londres
long comprido(a) ; longo(a)
  for a long time durante muito tempo
long-sighted presbíope
to look after cuidar de
to look at olhar
to look for procurar
loose solto(a)
  it's come loose soltou-se
lorry o camião
to lose perder
lost perdido(a)
  I have lost my wallet perdi a
  minha carteira
  I am lost estou perdido(a)
lost property office a secção
  de perdidos e achados
lot: a lot *(much)* muito(a)
  (many) muitos(as)
lotion a loção
lottery a lotaria
loud *(noisy)* ruidoso(a)
  (volume) alto(a)

lounge *(in hotel)* a sala de estar
  (in house) a sala de estar
  (in airport) o salão
to love amar
  I love swimming gosto muito
  de nadar
  I love you amo-te
lovely encantador(a)
low baixo(a)
low-fat magro
low tide a maré baixa
luck a sorte
lucky: to be lucky ter sorte
luggage a bagagem
luggage rack o porta-bagagens
luggage tag a etiqueta de bagagem
luggage trolley o carrinho
lump *(swelling)* o inchaço
  (on head) o galo
lunch o almoço
lunch break a hora do almoço
lung o pulmão
luxury o luxo

M

machine a máquina
mad *(insane)* louco(a)
  (angry) furioso(a)
madam a senhora
magazine a revista
maggot a larva
magnet o íman
magnifying glass a lupa
magpie a pega
maid a empregada
maiden name o nome de solteira
mail o correio
  by mail pelo correio
main principal
main course *(of meal)* o prato principal
main road a estrada principal
mains *(electrical)* a rede eléctrica
to make *(generally)* fazer
  (meal) preparar
make-up a maquilhagem
male masculino(a)
mallet o maço
man o homem
to manage *(cope)* arranjar-se
manager o/a gerente
managing director o/a director(a) geral
manual manual
many muitos(as)
map o mapa

marathon a maratona
marble o mármore
March Março
margarine a margarina
marina a marina
marinated marinado
marjoram o orégão
mark (stain) a nódoa
market o mercado
  where is the market? onde é que fica o mercado?
  when is the market? quando é que há mercado?
marketplace o mercado
marmalade o doce de laranja
married casado(a)
  I'm married sou casado(a)
  are you married? é casado(a)?
marry: to get married casar(-se)
marsh o pântano
marzipan o maçapão
mascara o rímel®
mashed potato o puré de batata
Mass (church service) a missa
mast o mastro
masterpiece a obra-prima
match o fósforo
  (game) o jogo
matches os fósforos
material o material
  (cloth) o tecido
to matter: it doesn't matter não tem importância
  what is the matter? o que é que se passa?
mattress o colchão
maximum o máximo
May Maio
mayonnaise a maionese
mayor o presidente do município
me me
  (after preposition) mim
meadow o prado
meal a refeição
to mean significar
  what does this mean? o que é que quer dizer isto?
measles o sarampo
to measure medir
meat a carne
  white meat as carnes brancas
  red meat as carnes vermelhas
  I don't eat meat não como carne
mechanic o/a mecânico(a)
medical insurance o seguro de doença
medicine o medicamento
medieval medieval

Mediterranean o Mediterrâneo
medium médio(a)
  medium rare (meat) meio-passado(a)
to meet (by chance) encontrar
  (by arrangement) encontrar-se com
  pleased to meet you prazer em conhecê-lo(a)
meeting a reunião
meeting point o ponto de encontro
melon o melão
to melt derreter
member (of club, etc) o/a sócio(a)
membership card o cartão de sócio(a)
memory a memória
  (thing remembered) a lembrança
  memory card (for digital camera) o cartão memória
men os homens
to mend arranjar ; consertar
meningitis a meningite
menu a ementa
  set menu a ementa fixa
  à la carte menu a ementa a la carte
meringue o merengue
message a mensagem
metal o metal
meter o contador
metre o metro
microwave oven o micro-ondas
midday o meio-dia
  at midday ao meio-dia
middle o meio
middle-aged de meia-idade
midge o mosquito
midnight a meia-noite
  at midnight à meia-noite
migraine a enxaqueca
  I've a migraine tenho uma enxaqueca
mild (climate) temperado(a)
  (taste) suave
mile a milha
milk o leite
  fresh milk o leite fresco
  full-cream milk o leite gordo
  hot milk o leite quente
  long-life milk o leite ultrapasteurizado
  powdered milk o leite em pó
  semi-skimmed milk o leite meio-gordo
  skimmed milk o leite magro
  soya milk o leite de soja
  with milk com leite
  without milk sem leite
milkshake o batido de leite
millenium o milénio
millimetre o milímetro
million o milhão

139

mince *(meat)* a carne picada
mind *n* a mente
to mind *vb (take care of)* ocupar-se de
   (object to) objectar
   do you mind if...? importa-se?
   I don't mind não me importo
mineral water a água mineral
minibar o minibar
minimum o mínimo
minister *(political)* o ministro
   (church) o pastor
mink o vison ; a manta
minor road a estrada secundária
mint *(herb)* a hortelã
   (sweet) o rebuçado de mentol
minute o minuto
mirror o espelho
to misbehave comportar-se mal
miscarriage o aborto (espontâneo)
Miss... Menina...
to miss *(plane, train, etc)* perder
missing *(lost)* perdido(a)
   my son is missing o meu filho
   desapareceu
mistake o erro
misty: *it's misty* há nevoeiro
misunderstanding o mal-entendido
to mix misturar
mixer a batedeira
mobile phone o telemóvel
modem o modem
modern moderno(a)
moisturizer o creme hidratante
mole *(on skin)* o sinal
moment: *just a moment* um momento
monastery o mosteiro
Monday a segunda-feira
money o dinheiro
   I've no money não tenho dinheiro
money order o vale postal
monkey o macaco
month o mês
   this month este mês
   last month o mês passado
   next month o mês que vem
monthly mensalmente
monument o monumento
moon a lua
mooring o atracadouro
mop a esfregona
moped a motocicleta
more mais
   more than 3 mais de três
   more bread mais pão
   more wine mais vinho

morning a manhã
   in the morning de manhã
   this morning esta manhã
   tomorrow morning amanhã de manhã
morning-after pill a pílula abortiva
mosque a mesquita
mosquito o mosquito
mosquito net o mosquiteiro
mosquito repellent o repelente contra
   mosquitos
most: *most of* a maioria de
moth a mariposa
   (clothes) a traça
mother a mãe
mother-in-law a sogra
motor o motor
motorbike a moto
motorboat o barco a motor
motorcycle a motocicleta
motorway a auto-estrada
mould *(mildew)* o bolor
mountain a montanha
mountain bike a bicicleta de montanha
mountain rescue o socorro para
   alpinistas
mountaineering o alpinismo
mouse o rato
mousse *(food)* a mousse
   (hair) a espuma
moustache o bigode
mouth a boca
mouthwash desinfectante para a boca
to move mexer ; mover
   it isn't moving não se mexe ;
   não se move
movie o filme
to mow cortar
Mr o Senhor
Mrs a Senhora
Ms a Senhora
much muito(a)
   too much demais
mud a lama
muddy *(road)* lamacento(a)
   (clothes) enlameado(a)
mugging o assalto
mumps a papeira
muscle o músculo
museum o museu
mushroom o cogumelo
music a música
musical o musical
mussel o mexilhão
must *(to have to)* dever
   I must devo
   we must devemos
   I mustn't não devo
   we mustn't não devemos

mustard a mostarda
mutton o carneiro
my meu (minha)

N

nail *(metal)* o prego
   (on finger) a unha
nailbrush a escova das unhas
nail clippers o corta-unhas
nail file a lima para as unhas
nail polish o verniz das unhas
nail polish remover a acetona
nail scissors as tesouras para as unhas
name o nome
   my name is... o meu nome é…
   what's your name? como é que
   te chamas?
nanny a ama
napkin o guardanapo
nappy a fralda
narrow estreito(a)
national nacional
national park o parque nacional
nationality a nacionalidade
natural natural
nature a natureza
nature reserve a reserva natural
navy blue azul-marinho
near perto
   near the bank perto do banco
   is it near? fica perto?
necessary necessário(a)
neck o pescoço
necklace o colar
nectarine a nectarina
to need precisar de
   I need... preciso de
   we need... precisamos de
   I need to go tenho que ir
needle a agulha
   a needle and thread uma agulha
   e a linha
negative *(photo)* o negativo
neighbour o/a vizinho(a)
nephew o sobrinho
nest o ninho
net a rede
nettle a urtiga
never nunca
   I never drink wine nunca bebo vinho
new novo(a)
news a notícia
   (on television) o noticiário ; telejornal
newsagent a tabacaria
newspaper o jornal
newsstand o quiosque

New Year o Ano Novo
   happy New Year! Feliz Ano Novo!
New Year's Eve a véspera de Ano
   Novo
New Zealand a Nova Zelândia
next próximo(a)
   next to ao lado de
   next week a semana que vem
   the next bus o próximo autocarro
   the next stop a próxima paragem
   the next train o próximo comboio
nice *(person, holiday)* agradável
   (place) bonito(a)
niece a sobrinha
night a noite
   at night à noite
   last night ontem à noite
   per night por noite
   tomorrow night amanhã à noite
nightclub a boite
nightdress a camisa de noite
night porter o porteiro da noite
no não
   no entry entrada proibida
   no smoking proibido fumar
   no thanks não, obrigado(a)
   (without) sem
   no sugar sem açúcar
   no ice sem gelo
nobody ninguém
noise o barulho
noisy barulhento(a)
   it's very noisy há muito barulho
non-alcoholic não-alcoólico(a)
none nenhum(a)
   there's none left não sobrou nada
non-smoker o/a não-fumador(a)
non-smoking não-fumador(a)
north o norte
Northern Ireland a Irlanda do Norte
North Sea o Mar do Norte
nose o nariz
not não
note *(banknote)* a nota
   (letter) a nota
note pad o bloco-notas
nothing nada
   nothing else mais nada
notice o aviso
noticeboard o quadro de avisos
novel o romance
November Novembro
now agora
nowhere *(be)* em nenhum lugar
   (go) a lugar nenhum
nuclear nuclear
nudist beach a praia para nudistas

number o número
numberplate *(car)* a matrícula
nurse o/a enfermeiro(a)
nursery *(creche)* a creche
nursery slope a rampa para principiantes
nut *(to eat)* a noz
(for bolt) a porca
nutmeg a noz moscada

O

oak o carvalho
oar o remo
oats a aveia
to obtain obter
obvious óbvio(a)
occasionally às vezes
occupation *(work)* a ocupação
ocean o oceano
October Outubro
octopus o polvo
odd *(number)* ímpar
of de
 a bottle of water uma garrafa de água
 a glass of wine um copo de vinho
 made of... feito de...
off *(radio, engine, etc)* desligado(a)
 (milk, food, etc) estragado(a)
 this meat is off esta carne está estragada
to offer oferecer
office o escritório
often muitas vezes
 how often? quantas vezes?
oil o óleo
oil filter o filtro do óleo
oil gauge o indicador do óleo
ointment a pomada
OK está bem
old velho(a)
 how old are you? quantos anos tem?
 I'm ... years old tenho ... anos
old age pensioner o/a reformado(a)
olive a azeitona
olive oil o azeite
omelette a omeleta
on *(light, TV)* aceso(a)
 (engine) a trabalhar
on em
 on the table na mesa
 on time a horas
once uma vez
 at once imediatamente
one um (uma)
one-way de sentido único
onion a cebola

only somente
 (adj) único(a)
open *adj* aberto(a)
to open abrir
opera a ópera
opera house o teatro da ópera
operation *(surgical)* a operação
operator *(phone)* o/a telefonista
opposite: *opposite (to)* em frente de
 opposite the hotel em frente do hotel
optician's o oculista
or ou
 tea or coffee? chá ou café?
orange *adj* cor-de-laranja
orange *(fruit)* a laranja
orange juice o sumo de laranja
orchestra a orquestra
order: *out of order* fora de serviço ; avariado
to order *(in restaurant)* pedir
 can I order? posso pedir?
oregano o orégão
organic biológico(a)
to organize organizar
original original
ornament o ornamento
other: *the other one* o/a outro(a)
 have you any others? tem outros(as)?
ounce = approx. 30 g
our nosso(a)
out fora
 he's gone out ele saiu
 he's out não está
out of order fora de serviço ; avariado
outdoor ao ar livre
outside: *it's outside* está lá fora
oven o forno
oven gloves as luvas de cozinha
ovenproof refratário(a)
over *(on top of)* sobre
to be overbooked ter mais reservas que lugares
to overcharge cobrar demais
overcoat o sobretudo
overdone *(food)* cozido demais
overdose a dose excessiva
to overheat aquecer demasiado
to overload sobrecarregar
to oversleep dormir além da hora
to overtake *(in car)* ultrapassar
to owe dever
 you owe me... deve-me...
 I owe you... devo-lhe...
owl o mocho
owner o/a dono(a)
oxygen o oxigénio
oyster a ostra

P

pace o passo
pacemaker o pacemaker
to pack bags fazer as malas
package o embrulho
package tour a viagem organizada
packet o pacote
padded envelope o envelope almofadado
paddling pool a piscina para crianças
padlock o cadeado
page a página
paid pago(a)
pain a dor
painful doloroso(a)
painkiller o analgésico
to paint pintar
paintbrush o pincel
painting a pintura
  (picture) o quadro
pair o par
palace o palácio
pale pálido
pan (frying) a frigideira
  (saucepan) o tacho
pancake a panqueca
panniers (for bike) as bolsas para a bicicleta
pants (briefs) as cuecas
panty liners os pensos higiénicos
paper o papel
  (newspaper) o jornal
paper hankies os lenços de papel
paper napkins os guardanapos de papel
papoose (for carrying baby) a mochila para levar o bebé
paracetamol o paracetamol
paraffin o óleo de parafina
paragliding para-pente
paralysed paralisado(a)
parcel a encomenda
pardon desculpe?
  I beg your pardon! desculpe-me!
parents os pais
park o parque
to park estacionar
parking disk o disco de estacionamento
parking meter o parquímetro
parking ticket a multa por estacionamento em lugar proibido
parsley a salsa
parsnip a cherivia

part a parte
partner (business) o/a sócio(a)
  (friend) o/a companheiro(a)
party (celebration) a festa
  (political) o partido
pass (mountain) o desfiladeiro
  (train, bus) o passe
passenger o/a passageiro(a)
passport o passaporte
passport control o controle de passaportes
pasta as massas
pastry (dough) a massa
  (cake) o bolo
pâté o paté
path o caminho
patient o/a paciente; o/a doente
  (adj) paciente
pavement o passeio
to pay pagar
  I'd like to pay quero pagar
  where do I pay? onde é que se paga?
  I've paid já paguei
payment o pagamento
payphone o telefone público
peace a paz
peach o pêssego
peak rate a taxa alta
peanut o amendoim
peanut allergy a alergia a amendoins
peanut butter a manteiga de amendoim
pear a pêra
pearls as pérolas
peas as ervilhas
pedal o pedal
pedal boat o barco de pedáis
pedestrian o/a peão
pedestrian crossing a passadeira para peões
to pee fazer xixi
to peel (fruit) descascar
peg (clothes) a mola
  (tent) a estaca
pen a caneta
pencil o lápis
penfriend o/a correspondente
penicillin a penicilina
penis o pénis
penknife o canivete
pension a pensão
pensioner o/a reformado(a)
people as pessoas
pepper (spice) a pimenta
  (vegetable) o pimento

per por
  per day por dia
  per hour por hora
  per week por semana
  per person por pessoa
  50 km per hour 50 km por hora
perch (fish) a perca
perfect perfeito(a)
performance a representação
  the next performance
  a próxima representação
perfume o perfume
perhaps talvez
period (menstruation) a menstruação
perm a permanente
permit a licença
person a pessoa
  per person por pessoa
personal organizer a agenda
personal stereo o Walkman®
pet o animal doméstico
pet food a comida para animais
  domésticos
pet shop a loja para animais
  domésticos
petrol a gasolina
  4-star petrol a gasolina super
  unleaded petrol a gasolina sem
  chumbo
petrol cap a tampa do depósito de
  gasolina
petrol pump a bomba de gasolina
petrol station a estação de serviço
petrol tank o depósito da gasolina
pewter o estanho
pharmacy a farmácia
pheasant o faisão
phone o telefone
  mobile telephone o telemóvel
to phone telefonar
phonebook a lista telefónica
phonebox a cabine telefónica
phonecard o credifone
photocopy a fotocópia
  I need a photocopy preciso duma
  fotocópia
photograph a fotografia
  to take a photograph tirar uma
  fotografia
phrase book o guia de conversação
piano o piano
to pick (fruit, flowers) colher
  (to choose) escolher
pickled de conserva
pickpocket o/a carteirista
picnic o piquenique
  to have a picnic fazer um piquenique

picnic area a zona de piqueniques
picnic hamper o cesto para
  piqueniques
picnic rug a manta
picnic table a mesa para piqueniques
picture (painting) o quadro
  (photo) a foto
pie (savoury) a empada
  (sweet) a torta
piece o bocado ; o pedaço
pier o cais
pig o porco
pill o comprimido
  to be on the Pill tomar a pílula
pillow a almofada
pillowcase a fronha
pilot o/a piloto(a)
pin o alfinete
  safety pin o alfinete de segurança
pineapple o ananás
pink cor-de-rosa
pint = approx. 0.5 litre
  a pint of beer uma caneca de cerveja
pipe (for smoking) o cachimbo
  (drain, etc) o tubo ; o cano
pity: what a pity! que pena!
pizza a pizza
place o lugar
place of birth o lugar de nascimento
plain (yoghurt, etc) natural
  (obvious) claro(a)
plait a trança
plan o plano
to plan planear
plane o avião
plant a planta
plaster (sticking) o adesivo
  (for broken limb) o gesso
plastic o plástico
plastic bag o saco de plástico
plate o prato
platform (railway) a linha
  which platform? qual é a linha?
play (at theatre) a peça
to play (sport) jogar
  (musical instrument) tocar
  (general play) brincar
playground o pátio de recreio
play park o parque infantil
playroom o quarto de brinquedos
pleasant agradável
please por favor ; faz favor
pleased: pleased to meet you prazer
  em conhecê-lo(a)
plenty: plenty of (much) muito(a)
  (many) muitos(as)
pliers o alicate

plug (electric) a ficha ; a tomada
  (for sink) a válvula
to plug in ligar
plum a ameixa
plumber o canalizador
plumbing (pipes) a canalização
plunger (for sink) o desentupidor
p.m. (afternoon/evening) de tarde
  (night) de noite
poached (fish) cozido(a)
  poached egg o ovo escalfado
pocket o bolso
points (in car) os platinados
poison o veneno
poisonous venenoso(a)
police (force) a polícia
police officer o/a polícia
police station a esquadra
polish (for shoes) a pomada
  para o calçado
  (for furniture) a cera
pollen o pólen
polluted poluído(a)
pollution a poluição
pony o pónei
pony trekking o passeio a cavalo
pool a piscina
pool attendant o/a empregado(a)
  da piscina
poor pobre
poorly: he feels poorly ele não se
  sente bem
pope o papa
poppy a papoila
pop socks as peúgas
popular popular
pork a carne de porco
port (wine) o vinho do porto
  (seaport) o porto
porter (for door) o porteiro
  (for luggage) o carregador
portion a porção
Portugal Portugal
Portuguese português (portuguesa)
  (language) o português
possible possível
post: by post pelo correio
to post pôr no correio
postbox o marco do correio
postcard o postal
postcode o código postal
poster o póster
  (advertising) o cartaz
postman/woman o/a carteiro(a)
post office os correios
to postpone adiar
pot (for cooking) a panela

potato a batata
  baked potato a batata assada
  boiled potatoes as batatas cozidas
  fried potatoes as batatas fritas
  mashed potatoes o puré de batata
  roast potatoes as batatas assadas
  sautéed potatoes as batatas salteadas
potato masher o passe-vite
potato peeler o descascador de
  batatas
potato salad a salada de batata
pothole o buraco
pottery a cerâmica
pound (money) a libra
  (weight) = approx. 0.5 kilo
to pour deitar
powdered: in powdered form em pó
powdered milk o leite em pó
power o poder
power cut o corte de energia
pram o carrinho do bebé
prawn o lagostim
to pray rezar
prayer a oração
to prefer preferir
pregnant grávida
  I'm pregnant estou grávida
to prepare preparar
to prescribe receitar
prescription a receita médica
present (gift) o presente; a oferta ;
  a prenda
preservative o preservativo
president o/a presidente
press (newspapers) a imprensa
pressure pressão
  blood pressure a tensão arterial
  tyre pressure a pressão dos pneus
pretty bonito(a)
price o preço
price list a lista de preços
priest o padre
prince o príncipe
princess a princesa
print (photo) a cópia
printer a impressora
prison a prisão
private privado(a)
prize o prémio
probably provavelmente
problem o problema
  no problem não tem problema
programme o programa
professor o/a professor(a) catedrático(a)
prohibited proibido(a)
promise a promessa
to promise prometer

145

pronounce pronunciar
  how is this pronounced? como se pronuncia isto?
protein a proteína
Protestant protestante
to provide fornecer
prune a ameixa seca
public público(a)
public holiday o feriado
publisher o/a editor(a)
pudding o pudim
to pull puxar
  I've pulled a muscle distendi o músculo
to pull over *(car)* encostar
pullover o pulóver
pump a bomba
pumpkin a abóbora
puncture o furo
puncture repair kit o estojo de ferramentas
puppet o fantoche
puppet show o teatro de marionetes; os fantoches
puppy o cachorro
purple roxo(a)
purpose: on purpose de propósito
purse o porta-moedas
to push empurrar
pushchair o carrinho
to put pôr
to put back repor
pyjamas o pijama

Q

quail a codorniz
quality a qualidade
quantity a quantidade
quarantine a quarentena
to quarrel discutir
quarter o quarto
quay o cais
queen a rainha
query a pergunta
question a pergunta
queue a fila ; a bicha
to queue fazer fila
quick rápido(a)
quickly depressa
quiet *(place)* sossegado(a)
  a quiet room um quarto tranquilo
quilt o edredão
quite: it's quite good é bastante bom
  quite expensive é muito caro
quiz o concurso
quiz show *(TV)* o concurso televisivo

R

rabbit o coelho
rabies a raiva
race *(sport)* a corrida
  (human) a raça
race course o hipódromo
rack *(luggage)* o porta-bagagens
racket a raqueta
radiator *(car)* o radiador
  (heater) o radiador
radio o rádio
radish o rabanete
raffle a rifa
rag o trapo
railcard o passe do comboio
railway o caminho de ferro
railway station a estação de comboio ; caminho de ferro
rain a chuva
to rain: it's raining está a chover
rainbow o arco-íris
raincoat o impermeável ; a gabardina
raisin a passa de uva
rake o ancinho
rape a violação
to rape violar
raped: I've been raped fui violado(a)
rare *(unique)* raro(a)
  (steak) mal passado(a)
rash *(skin)* a urticária
raspberries as framboesas
rat a ratazana
rate *(price)* a taxa
rate of exchange o câmbio
raw cru(a)
razor a máquina de barbear
razorblades as lâminas de barbear
to read ler
ready pronto(a)
  to get ready preparar-se
real real
to realize perceber
rearview mirror o retrovisor
reason a razão
receipt o recibo
receiver *(phone)* o auscultador
recently recentemente
reception *(desk)* a recepção
receptionist o/a recepcionista
to recharge recarregar
recipe a receita
to recognize reconhecer
to recommend recomendar
record *(music)* o disco
to record *(facts)* registar
  (music) gravar

to recover (from illness) recuperar
to recycle reciclar
red vermelho(a)
redcurrants as groselhas
to reduce reduzir
reduction o desconto
reel (fishing) o carretel
to refer to referir-se a
referee o/a árbitro(a)
refill (pen, lighter) a recarga
refund o reembolso
to refuse recusar
regarding com relação a
region a região
to register (at hotel) preencher o registo
registered (letter) registado(a)
registration form a folha de registo
regulations os regulamentos
to reimburse reembolsar
relation (family) o/a parente
relationship (personal) as relações
  (family) o parentesco
relative (family) o/a parente
to relax repousar ; relaxar
reliable de confiança
to remain ficar
to remember lembrar-se de
  I don't remember não me lembro
remote control o comando
removal firm a companhia de
  mudanças
to remove retirar
rent (house) a renda; o aluguer
  (car) o aluguer
to rent (house, car) alugar
rental o aluguer
repair a reparação
to repair reparar ; consertar
to repeat repetir
to reply responder
report o relatório
to report (crime, person) comunicar
request o pedido
to request pedir
to require precisar de
to rescue salvar
reservation a reserva
to reserve reservar
reserved reservado(a)
resident (at hotel) o/a hóspede
resort a estância
rest (repose) o descanso
  (remainder) o resto
  the rest of the wine o resto do vinho
to rest descansar
restaurant o restaurante
restaurant car o vagão restaurante

to retire reformar-se
retired reformado(a)
  I'm retired estou reformado(a)
to return (to go back) voltar
  (to give something back) devolver
return ticket o bilhete de ida e volta
to reverse fazer marcha atrás
to reverse the charges fazer uma
  chamada pagável no destino
reverse-charge call a chamada pagável
  no destino
reverse gear a marcha atrás
rheumatism o reumatismo
rhubarb o ruibarbo
rib a costela
ribbon a fita
rice o arroz
rich (person) rico(a)
  (food) suculento(a)
to ride (horse) montar a cavalo
  (in a car, bus, etc) viajar
right (correct) certo(a)
  to be right ter razão
right: *on/to the right* à direita
right-handed destro(a)
right of way a prioridade
ring (for finger) o anel
to ring (bell) tocar
  (phone) telefonar
  it's ringing está a tocar
ring road a circunvalação
ripe maduro(a)
river o rio
road a estrada
road map o mapa das estradas
road sign o sinal de trânsito
roadworks as obras na estrada
roast assado(a)
robber o ladrão (a ladra)
robin o pintarroxo
roll (bread) o pãozinho
rollerblades os patins em linha
rollers os rolos
roller skates os patins de rodas
rolling pin o rolo da massa
romance (novel) o romance
Romanesque românico(a)
romantic romântico(a)
roof o telhado
roof rack o porta-bagagens
room (in house, hotel) o quarto
  (space) espaço
  double room o quarto de casal
  family room o quarto de família
  single room o quarto individual
room number o número do quarto
room service o serviço de quarto

root a raíz
rope a corda
rose a rosa
rosemary o alecrim
rosé wine o vinho rosé
rotten *(fruit, etc)* podre ; estragado(a)
rough *(surface)* áspero(a)
 (sea) agitado(a)
round *(shape)* redondo(a)
roundabout *(traffic)* a rotunda
route a rota
row *(line)* a fila
to row *(boat)* remar
rowing *(sport)* o remo
rowing boat o barco a remos
royal real
rubber *(eraser)* a borracha
 (material) a borracha
rubber band o elástico
rubber gloves as luvas de borracha
rubbish o lixo
rubella a rubéola
rucksack a mochila
rudder o leme
rug o tapete
ruins as ruínas
ruler *(for measuring)* a régua
rum o rum
to run correr
rush hour a hora de ponta
rusty ferrugento(a)
rye o centeio

S
saccharin a sacarina
sad triste
saddle *(bike)* o selim
 (horse) a sela
safe *(for valuables)* o cofre
safe seguro(a)
 is it safe? é seguro?
safety belt o cinto de segurança
safety pin o alfinete de segurança
sage *(herb)* a salva
to sail *(sport, leisure)* velejar
sailboard a prancha
sail(ing) a vela
sailing boat o barco a vela
saint o/a santo(a)
salad a salada
 green salad a salada verde
 mixed salad a salada mista
 potato salad a salada de batatas
 tomato salad a salada de tomate
salad dressing o tempero da salada

salami o salame
salary o salário
sale(s) o saldo
salesman/woman o/a vendedor(a)
sales rep o/a representante de vendas
salmon o salmão
 smoked salmon o salmão fumado
salt o sal
salt water a água salgada
salty salgado(a)
same mesmo(a)
sample a amostra
sand a areia
sandals as sandálias
sandwich a sandes
 toasted sandwich a tosta
sanitary towel o penso higiénico
sardine a sardinha
satellite dish a antena parabólica
satellite TV a televisão via satélite
Saturday o sábado
sauce o molho
 tomato sauce o molho de tomate
saucepan a caçarola
saucer o pires
sauna a sauna
sausage a salsicha
to save *(life)* salvar
 (money) poupar
savoury saboroso(a)
savouries os salgados
saw a serra
to say dizer
scales *(weighing)* a balança
scallops as vieiras
scampi as gambas panadas
scan *(n)* o scan
to scan fazer um scan
scanner o scanner
scarf *(woollen)* o cachecol
 (headscarf) o lenço (de pescoço)
scenery a paisagem
schedule o programa
school a escola
 primary school a escola primária
 secondary school o colégio
scissors a tesoura
score *(of match)* o resultado
to score marcar
Scot o/a escocês (escocesa)
Scotland a Escócia
Scottish escocês (escocesa)
scouring pad a palha de aço
screen *(computer, TV)* o ecrã
screenwash o detergente para
 o pára-brisas

screw o parafuso
screwdriver a chave de parafusos
  phillips screwdriver® a chave phillips®
scuba diving mergulhar
sculpture a escultura
sea o mar
seafood os mariscos
seagull a gaivota
seal a foca
seam *(of dress)* a costura
to search for procurar
seasick enjoado(a)
  I get seasick enjoo
seasickness o enjoo
seaside a praia
  at the seaside na praia
season *(of year)* a estação
  (holiday) a temporada
  in season da época
season ticket o passe
seasoning o tempero
seat *(chair)* a cadeira
  (on bus, train, etc) o lugar
seatbelt o cinto de segurança
seaweed a alga marinha
second segundo(a)
second class a segunda classe
second-class *adj* de segunda classe
second-hand em segunda mão ;
  usado(a)
secretary o/a secretário(a)
security guard o guarda de segurança
sedative o sedativo
to see ver
seed a semente
to seize agarrar
self-catering com cozinha
self-employed que trabalha por conta
  própria
self-service o auto-serviço
to sell vender
  do you sell...? vende...?
sell-by date... usar antes de...
Sellotape® a fita-cola
semi-skimmed milk o leite meio-gordo
to send mandar
senior citizen o/a reformado(a)
sensible sensato(a)
separated separado(a)
separately: *to pay*
  separately pagar separadamente
September Setembro
septic tank a fossa séptica
sequel *(film, book)* a continuação;
  a sequela

serious sério(a)
  (illness) grave
to serve servir
service *(in church)* o serviço religioso
  (in restaurant) o serviço
  is service included? o serviço está
  incluído?
service charge o serviço
service station a estação de serviço
serviette o guardanapo
set menu a ementa fixa
settee o sofá
several vários(as)
to sew coser
sewer o esgoto
sex *(gender)* o sexo
  (intercourse) o sexo
shade a sombra
  in the shade à sombra
to shake *(bottle)* sacudir
shallow pouco profundo(a)
shampoo o champô
shampoo and set a lavagem e mise
to share dividir
to share out distribuir
sharp *(razor, knife)* afiado(a)
to shave fazer a barba
shaving cream o creme de barbear
shawl o xaile
she ela
sheep a ovelha
sheet *(for bed)* o lençol
shelf a prateleira
shell *(seashell)* a concha
  (egg, nut) a casca
shellfish o marisco
sheltered abrigado(a)
shepherd o pastor
sherry o xerez
to shine brilhar
shingles *(illness)* o herpes zóster
ship o barco
shirt a camisa
shock absorber o amortecedor
shoe o sapato
shoelaces os atacadores
shoe polish a graxa
shoe repairer's o sapateiro
shoe shop a sapataria
shop a loja
shop assistant o/a vendedor(a)
shop window a montra
shopping: *to go shopping* ir às
  compras
shopping centre o centro comercial
shore a costa
short curto(a)

149

short circuit o curto-circuito
short cut o atalho
shortage a escassez
shorts os calções
short-sighted míope
shoulder o ombro
to shout gritar
show o espectáculo
to show mostrar
shower o duche; o chuveiro
 to have a shower tomar um duche
 (rain) o chuveiro ; o aguaceiro
shower cap a touca de banho
shower curtain a cortina do chuveiro
shower gel o gel para banho
shrimps os camarões
to shrink encolher
shrub o arbusto
shut *(closed)* fechado(a)
to shut fechar
shutters as persianas ; as venezianas
shuttle service o serviço de ligação
shy tímido(a)
sick *(ill)* doente
 I feel sick sinto-me mal-disposto(a)
side o lado
side dish o acompanhamento
sidelight o farolim
sidewalk o passeio
sieve *(for liquids)* o coador
 (for flour) a peneira
to sightsee fazer turismo
sightseeing o turismo
 to go sightseeing fazer turismo
sightseeing tour a excursão
sign *(road-, notice, etc)* o sinal
to sign assinar
signature a assinatura
signpost a sinalização
silk a seda
silver a prata
similar: similar to semelhante a
simple simples
since *(time)* desde que
 (because) porque
 since Saturday desde sábado
to sing cantar
single *(not married)* solteiro(a)
 (not double) simples
single bed a cama de pessoa só
single room o quarto individual
single ticket o bilhete de ida ; simples
sink o lava-louça
sir senhor
sister a irmã
sister-in-law a cunhada

to sit sentar-se
 please, sit down faça o favor de
 se sentar
size *(clothes)* o tamanho
 (shoes) o número
to skate patinar
skates *(ice)* os patins de lâmina
 (roller) os patins de rodas
skating rink o rinque de patinagem
ski o esqui
 skis os esquis
to ski esquiar
ski boots as botas de esquiar
skiing o esqui
 to go skiing ir esquiar
ski instructor o/a instructor(a) de esqui
ski jump a pista para saltos de esqui
ski lift o ski lift
ski pole a vara de esqui
ski run a pista de esqui
ski stick a vara de esqui
ski suit o traje de esqui
skimmed milk o leite magro
skin a pele
skindiving mergulhar
skirt a saia
sky o céu
slang o calão
sledge o trenó
to sleep dormir
to sleep in dormir até tarde
sleeper *(on train)* a carruagem-cama
sleeping bag o saco cama
sleeping car a carruagem-cama
sleeping pill o comprimido para dormir
slice a fatia
slide *(photograph)* o diapositivo
to slip escorregar
slippers os chinelos
slow lento(a)
small pequeno(a)
smaller mais pequeno(a)
smell o cheiro
smile o sorriso
to smile sorrir
smoke o fumo
to smoke fumar
 I don't smoke não fumo
 can I smoke? posso fumar?
smoke alarm o alarme contra incêndios
smoked fumado(a)
smokers os fumadores
smoking: no smoking proibido fumar
smooth liso(a) ; macio(a)
snack o lanche
 to have a snack comer qualquer coisa
snack bar o snack-bar ; o café

snake a cobra
snake bite a mordedura de cobra
to sneeze espirrar
to snore ressonar
snorkel o tubo de ar
snow a neve
to snow nevar
  it's snowing está a nevar
snowboard o snowboard
snowboarding: to go snowboarding fazer snowboarding
snow chains as correntes para a neve
snowed up coberto de neve
snowman o boneco-de-neve
snowplough a máquina limpa-neve
snow tyres os pneus para a neve
so tão
  so much tanto(a)
  so then portanto
soap o sabão
soap powder o sabão em pó
sober sóbrio(a)
socket *(electrical)* a tomada
socks as peúgas
soda water a água com gás
sofa o sofá
sofa bed o sofá-cama
soft macio(a)
soft drink o refrigerante
software o software
soldier o soldado
sole *(fish)* o linguado
  (of shoe) a sola
soluble solúvel
some alguns (algumas)
someone alguém
something alguma coisa
sometimes às vezes
son o filho
son-in-law o genro
song a canção
soon em breve
  as soon as possible o antes possível
sore magoado(a)
sore throat: I have a sore throat dói-me a garganta
sorry: I'm sorry! lamento ; desculpe!
sort: what sort of cheese? que tipo de queijo?
sound o som
soup a sopa
sour azedo(a)
soured cream as natas azedas
south o sul
souvenir a recordação
spa as termas
space o espaço

spade a enxada
Spain a Espanha
Spanish espanhol(a)
  (language) o espanhol
spanner a chave inglesa
spare parts as peças sobressalentes
spare room o quarto de hóspedes
spare tyre o pneu sobressalente
spare wheel a roda sobressalente
sparkling espumoso(a)
  sparkling water a água com gás
  sparkling wine o espumante
spark plug a vela
to speak falar
  do you speak English? fala inglês?
  I don't speak Portuguese não falo português
special especial
specialist o/a especialista
speciality a especialidade
speech a fala
  (address) o discurso
speed a velocidade
speedboat a lancha
speeding o excesso de velocidade
speeding ticket a multa por excesso de velocidade
speed limit o limite de velocidade
  to exceed the speed limit ultrapassar o limite de velocidade
speedometer o conta-quilómetros
spell: how do you spell it? como se escreve?
to spend *(money)* gastar
spices as especiarias
spicy picante
spider a aranha
to spill entornar
spinach o espinafre
spin-dryer a secadora
spine a coluna
spirits as bebidas alcoólicas
splinter a lasca
spoke *(wheel)* o raio
sponge a esponja
spoon a colher
sport o desporto
sports centre o centro de desportos; centro desportivo
sports shop a loja de artigos desportivos
spot *(pimple)* a borbulha
to sprain: to sprain one's ankle torcer o tornozelo
spring *(season)* a primavera
  (coil) a mola
spring onion a cebolinha

square *(in town)* a praça
squash *(drink)* o sumo
  (game) o squash
to squeeze apertar
squid as lulas
stadium o estádio
staff o pessoal
stage o palco; a cena
stain a nódoa
stained glass o vitral
stain remover o tira-nódoas
stairs a escada
stale *(bread)* duro(a)
stalls *(in theatre)* a plateia
stamp *(postage)* o selo
to stand estar em pé
to stand up levantar-se
star *(in sky, in films)* a estrela
starfish a estrela-do-mar
to start começar
starter *(in meal)* a entrada
  (in car) o motor de arranque
station a estação
stationer's a papelaria
statue a estátua
stay a estadia; a visita
  enjoy your stay! desfrute a sua visita
to stay ficar
  I'm staying at a hotel fico num hotel
steak o bife
  medium steak o bife ao ponto
  well-done steak o bife bem-passado
  rare steak o bife mal-passado
to steal roubar
to steam cozer no vapor
steamed cozido(a) a vapor
steel aço
steep: is it steep? custa a subir?
steeple o campanário
steering wheel o volante
step *(stair)* o degrau
stepdaughter a enteada
stepfather o padrasto
stepmother a madrasta
stepson o enteado
stereo o estéreo
  personal stereo o Walkman®
sterling *(pounds)* esterlino(a)
stew o guisado
steward *(on plane)* o comissário de
  bordo
stewardess *(on plane)* a hospedeira de
  bordo
to stick *(with glue)* colar
sticking plaster o adesivo

still *(not moving)* imóvel
  (not sparkling) sem gás
  (yet) ainda
sting a picada
to sting picar
stitches *(surgical)* os pontos
stock cube o cubo de caldo
stockings as meias
stolen roubado(a)
stomach o estômago
stomach upset o mal-estar de
  estômago
stone a pedra
  (weight) = approx. 6.5 kg
to stop *(come to a halt)* parar
  (stop doing something) deixar de fazer
  alguma coisa
stop sign o sinal de paragem
store *(shop)* a loja
storey o andar
storm a tempestade
story a história
straightaway imediatamente
straight on sempre em frente
strainer o coador
strange estranho(a)
straw *(for drinking)* o canudo
strawberry o morango
stream o riacho
street a rua
street map o mapa das ruas
strength a força
stress o stress
strike *(of workers)* a greve
  to be on strike estar em greve
string o cordel
striped às riscas
stroke *(medical)* a trombose
  to have a stroke ter uma trombose
strong forte
  strong coffee o café forte
  strong tea o chá forte
stuck: it's stuck está preso(a)
student o/a estudante
student discount o desconto para
  estudantes
stuffed recheado(a)
stung picado(a)
stupid estúpido(a)
subscription a assinatura
subtitles as legendas
subway *(underpass)* a passagem
  subterrânea
suddenly de repente
suede a camurça

sugar o açúcar
  icing sugar o açúcar em pó
sugar-free sem açúcar
to suggest sugerir
suit *(men's and women's)* o fato ;
  o conjunto
suitcase a mala
sum a soma
summer o verão
summer holidays as férias de verão
summit o cume
sun o sol
to sunbathe tomar banhos de sol
sunblock o protector solar
sunburn a queimadura de sol
Sunday o domingo
sunflower o girassol
sunflower oil o óleo de girassol
sunglasses os óculos de sol
sunny: *it's sunny* está sol
sunrise o nascer do sol
sunroof o tecto de abrir
sunscreen o filtro solar
sunset o pôr do sol
sunshade o guarda-sol ; o toldo
sunstroke a insolação
suntan o bronzeado
suntan lotion a loção de bronzear
supermarket o supermercado
supper a ceia
supplement o suplemento
to supply abastecer
surcharge a sobretaxa
sure seguro(a)
  I'm sure estou seguro(a)
to surf fazer surfe
  to surf the Net navegar a Internet
surfboard a prancha de surf
surgery *(operation)* a cirurgia
  (building) o consultório
surname o apelido
  my surname is... o meu apelido é...
surprise a surpresa
surrounded by rodeado(a) por
suspension a suspensão
to survive sobreviver
to swallow engolir
swan o cisne
to swear *(bad language)* blasfemar;
  praguejar
  (in court) jurar
to sweat suar
sweater o pulóver
sweatshirt a sweatshirt
sweet *(not savoury)* doce
sweet *(dessert)* a sobremesa

sweetener o adoçante
sweets os rebuçados
to swell *(injury etc)* inchar
to swim nadar
swimming pool a piscina
swimsuit o fato de banho
swing *(for children)* o baloiço
Swiss suíço(a)
switch o interruptor
to switch off apagar ; desligar
to switch on acender ; ligar
Switzerland a Suíça
swollen *(finger, ankle, etc)* inchado(a)
swordfish o espadarte
synagogue a sinagoga
syringe a seringa

T

table a mesa
tablecloth a toalha de mesa
tablespoon a colher de sopa
tablet *(pill)* o comprimido
table tennis o ping-pong
table wine o vinho de mesa
tail o rabo ; a cauda
tailor's a alfaiataria
take *(carry)* levar ; transportar
  (to grab, seize) agarrar
  (medicine etc) tomar
  (to take someone to) levar
  how long does it take? quanto
  tempo demora?
take-away *(food)* para levar
to take off levantar voo
to take out *(of bag etc)* tirar
talc o talco
to talk to conversar com
tall alto(a)
tame *(animal)* manso(a)
tampons os tampões
tangerine a tangerina
tank *(car)* o depósito
  (fish) o aquário
tap a torneira
tap water a água da torneira
tape *(video)* a cassette de vídeo
tape measure a fita métrica
tape recorder o gravador
target o alvo
tarragon o estragão
tart a tarte
tartar sauce o molho tártaro
taste o sabor
to taste provar
  can I taste it? posso provar?

tax o imposto
taxi o táxi
taxi driver o/a taxista
taxi rank a praça de táxis
tea o chá
  herbal tea a tisana
  lemon tea o chá de limão
  strong tea o chá forte
  tea with milk o chá com leite
teabag o saquinho de chá
teapot o bule (de chá)
to teach ensinar
teacher o/a professor(a)
team a equipa
tear *(in eye)* a lágrima
  (in material) o rasgão
teaspoon a colher de chá
teat *(on baby's bottle)* o tetina
tea towel o pano de cozinha
teenager o/a adolescente
teeshirt a 'T-shirt' ; camiseta
teeth os dentes
teething dentição
telegram o telegrama
telephone o telefone
  mobile telephone o telemóvel
to telephone telefonar
telephone box a cabine telefónica
telephone call a chamada
telephone card o cartão telefónico
telephone directory a lista telefónica
telephone number o número de
  telefone
television a televisão
television set o televisor
telex o telex
to tell dizer
temperature a temperatura
  to have a temperature ter febre
temple o templo
temporary temporário(a)
tenant o/a inquilino(a)
tendon o tendão
tennis o ténis
tennis ball a bola de ténis
tennis court o campo de ténis
tennis racket a raqueta de ténis
tent a tenda
tent peg a estaca
terminal *(airport)* o terminal
terrace a esplanada
terracotta a terracota; o barro
terrorist o/a terrorista
to test *(try out)* testar
testicles os testículos
tetanus o tétano

than que
  better than melhor do que
  more than you mais do que tu
  more than five mais de cinco
to thank agradecer
thank you/thanks obrigado(a)
  thank you very much muito
  obrigado(a)
  no thanks não, obrigado(a)
that aquele (aquela)
that one esse (essa)
the *(sing)* o (a)
  (plural) os (as)
theatre o teatro
theft o roubo
their seu (sua)
them *(direct object)* os (as)
  (indirect object) lhes
  (after preposition) eles (elas)
then então
there *(over there)* ali
there is/there are há
thermometer o termómetro
these estes (estas)
  these ones estes (estas)
they eles (elas)
thick grosso(a)
thief o/a ladrão (ladra)
thigh a coxa
thin magro(a)
thing a coisa
  my things as minhas coisas
to think pensar
  (to be of opinion) achar
third terceiro(a)
thirsty: *I'm thirsty* tenho sede
this este (esta)
  this one este (esta)
thorn o espinho
those aqueles (aquelas)
  those ones aqueles (aquelas)
thousand mil
thread a linha
thriller *(film)* o filme de suspense
  (book) o livro de suspense
throat a garganta
throat lozenges as pastilhas para
  a garganta
through através de
to throw away deitar fora; descartar
thrush *(candida)* a candidíase vaginal
thumb o polegar
thunder o trovão
thunderstorm o temporal;
  a tempestade
Thursday a quinta-feira
thyme o tomilho

ticket *(bus, train, etc)* o bilhete
　(for cinema, theatre etc) a entrada
　a single ticket um bilhete de ida
　a return ticket um bilhete de ida
　e volta
　a tourist ticket um bilhete de turista
　a book of tickets uma caderneta de
　bilhetes
ticket collector o/a revisor(a)
ticket inspector o/a inspector(a)
　de bilhetes
ticket office a bilheteira
tide *(sea)* a maré
　low tide a maré baixa
　high tide a maré alta
tidy arrumado(a)
to tidy up arrumar
tie a gravata
tight apertado(a)
tights os collants
tile *(floor)* o ladrilho
　(wall) o azulejo
till *(cash desk)* a caixa
till *(until)* até
　till 2 o'clock até às duas
time o tempo
　(clock) as horas
　what time is it? que horas são?
　this time esta vez
timetable o horário
tin *(can)* a lata
tinfoil a folha de alumínio
tin-opener o abre-latas
tip a gorjeta
to tip dar uma gorjeta
tipped *(cigarette)* com filtro
Tippex® o fluido corrector
tired cansado(a)
tissues os lenços de papel
to a
　to London para Londres
　to the airport ao aeroporto
toadstool o cogumelo venenoso
toast *(to eat)* a torrada
　(raising glass) brindar
tobacco o tabaco
tobacconist's a tabacaria
today hoje
toddler a criança jovem (que começa
　a andar)
toe o dedo
together juntos
toilet a casa de banho ; o lavabo
　disabled toilets a casa de banho
　para deficientes
toilet brush a escova da sanita
toilet paper o papel higiénico

toiletries os artigos de toilette
token *(for bus)* o bilhete ; a senha
toll *(motorway)* a portagem
tomato o tomate
　tinned tomatoes os tomates em lata
tomato juice o sumo de tomate
tomato purée o concentrado de
　tomate
tomato sauce o molho de tomate
tomato soup a sopa de tomate
tomorrow amanhã
　tomorrow morning amanhã de manhã
　tomorrow afternoon amanhã à tarde
　tomorrow evening amanhã ao fim da
　tarde/à noite
　tomorrow night amanhã à noite
tongue a língua
tonic water a água tónica
tonight esta noite
tonsillitis a amigdalite
too *(also)* também
　too big grande demais
　too small pequeno(a) demais
　too hot *(food)* quente demais
　too noisy demasiado barulhento(a)
tool a ferramenta
toolkit o jogo de ferramentas
tooth o dente
toothache a dor de dentes
toothbrush a escova de dentes
toothpaste a pasta dentífrica
toothpick o palito
top: *the top floor* o último andar
top *(of hill)* a parte de cima
　on top of... em cima de...
topless: *to go topless* fazer topless
torch *(flashlight)* a lanterna
torn rasgado(a)
total *(amount)* o total
to touch tocar
tough *(meat)* duro(a)
tour *(trip)* a excursão
　(of museum etc) a visita
　guided tour a visita guiada
tour guide o/a guia turístico(a)
tour operator a empresa de viagens
tourist o/a turista
tourist information a informação
　turística
tourist office o posto de turismo
tourist route a rota turística
tourist ticket o bilhete turístico
to tow rebocar
towbar o gancho de reboque
towel o toalha
tower a torre

town a cidade
town centre o centro da cidade
town hall a Câmara Municipal
town plan o mapa da cidade
towrope o cabo de reboque
toxic tóxico(a)
toy o brinquedo
toy shop a loja de brinquedos
tracksuit o fato de treino
traditional tradicional
traffic o trânsito
traffic jam o engarrafamento
traffic lights o semáforo
traffic warden o/a guarda de trânsito
trailer o reboque
train o comboio
  by train de comboio
  the next train o próximo comboio
  the first train o primeiro comboio
  the last train o último comboio
trainers os ténis ; as sapatilhas
tram o eléctrico
tranquillizer o calmante
to transfer transferir
to translate traduzir
translation a tradução
to travel viajar
travel agent o agente de viagens
travel documents os documentos
  de viagem
travel guide o/a guia turístico(a)
travel insurance o seguro de viagem
travel sickness o enjoo
traveller's cheque o cheque de viagem
tray o tabuleiro ; a bandeja
tree a árvore
trip a viagem
trolley *(luggage, shopping)* o carrinho
trouble os problemas
  to be in trouble estar em dificuldades
trousers as calças
trout a truta
truck o camião
true verdadeiro(a)
trunk *(luggage)* o baú ; a mala grande
trunks *(swimming)* os calções de banho
truth a verdade
to try *(attempt)* tentar
to try on *(clothes, shoes)* provar
T-shirt a T-shirt ; camiseta
Tuesday a terça-feira
tulip a túlipa
tumble dryer a máquina de secar roupa
tuna o atum
tunnel o túnel
turkey o peru

to turn voltar ; girar
  to turn around voltar-se
to turn off *(light etc)* apagar
  (engine) desligar
  (tap) fechar
to turn on *(light etc)* acender
  (engine) ligar
  (tap) abrir
turnip o nabo
turquoise *(colour)* turquesa
tweezers a pinça
twice duas vezes
twin-bedded room o quarto com
  duas camas
twins os gémeos
  identical twins os gémeos idênticos
to type escrever à máquina
typical típico
tyre o pneu
tyre pressure a pressão dos pneus

U

ugly feio(a)
ulcer a úlcera
umbrella o guarda-chuva; a sombrinha
  (sunshade) o guarda-sol
uncle o tio
uncomfortable incómodo(a)
unconscious inconsciente
under debaixo de
undercooked mal cozido(a)
underground *(metro)* o metropolitano
underpants as cuecas
underpass a passagem subterrânea
to understand compreender
  I don't understand não percebo
  do you understand? percebe?
underwear a roupa interior
underwater debaixo da água
undo desfazer
to undress despir-se
unemployed desempregado(a)
to unfasten desatar
unhappy triste; infeliz
  to be unhappy with... não estar
  satisfeito(a) com...
United Kingdom o Reino Unido
United States os Estados Unidos
university a universidade
unleaded petrol a gasolina sem
  chumbo
unlikely improvável
to unlock destrancar
unlucky infeliz; sem sorte
to unpack *(suitcases)* desfazer as malas

unpleasant desagradável
   (person) antipático(a)
to unplug desligar
to unscrew desaparafusar
until até
   until 2 o'clock até às duas
unusual insólito(a)
up: *to get up* levantar-se
upside down invertido(a)
upstairs em cima
urgent urgente
urine a urina
us nos
   (after preposition) nós
USA os EUA
to use utilizar
useful útil
usual habitual
usually geralmente
U-turn a meia-volta

V

vacancies *(in hotel etc)* os quartos vagos
   (jobs) as vagas
vacant livre
   (hotel room) o quarto vago
vacation as férias
   on vacation de férias
vaccination a vacinação
vacuum cleaner o aspirador
vagina a vagina
valid válido(a)
valley o vale
valuable valioso(a)
valuables os objetos de valor
value o valor
valve a válvula
van a carrinha
vanilla a baunilha
vase *(for flowers)* a jarra
VAT o IVA
veal a carne de vitela
vegan vegetalista
   I'm vegan sou vegetalista
vegetables os legumes; os vegetais
vegetarian vegetariano(a)
   I'm vegetarian sou vegetariano(a)
vehicle o veículo
vein a veia
Velcro® o Velcro®
velvet o veludo
vending machine a máquina de
   venda automática
venereal disease a doença venérea
venison a carne de veado
ventilator o ventilador

very muito
vest a camisola interior
vet o/a veterinário(a)
via por
video o vídeo
to video *(from TV)* gravar
video camera a câmara de vídeo
video cassette a videocassete
video game o jogo de vídeo
video phone o videofone
video recorder o gravador de vídeo
view a vista
village a aldeia
vinaigrette a vinagreta
vinegar o vinagre
vineyard a vinha
violet *(flower)* a violeta
viper a víbora
virus o vírus
visa o visto
visit a visita
to visit visitar
visiting hours *(hospital)* as horas de visita
visitor a visita
vitamin a vitamina
vodka a vodka
voice a voz
volcano o vulcão
volleyball o voleibol
voltage a voltagem
to vomit vomitar
voucher o vale ; o recibo

W

wage o salário
waist a cintura
waistcoat o colete
to wait for esperar por
waiter o empregado de mesa
waiting room a sala de espera
waitress a empregada de mesa
to wake up acordar
Wales o País de Gales
to walk andar
walk o passeio
Walkman® o Walkman®
walking boots as botas de montanha
walking stick a bengala
wall *(inside)* a parede
   (outside) o muro
wallet a carteira
walnut a noz
to want querer
   I want... quero...
   we want... queremos...
war a guerra

ward *(in hospital)* a enfermaria
wardrobe o guarda-fato
warehouse o armazém
warm quente
 I'm warm estou com calor
 it's warm (weather) está calor
to warm up aquecer
warning triangle o triângulo
 de sinalização
wash: to have a wash lavar-se
to wash lavar
wash and blow-dry lavar e secar
washbasin o lavatório
washing machine a máquina de lavar
 roupa
washing powder o detergente para
 a roupa
washing-up bowl a bacia
washing-up liquid o detergente
 para a louça
wasp a vespa
waste bin o balde do lixo
watch o relógio
to watch ver ; observar
watchstrap a pulseira de relógio
water a água
 bottled water a água mineral
 (engarrafada)
 cold water a água fria
 drinking water a água potável
 fresh water a água corrente
 hot water a água quente
 mineral water a água mineral
 salt water a água salgada
 sparkling water a água com gás
 still water a água sem gás
watercress o agrião
waterfall a queda de água
water heater o esquentador
watermelon a melancia
waterproof impermeável
to waterski fazer esqui aquático
water-skiing o esqui aquático
waterwings as braçadeiras
waves as ondas
wax a cera
waxing *(hair removal)* depilação com cera
way *(path)* o caminho
 (manner) a maneira
way in *(entrance)* a entrada
way out *(exit)* a saída
we nós
weak fraco(a)
 (tea, etc) aguado(a)
to wear vestir
weather o tempo
weather forecast a previsão do tempo

website o website
wedding o casamento
wedding anniversary o aniversário
 de casamento
wedding cake o bolo de noiva
wedding dress o vestido de noiva
wedding present a prenda de
 casamento
wedding ring a aliança de casamento
Wednesday a quarta-feira
week a semana
 last week a semana passada
 next week a semana que vem
 per week por semana
 this week esta semana
 during the week durante a semana
weekday o dia útil
weekend o fim-de-semana
 next weekend o próximo
 fim-de-semana
 this weekend este fim-de-semana
weekly por semana
 weekly ticket o bilhete semanal
to weigh pesar
weight o peso
welcome bem-vindo(a)
well bem
 he's not well ele não se sente bem
well *(for water)* o poço
well-done *(steak)* bem-passado
wellington boots as galochas
Welsh galês (galesa)
 (language) o galês
west o oeste
wet molhado(a)
 (weather) chuvoso(a)
wetsuit o fato de mergulhador
what que
 what is it? o que é?
wheat o trigo
wheel a roda
wheelchair a cadeira de rodas
wheel clamp o imobilizador
when? quando?
where? onde?
which: which is it? qual é?
while enquanto
 in a while dentro de pouco
whipped cream o chantilly
whisky o uísque
white branco(a)
who: who is it? quem é?
whole inteiro(a)
wholemeal bread o pão integral
whose: whose is it? de quem é?
why? porquê?
wide largo(a)

widow a viúva
widower o viúvo
width a largura
wife a mulher ; a esposa
wig a peruca
to win ganhar
wind o vento
windbreak o guarda-vento
windmill o moínho
window a janela
  (shop) a montra
windscreen o pára-brisas
windscreen wipers o limpa-pára-brisas
to windsurf fazer windsurf
windsurfing o wind-surf
windy: *it's windy* está vento
wine o vinho
  red wine o vinho tinto
  white wine o vinho branco
  rosé wine o vinho rosé
  dry wine o vinho seco
  sweet wine o vinho doce
  sparkling wine o vinho espumante
  house wine o vinho da casa
  table wine o vinho de mesa
wine list a lista de vinhos
wing a asa
wing mirror o retrovisor exterior
winter o inverno
wire a arame
  (electric) o fio (eléctrico)
with com
  with ice com gelo
  with milk com leite
  with sugar com açúcar
without *milk* sem leite
  without sugar sem açúcar
witness a testemunha
wolf o lobo
woman a mulher
wonderful maravilhoso(a)
wood *(substance)* a madeira
woods a floresta
wool a lã
word a palavra
to work *(person)* trabalhar
  (machine) funcionar
  it doesn't work não está a funcionar;
  não funciona
work permit a autorização
  de trabalho
world o mundo

worldwide no mundo inteiro
worried preocupado(a)
worse pior
worth: *it's worth...* vale...
to wrap *(parcel, etc)* embrulhar
wrapping paper o papel de embrulho
wrinkles as rugas
wrist o pulso
to write escrever
  please write it down escreve-o,
  por favor
writing paper o papel de carta
wrong errado(a)
wrought iron o ferro forjado

X
x-ray a radiografia
to x-ray radiografar

Y
yacht o iate
year o ano
  last year o ano passado
  next year o ano que vem
  this year este ano
yearly: *twice yearly* duas vezes
  por ano
yellow amarelo(a)
Yellow Pages as Páginas Amarelas
yes sim
yesterday ontem
yet: *not yet* ainda não
yoghurt o iogurte
  plain yoghurt o iogurte natural
yolk a gema
you você/tu/vocês/vós
young novo(a)
  (person) o/a jovem
your teu (tua)
youth hostel o albergue da juventude

Z
zebra crossing a passadeira para peões
zero o zero
zip o fecho éclair
zone a zona
zoo o jardim zoológico
zoom lens o zoom

A

a to ; the *(feminine)*
abadia *f* abbey
abaixo down ; below
aberto open
  aberto todo o ano open all year round
abre-garrafas *m* bottle-opener
abre-latas *m* tin/can-opener
Abril *m* April
abrir to open; to unlock *(door)*
acabar to end ; to finish
acampar to camp
aceitar to accept
acelerador *m* accelerator
acender to switch/turn on ; to light *(fire, cigarette)* **acenda as luzes** switch on the lights
acepipe *m* titbit
  acepipes starters ; hors d'œuvres
aceso(a) on *(light, etc)*
acesso *m* access
achar to think ; to find
  acha bem? do you think it's all right?
acidente *m* accident
acima above
aço *m* steel
  aço inoxidável stainless steel
açorda *f* bread-based dish
acordo *m* agreement
Açores *mpl* the Azores archipelago
actual present(-day)
actualizar to modernize ; to update
açúcar *m* sugar
adega *f* wine cellar
adesivo *m* plaster *(for cut)*
adeus goodbye
adiantado(a) fast *(watch)* ; early *(train, etc)*
adulto(a) adult
advogado(a) *m/f* lawyer
aéreo(a): a linha aérea airline
  via aérea air mail
aeroporto *m* airport
agência *f* agency
  agência de viagens travel agents
agente *m/f* agent
agora now
Agosto *m* August
agradável pleasant
agradecer to thank
água *f* water

água destilada distilled water
água potável drinking water
água com gás fizzy water
água sem gás still water
aguardente *f* spirit brandy
agudo(a) sharp *(pain)*
ajudar to help
albergue *m* hostel
  albergue da juventude youth hostel
alcoólico(a) alcoholic
aldeia *f* small village
alegre jolly
Alemanha *f* Germany
alemão (alemã) German
alérgico(a) a allergic to
alface *f* lettuce
alfaiate *m* tailor
alfândega *f* customs
alfinete *m* pin
alforreca *f* jellyfish
algodão *m* cotton
algum(a) some ; any
  alguns (algumas) a few ; some
  mais alguma coisa? anything else?
alho *m* garlic
alhos-porros *mpl* leeks
ali there
alimentação *f* food
alívio *m* relief
almoço *m* lunch
  pequeno-almoço breakfast
almofada *f* pillow ; cushion
alojamento *m* accommodation
alpinismo *m* climbing
alto! stop!
alto(a) high ; tall ; loud
  a estação alta high season
altura *f* height
alugar to hire ; to rent
  aluga-se to rent
  alugam-se quartos rooms to let
aluguer *m* rental
amanhã tomorrow
amarelo(a) yellow
amargo(a) bitter
ambulância *f* ambulance
amêijoa *f* clam ; cockle
ameixa *f* plum
  ameixa seca prune
amêndoa *f* almond
  amêndoa amarga bitter almond liqueur

amendoim m peanut
amigo(a) m/f friend
amora f blackberry ; mulberry
amortecedor m shock absorber
amostra f sample
analgésico m painkiller
ananás m pineapple
anchovas fpl anchovies
andar to walk
andar m floor ; storey
  o primeiro andar first floor
anel m ring
anis m aniseed liqueur
aniversário m anniversary ; birthday
ano m year
  Ano Novo New Year
antes (de) before
antiguidades fpl antiques
apagado(a) off (radio, etc) ; out (light, etc)
apagar to switch/turn off (light, etc)
aparelho m gadget ; machine ; apparatus
  aparelho para a surdez hearing aid
apartamento m apartment ; flat
apelido m surname
  apelido de solteira maiden name
apenas only
apertado(a) tight
apetite m appetite
  bom apetite! enjoy your meal!
apólice de seguro f insurance certificate
aquecedor m heater ; electric fire
aquecimento m heating
aqui here
ar m air ; choke (car)
  ar condicionado air conditioning
arder to burn
areia f sand
arenque m herring
armário m cupboard ; closet
armazém m warehouse
  grande armazém department store
arrendar to let
arroz m rice
  arroz doce rice pudding
artesanato m handicrafts
artigo m item
  artigos de ménage household goods
  artigos de vime wickerwork
árvore f tree
ascensor m lift

assado(a) roast ; baked
assinar to sign
assinatura f signature
assistência f audience ; assistance
atacadores mpl laces
até until ; as far as
aterrar to land
atrás behind
atrasado(a) late (for appointment)
atrasar to delay
atraso m delay
atravessar to cross
atum m tuna (fish)
autocarro m bus ; coach
  a paragem de autocarro bus stop
auto-estrada f motorway
automobilista m/f driver
automóvel m car
autorização f licence ; permit
avaria f breakdown
avariado(a) out of order (machine) ; broken down (car)
ave f bird
avelã f hazelnut
avenida f avenue
avião m plane
aviso m warning
avô m grandfather
avó f grandmother
azedo(a) sour
azeite m olive oil
azeitona f olive
azul blue
azulejo m ornamental tile

B

bacalhau m dried salt cod
  bacalhau à Brás dried salt cod with eggs, onion and potatoes
bagaceira f eau de vie
bagaço m eau de vie
bagagem f luggage ; baggage
Bairrada region producing full-bodied red and aromatic white wines
bairro m quarter ; district
Baixa f commercial centre of Lisbon
baixar to lower
baixo: em baixo below
balança f scales (weighing machine)
balcão m shop counter ; circle in theatre
banco m bank ; seat (in car, etc)

bandeira f flag ; banner
bandeja f tray ; salver
bandido m gangster ; robber
banheira f bath-tub
banheiro m lifeguard
banho m bath
  a casa de banho bathroom
  tomar banho to have a bath
banquete m banquet ; sumptuous dinner
barato(a) cheap
barba f beard
  fazer a barba to shave
barbeiro m barber
barco m boat ; ship
  barco a remos rowing boat
  barco a vela sailing boat
barraca f hut (shed) ; beach hut
barreira f trench ; obstacle ; barrier
barriga f belly
barro m pottery ; terracotta
barulho m noise
bastante enough
batata f potato
  batatas fritas chips ; crisps
bater to beat ; to knock
  bata à porta please knock
bateria f battery (for car)
batido de leite m milk shake
baunilha f vanilla
bebé m baby
beber to drink
bebida f drink
beco m alley
belo(a) beautiful
bem well
  está bem OK
  bem passado well done (steak)
bem-vindo(a) welcome
bengaleiro m cloakroom (at theatre) ; hat and umbrella stand
benzer to bless
beringela f aubergine
berma f hard shoulder
  bermas baixas steep verge – no hard shoulder
berço m crib; cradle; cot
besugo m sea bream
beterraba f beetroot
bexiga f bladder
bica f espresso coffee
bicha f queue
  fazer bicha to queue

bicicleta f bicycle
bife m steak
  bife com batatas fritas steak and chips
bifurcação f junction
bilhar m billiards
bilhete m ticket ; fare
  bilhete de entrada admission ticket
  bilhete de identidade identity card
bilheteira f ticket office
binóculos mpl binoculars
boa see bom
boca f mouth
bocado: um bocado a bit ; a portion
boîte f nightclub
bola f ball
  bola de Berlim doughnut
bolacha f biscuit
bolo m cake
  bolo-rei ring-shaped fruit cake eaten at Christmas
bolsa f stock exchange ; handbag
bom (boa) good ; fine (weather) ; kind
  bom dia good morning
  boa tarde good afternoon
  boa noite good evening ; good night
bomba f bomb ; pump (petrol)
bombeiros mpl fire brigade
bondade f kindness
boneco(a) doll ; puppet toy
bonito(a) pretty
borbulha f spot ; pimple
bordados mpl embroidered items
borrego m lamb
bosque m small forest ; woodland
bota f boot (to wear)
botão m button; bud
braço m arm
branco(a) white
  vinho branco white wine
breve brief
  em breve soon
brigada de trânsito f traffic police
brincos mpl earrings
brinquedo m toy
britânico(a) British
broa f corn (maize) bread
  broas corn (maize) cakes
bronzeador m suntan oil
brushing m blow-dry
bugigangas fpl bric-à-brac
burro(a) m/f ass ; donkey ; stupid person

buscar to look for
bússola f compass
buzinar to toot (car horn)

C

cá here ; in this place
cabana f shack ; hut
cabeça f head
cabedais mpl leather goods
cabeleireiro(a) m/f hairdresser
cabelo m hair
cabide m coat hanger ; peg (for clothes)
cabine f cabin ; booth
  cabine telefónica phone box
cabo m knife handle ; electric lead
  cabos de emergência jump leads
  cabo de reboque tow rope
cabra f goat
  queijo de cabra goat's cheese
cabrito m kid (goat)
caça f game (to eat) ; hunting
caçador m hunter
cachorro m hot dog ; puppy
cada each ; every
cadeado m padlock
cadeia f jail ; chain
cadeira f chair
  cadeira de bebé high chair ; push chair
  cadeira de lona deck chair
  cadeira de rodas wheelchair
cadela f female dog
café m (black) coffee ; café
cãibra f cramp
cair to fall ; to fall over
cais m quay
caixa f cash desk
  caixa automática cash machine
  caixa do correio letterbox
caixão m coffin
caixote m bin ; wooden box ; container
calar to stop talking ; to keep silent
calçado m footwear
calças fpl trousers
calções mpl shorts
  calções de banho swimming trunks
calços para travões mpl brake pads
calcular to estimate ; to calculate
caldeirada f fish stew
caldo m stock (for soup)
  caldo verde cabbage soup

calor m heat
cama f bed
  cama de casal double bed
  cama de bebé cot
  cama de criança child's bed
  cama de solteiro single bed
  a roupa de cama bedding
câmara de ar f inner tube
câmara municipal f town hall
camarão m shrimp
camarote m cabin ; box (theatre)
cambiar to exchange ; to change money
câmbio m exchange rate
  casa de câmbios f money exchange shop
camião m lorry
caminho m path ; way ; route
camioneta f coach
camisa f shirt
  camisa de noite nightdress
camomila f camomile (tea)
campaínha f bell (on door)
campismo m camping
campo m field ; countryside
campo de golfe golf course
camurça f suede
cancelar to cancel
canela f cinnamon
caneta f pen
cano de esgoto m drain
canoagem f canoeing
cansaço m fatigue
cansado(a) tired
cantar to sing
cantina f canteen
canto m corner (inside)
cão m dog
capacete m crash helmet
capela f chapel
capitão m captain
capota f bonnet (of car)
cara f face
caracóis mpl snails ; curls (hair)
caramelos mpl toffees
caranguejo m crab
carapau m horse mackerel
caravana f caravan
carburador m carburettor
carga f refill ; load
caril m curry
carioca m weak coffee
  carioca de limão lemon infusion

carne f meat
 carne de borrego spring lamb
 carne picada mince
 carne de porco pork
 carne de vaca beef
 carne de vitela veal
 carnes frias cold meats
carneiro m mutton ; lamb
caro(a) expensive
 caro(a) amigo(a) dear friend
caroço m kernel ; pip
carregamento m cargo ; load
carrinha f van
carrinho m trolley
 carrinho de bebé pram ; carry cot
carro m car
carruagem f carriage *(railway)*
 carruagem-cama sleeper *(railway)*
carruagem-restaurante f restaurant car
carta f letter
cartão m card ; business card
 cartão bancário cheque card
 cartão de crédito credit card
 cartão de embarque boarding card
 cartão de felicitações greetings card
 cartão garantia cheque card
cartaz m poster ; billboard
carteira f wallet
carteirista m pickpocket
carteiro m postman
carvalho m oak tree
carvão m coal
casa f home ; house
 casa de banho toilet ; bathroom
casaco m jacket ; coat
casado(a) married
casal m couple
casamento m wedding
caso m case
 em caso de... in case of...
castanha f chestnut
 castanhas assadas roast chestnuts
 castanhas piladas dried chestnuts
castanho(a) brown
castelo m castle
catedral f cathedral
causa f cause
 por causa de because of
cautela take care
cavala f mackerel
cavalheiro m gentleman
cavalo m horse
cave f cellar

cebola f onion
cedo early
cego(a) adj blind
 m/f blind man/woman
ceia f supper
célebre famous
cem one hundred
cemitério m cemetery
cenoura f carrot
centígrado m centigrade
centímetro m centimetre
cêntimo m cent
cento: *por cento* per cent
centro m centre
 centro da cidade city centre
 centro comercial shopping centre
 centro de saúde health centre
cera f wax
cerâmica f pottery
cérebro m brain
cereja f cherry
certeza f certainty
 ter a certeza to be sure
certificado m certificate
certo(a) right *(correct, accurate)* ; certain
cerveja f beer ; lager
 cerveja preta bitter *(beer)*
cervejaria f beer house
cesto m basket
céu m sky
chá f tea
 chá de limão lemon tea
chamada f telephone call
 chamada gratuita free call
 chamada internacional international call
 chamada pagável no destino reverse charge call
chamar to call
champô m shampoo
chão m floor
chapa de matrícula f number plate
chapéu m hat
 chapéu de sol sunhat ; sunshade
charcutaria f delicatessen
chave f key
 fechar à chave to lock up
chávena f cup
chefe m boss
 chefe de cozinha chef
chega! that's enough!
chegadas fpl arrivals
chegar to arrive

cheio(a) full
cheirar to smell
cheiro m smell
  mau cheiro bad smell
cheque m cheque
  cheque de viagem traveller's cheque
  levantar um cheque to cash a cheque
cherne m black jewfish or grouper
chispalhada f bean stew with pig's trotters
chispe m pig's trotters
chocos mpl cuttlefish
  chocos com tinta cuttlefish cooked in their ink
chouriço m spicy sausage
churrascaria f barbecue restaurant
churrasco m barbecue
  no churrasco barbecued
chuva f rain
chuveiro m shower (bath)
Cia. see companhia
cidadão (cidadã) m/f citizen
cidade f town ; city
cigarro m cigarette
cima: em cima de on (top of)
cinco five
cinto m belt
  cinto de salvação lifebelt
  cinto de segurança seat belt
cinzento(a) grey
circuito m circuit
cirurgia f surgery (operation)
claro(a) light (colour) ; bright
classe f class
cliente m/f client
clínica f clinic
clube m club
cobertor m blanket
cobrar to cash ; charge
cobrir to cover
código m code ; dialling code
  código postal postcode
codorniz f quail
coelho m rabbit
coentro m coriander
cofre m safe
cogumelo m mushroom
coisa f thing
cola f glue
colar n necklace
colar vb to stick
colcha f bedspread

colchão m mattress
colecção f collection (of stamps etc)
colégio m (secondary) school
colete de salvação m life jacket
colher f spoon
colina f hill
collants mpl tights
colorau m paprika
coluna f pillar
  coluna vertebral spine
com with
comando m TV remote control
comandos mpl controls
comboio m train
combustível m fuel
começar to begin ; to start
comer to eat
comida f food
comissário de bordo m steward ; purser
como as ; how
  como disse? I beg your pardon?
  como está? how are you?
comodidade f comfort
companheiro(a) m/f live-in partner
companhia (Cia.) f company
compartimento m compartment
completar to complete
completo no vacancies (sign in hotel etc)
compota f jam
compra f purchase
  ir às compras to go shopping
comprar to buy
compreender to understand
comprido(a) long
comprimento m length
comprimido m pill ; tablet
computador m computer
concelho m council
concordar to agree
concorrente m/f candidate
concurso m competition
condução f driving
  a carta de condução driving licence
condutor m driver ; chauffeur
conduzir to drive
conferência f conference
conferir to check
congelado(a) frozen (food)
congelar to freeze
  não congelar do not freeze
conhaque m cognac

conhecer to know *(person, place)*
conselho *m* advice
consertos *mpl* repairs
conservar to keep ; to preserve
  conservar no frio store in a cold place
constipação *f* cold *(illness)*
consulado *m* consulate
consulta *f* consultation ; appointment
consultório *m* surgery
consumir antes de... best before...
  (label on food)
conta *f* account; bill
contador *m* meter *(electricity, water)*
conter to contain
  não contem... does not contain...
contra against
contraceptivo *m* contraceptive
contrato *m* contract
convidado(a) *m/f* guest
convidar to invite ; to ask *(invite)*
convite *m* invitation
copo *m* glass *(container)*
cor *f* colour
coração *m* heart
cordeiro *m* lamb
cor-de-laranja orange *(colour)*
cor-de-rosa pink
corpo *m* body
correia *f* strap
  correia de ventoinha fan belt
correio *m* post office
  pelo correio by post
corrente *f* chain ; current
correr to flow ; to run *(person)*
correspondência *f* mail
corrida *f* race
  corrida de touros bullfight
  corridas de cavalos races
cortar to cut ; to cut off
  cortar e fazer brushing to cut
  and blow-dry
corte *m* cut
cortiça *f* cork
costa *f* shore ; coastline
costela *f* rib
costeleta *f* chop *(meat)* ; cutlet
cotovelo *m* elbow
couro *m* leather
couve *f* cabbage
  couves-de-Bruxelas Brussels sprouts
couve-flor *f* cauliflower
couvert *m* cover charge

coxia *f* aisle
cozer to boil
cozido(a) boiled
  mal cozido underdone
cozinha *f* kitchen
cozinhar to cook
cozinheiro(a) *m/f* cook
cravinhos *mpl* cloves
cravo *m* carnation
creme *m* custard
  creme de barbear shaving cream
  creme para bronzear suntan cream
  creme hidratante moisturizer
  creme de limpeza cleansing cream
criança *f* child
cru(a) raw
cruz *f* cross
cruzamento *m* junction *(crossroads)*
cruzar to cross
cruzeiro *m* cruise
cuecas *fpl* briefs ; pants
cuidado *m* care *(caution)*
cumprimento *m* greeting
  cumprimentos regards
cunhado(a) *m/f* brother-in-law/
  sister-in-law
curso *m* course
curto(a) short
curva *f* bend ; turning ; curve
  curva perigosa dangerous bend
custar to cost
custo *m* charge ; cost

D

damasco *m* apricot
dança *f* dance
dano *m* damage
Dão fruity red and white wines from
  the north of Portugal
dar to give
  dar prioridade to give way
data *f* date
  data de nascimento date of birth
de of ; from
debaixo de under
decidir to decide
dedo *m* finger
dedo do pé toe
defeito *m* flaw
deficiente disabled
degrau *m* step *(stair)*

deitar-se to lie down
deixar to let *(allow)* ; to leave behind
delito *m* crime
demais too much ; too many
demasia *f* change *(money)* ; excess
demorado(a) late
demorar to delay
dente *m* tooth
dentes teeth
dentes postiços false teeth
dentista *m* dentist
dentro inside
depois after(wards)
depósito *m* deposit *(in bank)*
  depósito de bagagens left-luggage
  depósito da gasolina petrol tank
depressa quickly
desafio *m* match ; game *(sport)* ;
  challenge
desaparecido(a) missing
desapertar to loosen
descafeinado *m* decaffeinated
descansar to rest
descartável throw-away ; disposable
descer to go down
descoberta *f* discovery
descongelar to defrost *(food)* ;
  to de-ice
desconhecido(a) *m/f* stranger
desconhecido(a) *adj* unknown
desconto *m* discount ; reduction
desculpe excuse me ; sorry
desejar to desire ; to wish
desembarcar to disembark
desempregado(a) unemployed
desenho *m* design ; drawing
desinchar to go down *(swelling)*
desinfectante *m* disinfectant
desligado(a) off *(engine, gas)*
desligar to hang up *(phone)* ;
  to switch off *(engine, radio)*
desligue o motor switch off your
  engine
desmaiar to faint
desodorizante *m* deodorant
despachante *m* shipper ; (transport)
  agent
despesa *f* expense
desporto *m* sport
destinatário *m* addressee
desvio *m* bypass ; detour ; diversion
detergente *m* detergent

detergente para a louça washing-up
  liquid
detergente para a roupa washing
  powder
devagar slowly ; slow down *(sign)*
dever: eu devo I must
deve-me... you owe me...
devolver to give back ; to return
Dezembro *m* December
dia *m* day
  dias da semana weekdays
  dia útil working day
  dia de anos birthday
diabético(a) diabetic
diante de in front of *(place)*
diário daily
diarreia *f* diarrhoea
dieta *f* diet ; special diet
diferença *f* difference
difícil difficult
digestão *f* digestion
diluir to dilute
diminuir to reduce
dínamo *m* dynamo
dinheiro *m* money ; cash
direcção *f* direction ; address ; steering
directo(a) direct
direita *f* right(-hand side)
  à direita on the right
  para a direita to the right
direito(a) straight ; right(-hand)
  Dto. on right-hand side *(address)*
direitos *mpl* duty *(tax)* ; rights
dirigir to direct
disco *m* record *(music, etc)*
  disco de estacionamento parking disk
disponível available
dissolver to dissolve
distância *f* distance
distrito *m* district
divã-cama *m* bed settee
diversões *fpl* entertainment
divertir-se to enjoy oneself ;
  to have fun
dívida *f* debt
divisas *fpl* foreign currency
dizer to say
dobrada *f* tripe
dobrado(a) bent
dobro *m* double
doce *adj* sweet *(taste)*
doce *m* dessert ; jam

documentos mpl documents
doente ill ; sick
doer to ache ; to hurt
dólar m dollar
domicílio m residence
domingo m Sunday
dono(a) m/f owner
  dona de casa housewife
dor f ache ; pain
dormir to sleep
Douro region producing port
Dto. see direito(a)
duche m shower
duplo(a) double
durante during
durar to last
duro(a) hard ; stiff ; tough (meat)
dúzia f dozen

E

e and
é he/she/it is ; you are
economizar to save
écrã m screen
edifício m building
edredão m duvet ; quilt
educado(a) polite
eixo de roda m axle
ela she ; her ; it
elas they (feminine)
elástico m elastic band
ele he ; him ; it
eles they (masculine)
electricista m electrician
eléctrico m tram
electrodomésticos mpl electrical
  appliances
elevador m lift
em at ; in (with towns, countries) ; into
embaixada f embassy
embarcar to board (ship, plane)
embarque m embarkation ; time
  of sailing
embraiagem f clutch
ementa f menu
  ementa fixa set menu
emergência f emergency
empregado(a) m/f waiter(ess) ;
  maid ; attendant (at petrol station) ;
  assistant (in shop) ; office worker
emprego m job ; employment

empurrar to push
  empurre push (sign)
EN see estrada
encaracolado(a) curly
encarnado(a) red
encerrado(a) closed
encher to fill up ; to pump up (tyre)
enchidos mpl processed meats ;
  sausages
encomenda f parcel
encontrar to meet ; to find
encontro m date ; meeting
encosta f hill (slope)
endereço m address
energia f energy
  o corte de energia power cut
enfermeiro(a) m/f nurse
enganar-se to make a mistake
engano m mistake
engolir to swallow
  não engolir do not swallow
engraxar to polish (shoes)
enguia f eel
enjoar to be sick
ensinar to teach
ensopado m stew served on slice
  of bread
enorme big ; huge
entender to understand
entorse f sprain
entrada f entrance ; starter (in meal)
  entrada livre admission free
entrar to go in ; to come in ;
  to get into (car, etc)
entre among ; between
entregar to deliver
entrevista f interview
enviar to send
enxaqueca f migraine
época f period
equipamento m equipment
equitação f horse riding
erro m mistake
erva f grass ; herb
ervilhas fpl peas
esc. see escudo
escada f ladder ; stairs
  escada rolante escalator
escalfado(a) poached (egg)
escape m exhaust
escocês (escocesa) Scottish
Escócia f Scotland

escola f school

escova f brush

escova de dentes toothbrush

escrever to write

escrito: por escrito in writing

escritório m office

escudo (esc.) m escudo *(former Portuguese currency)*

escuro(a) dark *(colour)*

escutar to listen to

esferográfica f ballpoint pen

esgotado(a) sold out *(tickets)* ; exhausted

esgoto m drain

esmalte m enamel

espaço m space

espadarte m swordfish

espalhar to scatter

Espanha f Spain

espanhol m Spanish *(language)*

espanhol(a) Spanish

espargo m asparagus

esparguete m spaghetti

esparregado m puréed spinach

especialidade f speciality

especiarias fpl spices

espectáculo m show *(in theatre etc)*

espelho m mirror
 espelho retrovisor driving mirror

esperar to expect ; to hope
 esperar por to wait for

espetada f kebab

espinafre m spinach

esplanada f terrace

esposa f wife

espumante m sparkling wine

espumoso(a) sparkling *(wine)*

Esq. *see* esquerda

esquadra f police station

esquentador m water heater

esquerda f left(-hand side)
 à esquerda on the left
 Esq. on left(-hand) side *(address)*

esqui m ski

esquina f corner *(outside)*

está he/she/it is ; you are

estação f station
 estação alta high season
 estação baixa low season
 estação do ano season
 estação de autocarros bus station
 estação de serviço service station

estação do comboio railway station

estacionamento m parking

estacionar to park *(car)*

estádio m stadium

estado m state
 estado civil marital status

Estados Unidos (EUA) mpl United States

estalagem f inn

estância termal f spa

estar to be

este/esta m/f this
 estes/estas m/f these

estômago m stomach
 o mal-estar de estômago stomach upset

estores mpl blinds

estrada f road
 estrada em mau estado uneven road surface
 estrada nacional (EN) major road ; national highway
 estrada sem saída no through road
 estrada secundária minor road

estrangeiro(a) m/f foreigner

estranho(a) strange

estreito(a) narrow

estudante m/f student

estufado(a) braised

etiqueta f ticket ; label ; etiquette

eu I

EUA *see* Estados Unidos

euro m euro

europeu (europeia) European

evitar to avoid

excepto except
 excepto aos domingos Sundays excepted

excesso de bagagem m excess luggage ; excess baggage

excursão f excursion ; tour
 excursão guiada guided tour

exemplo m example
 por exemplo for example

expirar to expire

explicar to explain

exportação f exportation

exportar to export

exposição f exhibition

extintor m fire extinguisher

extremidade f edge ; extremity

F

fábrica f factory
fabricado(a) em ... made in ...
faca f knife
fácil easy
facilidade f facility ; ease
factura f invoice
fado m traditional Portuguese song
faiança f pottery
faisão m pheasant
faixa f lane (in road)
falar to speak
falecido(a) deceased
falésias fpl cliffs
falta f lack
  falta de corrente power cut
família f family
farinha f flour
farinheira f sausage made with pork fat and flour
farmácia f chemist's
  farmácia permanente duty chemist
  farmácias de serviço emergency chemists'
faróis mpl headlights
farol m headlight ; lighthouse
farolim m sidelight
fatia f slice
fato m suit (man's)
  fato de banho swimsuit
  fato de treino tracksuit
favas fpl broad beans
favor m favour
  faz favor please
  por favor please
fazer to do ; to make
febras de porco fpl slices of roast pork
febre f fever
  febre dos fenos hay fever
  ter febre to have a temperature
fechado closed
  fechado Domingos e Feriados closed Sundays and Bank holidays
fechar to shut ; to close
feijão m beans
feijão-verde m French beans
feijoada f bean stew with pork and spicy sausage
feio(a) awful ; ugly

feira f fair (commercial) ; market
feito(a) à mão handmade
feliz happy
feriado m public holiday
  feriado nacional bank holiday
férias fpl holidays
ferido(a) injured
ferragens fpl ironware
ferro m iron
  ferro de engomar iron (for clothes)
ferver to boil
festa f party (celebration)
Fevereiro m February
fiambre m ham (boiled)
ficar to stay ; to be ; to remain
  ficar bem to suit
ficha f plug (electrical) ; registration card (in hotel, clinic)
  ficha dupla/tripla adaptor (electrical)
fígado m liver
figo m fig
  figos secos dried figs
fila f row (line) ; queue
filete m fillet steak ; tenderloin
filha f daughter
filho m son
filial f branch (of bank, etc)
filigranas fpl filigree work
fim m end
  fim-de-semana weekend
fio m wire
fita f tape ; ribbon
  fita métrica tape measure
flor f flower
floresta f forest
florista f florist
fogão m cooker
fogo m fire
  fogos de artifício fireworks
folha f leaf
  folha de alumínio aluminium foil
  folha de estanho tinfoil
folhados mpl puff pastries
folheto m leaflet
fome f hunger
  tenho fome I'm hungry
fonte f fountain ; source
fora out ; outside
força f power (strength) ; force

formiga f ant
fornecer to supply
forno m oven
fortaleza f fortress
forte strong
forte m fortress
fósforo m match
fotografia f photograph ; print
fraco(a) weak
fralda f nappy
framboesa f raspberry
França f France
francês m French (language)
francês (francesa) French
frango m chicken (young and tender)
 frango assado roast chicken
frase f sentence
freguês (freguesa) m/f customer
frente f front
 em frente de in front of ; opposite
fresco(a) fresh ; cool ; crisp
 sirva fresco serve cool
frigorífico m fridge
frio(a) cold
fritar to fry
frito(a) fried
fronha f pillow case
fronteira f border (frontier)
fruta f fruit
frutaria f fruit shop
fruto m fruit
fuga f leak ; escape
fugir to run away
fumadores mpl smokers
 para não fumadores non-smoking
 (compartment, etc)
fumar to smoke
 não fumar no smoking
fumo m smoke
funcionar to work (machine)
 não funciona out of order (sign)
funcionário(a) m/f employee ;
 civil servant
fundo m bottom
fundo(a) deep
furar to pierce
furnas fpl caverns
furto m theft
fusível m fuse
futebol m football

G

gabinete de provas m changing room
gado m cattle
 gado bravo beware – unfenced bulls
gaivota f seagull ; pedal boat
galão m large white coffee ; gallon
galeria f gallery
Gales: o País de Gales Wales
galês (galesa) Welsh
galinha f hen ; chicken
gamba f prawn
ganhar to earn ; to win
ganso m goose
garagem f garage
garantia f guarantee
gare f platform
garfo m fork
garganta f throat
garoto m boy ; small white coffee
garrafa f bottle
garrafão m two or five-litre bottle
gás m gas
 a botija de gás gas cylinder
gasóleo m diesel
gasolina f petrol
gasosa f fizzy sweetened water
gastar to spend
gaveta f drawer
gelado m ice cream ; ice lolly
gelar to freeze
gelataria f ice cream parlour
geleia f jelly
gelo m ice
gémeo(a) m/f twin
género m kind ; type
 o meu género de filme my kind
 of film
gengibre m ginger
gengivas fpl gums
genro m son-in-law
gente f people
 toda a gente everybody
geral f gallery (in theatre)
geral adj general
 em geral generally
geralmente usually
gerente m manager
ginjinha f morello cherry liqueur
gira-discos m record player
girassol m sunflower

gola f collar
golfe m golf
 o taco de golfe golf club (stick)
gordo(a) fat
gorjeta f tip (to waiter, etc)
gostar de to like
gosto m taste
governo m government
Grã-Bretanha f Britain
grama m gramme
grande big ; large ; great
grão m chickpeas
grátis free (costing nothing)
gravador m tape recorder
gravata f tie
grávida pregnant
gravura f print (picture)
grelhado(a) grilled
greve f strike (industrial)
 em greve on strike
gripe f flu
groselha f (red)currant
grosso(a) thick
grupo m group ; party (group)
 grupo sanguíneo blood group
grutas fpl caves
guarda m/f police officer
guarda-chuva m umbrella
guarda-lamas m mudguard
guardanapo m napkin
guardar to keep ; to watch over
guarda-sol m sunshade
guia m/f guide
guiché m window (at post office, bank)
guisado m stew
guitarra f guitar

H

há there is ; there are
habitação f residence ; home
habitar to reside
história f history ; story
hoje today
homem m man
 o wc dos Homens gents' toilet
hora f hour ; time (by the clock)
 hora de chegada time of arrival
 hora de partida departure time
 hora de ponta rush hour
horário m timetable
hortelã f mint (herb)

hortelã-pimenta f peppermint
hóspede m/f guest
hospedeira f hostess
 hospedeira de bordo flight attendant

I

iate m yacht
icterícia f jaundice
ida f visit ; trip ; single trip
 ida e volta return trip
idade f age
identificação f identification
idosos mpl the elderly ; old people
ignição f ignition ; starter (in car)
igreja f church
igual equal ; the same as
ilha f island
impedir to prevent
impedido(a) engaged (phone)
imperial m draught beer
impermeável m raincoat
 adj waterproof
importação f importation
importância f importance ;
 amount (money)
importante important
imposto m tax ; duty
 impostos duty ; tax
impressão digital f fingerprint
impresso m form (to fill in)
imprevisto(a) unexpected
impulso m unit of charge (for phone) ;
 impulse
incêndio m fire
inchado(a) swollen
incluído(a) included
incomodar to disturb
 não incomodar do not disturb
indicativo m dialling code
indigestão f indigestion
infecção f infection
infeccioso(a) infectious (illness)
inflamação f inflammation
informação f information
infracção f offence
Inglaterra f England
inglês m English (language)
inglês (inglesa) English
iniciais fpl initials
iniciar to begin
início m beginning

inquilino m tenant
inscrever to register
insecto m insect
insolação f heatstroke ; sunstroke
instalações fpl facilities
instituto m institute
insuflável inflatable
inteiro(a) whole
interdito(a) forbidden
interessante interesting
interior inside
interno(a) internal
intérprete m/f interpreter
interruptor m switch
intervalo m interval (in theatre)
intestinos mpl bowels
intoxicação f food poisoning
introduzir to introduce ; insert
inundação f flood
inverno m winter
iogurte m yoghurt
ir to go
Irlanda f Ireland
  a Irlanda do Norte Northern Ireland
irlandês (irlandesa) Irish
irmã f sister
irmão m brother
iscas fpl marinated pig's liver
  with potatoes
isqueiro m lighter
isso that
isto this
Itália f Italy
italiano(a) Italian
itinerário m route ; itinerary
IVA m VAT

J
já already ; now
jamais never
Janeiro m January
janela f window
jantar m dinner ; evening meal
jardim m garden
joalharia f jeweller's ; jewellery
joelho m knee
jogar to play (sport)
jogo m match ; game; play
jóia f jewel
jornal m newspaper
jovem young

judeu (judia) m/f Jew ; Jewish
juiz(a) m/f judge
julgamento m verdict ; sentence
Julho m July
Junho m June
juntar to join
junto near
justiça f justice
juventude f youth

K
kg. see quilo(grama)

L
lã f wool
lábio m lip
laço m bow (ribbon, string) ; bow-tie
lado m side
ao lado de next to
ladrão (ladra) m/f thief
lagarto m lizard
lago m lake
lagosta f lobster
lagostim m king prawn
lâminas de barbear fpl razor blades
lâmpada f light bulb
lampreia f lamprey
lançar to throw
lanchar to go for a snack
lanche m light mid-afternoon snack
lápis m pencil
  lápis de cera crayons (wax)
lar m home
laranja f orange
  o doce de laranja marmalade
largo m small square
largo(a) broad ; loose (clothes) ; wide
largura f width
lata f tin ; can (of food)
latão m brass
lavabo m lavatory ; toilet
lava-louça m sink
lavandaria f laundry
  lavandaria automática launderette
  lavandaria a seco dry-cleaner's
lavar to wash (clothes, etc)
lavar a louça to wash up
lavar à mão to handwash
lavável washable
lebre f hare

legumes *mpl* vegetables
lei *f* law
leilão *m* auction
leitão *m* sucking pig
leite *m* milk
  com leite white *(coffee)*
  leite desnatado skimmed milk
  leite evaporado evaporated milk
  leite gordo full-cream milk
  leite magro skimmed milk
  leite meio-gordo semi-skimmed milk
lembranças *fpl* souvenirs
lembrar-se to remember
leme *m* rudder ; helm
lenço *m* handkerchief ; tissue
lençol *m* sheet
lente *f* lens
  lentes de contacto contact lenses
lento(a) slow
leque *m* fan *(hand-held)*
ler to read
leste *m* east
letra *f* letter *(of alphabet)*
  letra maiúscula capital letter
levantar to draw *(money)* ; to lift
levantar-se to stand up ; get up *(from bed)*
levar to take ; to carry
leve light *(not heavy)*
libra *f* pound
  libras esterlinas pounds sterling
lição *f* lesson
licença *f* permit
liceu *m* secondary school
licor *m* liqueur
ligação *f* connection *(trains, etc)*
ligado(a) on *(engine, gas, etc)*
ligeiro(a) light
lima *f* lime *(fruit)*
lima *f* file
  lima das unhas nail file
limão *m* lemon
limite *m* limit
  limite de velocidade speed limit
limonada *f* lemonade
limpar to wipe ; to clean
limpeza *f* cleaning
  limpeza a seco dry-cleaning
limpo(a) clean
língua *f* language ; tongue
linguado *m* sole *(fish)*
linguiça *f* narrow spicy pork sausage

linha *f* line ; thread ; platform *(railway)*
linho *m* linen
liquidação *f* (clearance) sale
Lisboa (Lx) Lisbon
liso(a) smooth ; straight
lista *f* list
  lista de preços price list
  lista telefónica telephone directory
litro *m* litre
livraria *f* bookshop
livre free ; vacant ; for hire
livro *m* book
lixívia *f* bleach
lixo *m* rubbish
loção *f* lotion
loja *f* shop
lombo *m* loin *(cut of meat)*
Londres London
longe far
  é longe? is it far?
longo(a) long
lotaria *f* lottery
louça *f* dishes ; crockery
louro(a) fair *(hair)*
louro *m* bay leaf *(herb)*
lua *f* moon
lua-de-mel *f* honeymoon
lugar *m* seat *(theatre)* ; place
lulas *fpl* squid
luvas *fpl* gloves
luxo *m* luxury
luz *f* light
  luzes de presença sidelights
  luzes de perigo hazard lights
Lx see Lisboa

M

M. underground *(metro)*
má *see* mau
maçã *f* apple
macho *m* male *(animal)*
macio(a) soft ; smooth
maço *m* packet *(of cigarettes)*
Madeira *f* Madeira
madeira *f* wood
Madeira *m* Madeira wine
madrugada *f* early morning
maduro(a) ripe
mãe *f* mother
magro(a) thin
Maio *m* May

maior larger
  a maior parte de the majority of
mais more
  o/a mais the most
mal wrong ; evil
mala f suitcase ; bag ; trunk
malagueta f chilli
mal-entendido m misunderstanding
mal-estar m discomfort
mancha f stain
mandar to send ; to order
maneira f way (method)
manga f sleeve ; mango
manhã f morning
manteiga f butter
manter to keep ; to maintain
mão f hand
mapa m map
  mapa das estradas road map
  mapa das ruas street plan
máquina f machine
  máquina fotográfica camera
mar m sea
maracujá m passion fruit
marca f brand ; mark
marcação f booking ; dialling
marcar to dial (phone) ; to mark
marcha-atrás f reverse (gear)
Março m March
marco do correio m pillar box
maré f tide
  maré alta high tide
  maré baixa low tide
marfim m ivory
marido m husband
marisco m seafood ; shellfish
marmelada f quince jam
marmelo m quince
mármore m marble (substance)
Marrocos Morocco
marroquinaria f leather goods
mas but
massa f dough
  massas pasta
  massa folhada puff pastry
matrícula f number plate
mau (má) bad ; evil
máximo(a) maximum
mazagrã m iced coffee and lemon
me me
mecânico m mechanic
média f average

medicamento m medicine
médico(a) m/f doctor
medida f measure ; size
médio(a) medium
medusa f jellyfish
meia f stocking ; half
meia-hora f half-hour
meia-noite f midnight
meio m middle
  no meio de in the middle of
meio(a) half
  meia garrafa a half bottle
  meia de leite cup of milky coffee
  (half milk, half coffee)
  meia pensão half board
meio-dia m midday ; noon
meio-seco medium sweet (wine)
mel m honey
melancia f watermelon
melão m melon
melhor better
  o/a melhor the best
meloa f small round melon
menina f Miss ; girl
menino m boy
menor smaller ; minor (underage)
menos least ; less
mensagem f message
mensal monthly
menstruação f period (menstruation)
mercado m market
mercearia f grocer's
merengue m meringue
mês m month
mesa f table
mesmo(a) same
mesquita f mosque
metade f half
  pela metade do preço half-price
meter to put in
metro m metre ; underground (rail)
metropolitano m tube (underground)
meu (minha) my ; mine
mexer to move
  não mexer do not touch
mexilhão m mussel
migas à alentejana bread dish with
  pork meats
mil thousand
milhão m million
milho m maize ; corn
mim me

minha *see* meu
mínimo(a) minimum
minúsculo(a) tiny
missa *f* Mass *(church service)*
mobília *f* furniture
mochila *f* backpack ; rucksack
moda *f* fashion
moeda *f* coin ; currency
moído(a) ground *(coffee, etc)*
moinho *m* windmill
  moinho de café coffee grinder
mola *f* peg ; spring *(coiled metal)*
molhado(a) wet
molho *m* sauce ; gravy
momento *m* moment
montanha *f* mountain
montante *m* amount *(total)*
montra *f* shop window
morada *f* address
moradia *f* villa
morango *m* strawberry
morar to live ; to reside
morcela *f* black pudding
mordedura *f* bite *(animal)*
morder to bite
  fui mordido(a) por um cão I was
  bitten by a dog
moreno(a) tanned ; dark-skinned
morrer to die
mortadela *f* cold meat *(salami)*
mosaicos *mpl* mosaic tiles
mosca *f* fly *(insect)*
mostarda *f* mustard
mosteiro *m* monastery
mostrador *m* dial ; glass counter
mostrar to show
motocicleta *f* motorbike
motor *m* engine ; motor
  motor de arranque starter motor
motorista *m* driver
motorizada *f* motorbike
muçulmano(a) *m/f* Muslim
mudar to change
  mudar-se to move house
muito very ; much ; quite *(rather)*
muitos(as) a lot (of) ; many ;
  plenty (of)
mulher *f* female ; woman ; wife
multa *f* fine
multidão *f* crowd
mundial worldwide
mundo *m* world

muralhas *fpl* ramparts
muro *m* wall
museu *m* museum
música *f* music

N
nabo *m* turnip
nacional national
nacionalidade *f* nationality ; citizenship
nada nothing
  nada a declarar nothing to declare
nadar to swim
namorada *f* girlfriend
namorado *m* boyfriend
não no ; not
nariz *m* nose
nascer to be born
nascimento *m* birth
nata *f* cream
natação *f* swimming
Natal *m* Christmas
natureza *f* nature
navio *m* ship
neblina *f* mist
negar to refuse
negativo(a) negative
negócios *mpl* business
negro(a) black
nem: nem... nem... neither... nor...
nenhum(a) none
neta *f* granddaughter
neto *m* grandson
neve *f* snow
nevoeiro *m* fog
ninguém nobody
nível *m* level
nó *m* knot
No. *see* número
nocivo(a) harmful
nódoa *f* stain
noite *f* evening ; night
  à noite in the evening/at night
  boa noite good evening/night
noivo(a) *adj* engaged (to be married)
  m/f bride/groom; fiancé(e)
nome *m* name
  nome próprio first name
nora *f* daughter-in-law
nordeste *m* north east
normalmente usually
noroeste *m* north west

norte m north
nós we ; us
nosso(a) our
nota f note ; banknote
notar to notice
notícia f piece of news
Nova Zelândia f New Zealand
Novembro m November
novo(a) new ; young ; recent
noz f nut ; walnut
noz-moscada f nutmeg
nu(a) naked
nublado(a) dull (weather) ; cloudy
número (No.) m number ; size
  (of clothes, shoes)
nunca never
nuvem f cloud

O

o the (masculine)
objeto m object
  objetos perdidos lost property
obra-prima f masterpiece
obras fpl roadworks ; repairs
obrigado(a) thank you
oceano m ocean
ocidental western
oculista m optician
óculos mpl glasses
  óculos de sol sunglasses
ocupado(a) engaged (phone, toilet)
oeste m west
oferecer to offer ; to give something
  ofereço este livro I give this book
oferta f offer ; gift
olá hello
olaria f pottery
óleo m oil
  óleo dos travões brake fluid
oleoso(a) greasy ; oily
olhar para/por to look at/after
olho m eye
onda f wave (on sea)
onde where
ontem yesterday
óptimo(a) excellent
ora now ; well now
orçamento m budget
ordem f order
ordenado m wage
orelha f ear

organizado(a) organized
orquídea f orchid
osso m bone
ostra f oyster
ou or
ourivesaria e joalharia goldsmith's and
  jeweller's
ouro m gold
  de ouro gold (made of gold)
outono m autumn
outro(a) other
  outra vez again
Outubro m October
ouvido m ear (inner)
ouvir to hear ; to listen (to)
ovelha f sheep
ovo m egg
oxigénio m oxygen

P

padaria f baker's
pagamento m payment
  pagamento a pronto cash payment
pagar to pay
página f page
  páginas amarelas Yellow Pages
pago(a) paid
pai m father
  pais parents
país m country
palácio m palace
palavra f word
pálido(a) pale
palito m toothpick
panado(a) fried in egg and
  breadcrumbs
pane f breakdown
panela f pan ; pot
pano m cloth
pão m bread ; loaf
  pão de centeio rye bread
  pão integral wholemeal bread
  pão de ló sponge cake
  pão de milho maize bread
  pão torrado toasted bread
  pão de trigo wheat bread
papel m paper
  papel de carta writing paper
  papel de embrulho wrapping paper
  papel higiénico toilet paper
papelaria f stationer's
papo-seco m roll (of bread)

par m pair ; couple
para for ; towards ; to
parabéns mpl congratulations ; happy birthday
pára-brisas f windscreen
pára-choques m bumper
parafuso m screw
paragem f stop (for bus, etc)
parar to stop
pare stop (sign)
  pare ao sinal vermelho stop when lights are red
parede f wall
parente m/f relation (family)
pargo m sea bream
parque m park
parquímetro m parking meter
parte f part
  parte de frente front
  parte de trás back
particular private
partidas fpl departures
partir to break ; to leave
  a partir de... from...
Páscoa f Easter
passa f raisin
passadeira f zebra crossing
passado m the past
passado(a): mal passado(a) rare (steak)
  bem passado(a) well done (steak)
passageiro m passenger
passagem f fare ; crossing
  passagem de nível level-crossing
  passagem de peões pedestrian crossing
  passagem proibida no right of way
  passagem subterrânea underpass
passaporte m passport
passar to pass ; to go by
pássaro m bird
passatempos mpl hobbies
passe m season ticket
passe go (when crossing road) ; walk
passear to go for a walk
passeio m walk ; pavement
pasta f paste
  pasta dentífrica toothpaste
pastéis mpl pastries
pastel m pie ; pastry (cake)
  pastel folhado puff pastry
pastelaria f pastries ; café ; cake shop
pastilha f pastille
  pastilha elástica chewing gum

  pastilhas para a garganta throat lozenges
pataniscas fpl salted cod fritters
patinagem f skating (ice) ; roller-skating
patinar to skate
pátio m courtyard
pato m duck
pau m stick
pé m foot
  a pé on foot
peão m pedestrian
peça f part ; play
  peças e acessórios spares and accessories
peça... ask for...
pediatra m/f paediatrician
pedir to ask (for)
  pedir alguma coisa to ask for something
  pedir emprestado(a) to borrow
peito m breast ; chest
peixaria f fishmonger's
peixe m fish
  peixe congelado frozen fish
peixe-espada m scabbard fish
pele f fur ; skin
pensão m guesthouse
  pensão completa full board
  pensão residencial boarding house
  meia pensão half board
pensar to think
penso m sticking plaster
  penso higiénico sanitary towel
pente m comb
peões mpl pedestrians
pepino m cucumber
  pepino de conserva gherkin
pequeno(a) little ; small
  pequeno-almoço breakfast
pêra f pear
  pêra abacate avocado pear
percebes mpl edible barnacles
percurso m route
perdão I beg your pardon ; I'm sorry
perder to lose ; to miss (train, etc)
perdido(a) lost
  perdidos e achados lost and found ; lost property
perdiz f partridge
pergunta f question
  fazer uma pergunta to ask a question

178

perigo *m* danger
  perigo de incêndio fire hazard
perigoso(a) dangerous
permitir to allow
perna *f* leg
pérola *f* pearl
pertencer: *pertencer a* to belong to
perto (de) near
peru *m* turkey
pesado(a) heavy
pêsames *mpl* condolences
pesar to weigh
pesca *f* fishing
pescada *f* hake
pescadinhas *fpl* whiting
pescar to fish
peso *m* weight
pêssego *m* peach
pessoa *f* person
pessoal *adj* personal
pessoal *m* staff ; personnel
petiscos *mpl* snacks ; titbits
petróleo *m* oil
peúgas *fpl* socks
picada *f* sting
picado(a) chopped ; minced
picante spicy
picar to sting
  uma picada de mosquito
  a mosquito bite
pilha *f* pile ; battery *(for torch)*
pílula *f* the pill
pimenta *f* pepper
pimento *m* pepper *(vegetable)*
pintar to paint
pintura *f* painting
pior worse
piripiri *m* hot chilli dressing
pisca-pisca *m* indicator *(on car)*
piscina *f* swimming pool
  piscina aberta outdoor swimming
  pool
  piscina para crianças paddling pool
piso *m* floor ; level ; surface
  piso escorregadio slippery surface
pista *f* track ; runway
planta *f* plant ; map
plataforma *f* platform
plateia *f* stalls *(in theatre)*
platinados *fpl* points *(in car)*
pneu *m* tyre
  a pressão dos pneus tyre pressure

pó *m* dust ; powder
  pó de talco talcum powder
poço *m* well
poder to be able
polegar *m* thumb
polícia *f* police
polícia *m* policeman ; police officer
  mulher-polícia *f* policewoman
poluição *f* pollution
polvo *m* octopus
pomada *f* ointment
  pomada para o calçado shoe polish
pomar *m* orchard
pombo *m* pigeon
ponte *f* bridge
população *f* population
por by *(through)*
  por aqui/por ali this/that way
  por hora per hour
  por pessoa per person
pôr to put
porção *f* portion
porco *m* pig ; pork
por favor please
pormenores *mpl* details
porque because
porquê why
porta *f* door
  a porta No. ... gate number ...
porta-bagagens *m* boot *(of car)* ;
  luggage rack
porta-chaves *m* key ring
portagem *f* motorway toll
porta-moedas *m* purse
porteiro *m* porter
porto *m* harbour
Porto : *o Porto* Oporto
  o vinho do Porto Port wine
português *m* Portuguese *(language)*
português (portuguesa) Portuguese
posologia *f* dose *(medicine)*
postal *m* postcard
posto *m* post ; job
  posto clínico first aid post
  posto de socorros first aid centre
pouco(a) little
pousada *f* state-run hotel ; inn
povo *m* people
povoação *f* small village
praça *f* square *(in town)* ; market
  praça de táxis taxi rank
  praça de touros bullring

praia f beach ; seaside
prata f silver
prateleira f shelf
praticar to practise
prato m dish ; plate ; course of meal
  prato da casa speciality of the house
  prato do dia today's special
prazer m pleasure
  prazer em conhecê-lo pleased
  to meet you
precipício m cliff ; precipice
precisar de to need
preciso(a): é preciso it is necessary
preço m price
  preços de ocasião bargain prices
  preços reduzidos reduced prices
preencher to fill in
preferir to prefer
prejuízo m damage
prémio m prize
prenda f gift
preocupado(a) worried
preparado(a) ready
presente m gift ; present
preservativo m condom
pressão f pressure
  pressão dos pneus tyre pressure
presunto m cured ham
preto(a) black
primavera f spring (season)
primeiro(a) first
  primeiro andar first floor
  de primeira classe first-class
primo(a) m/f cousin
princípio m beginning
prioridade f priority
  prioridade à direita give way
  to the right
prisão f prison
  ter prisão de ventre to be
  constipated
privado(a) adj private
procurar to look for
produto m product ; proceeds
  produtos alimentares foodstuffs
professor(a) m/f teacher
profissão f profession
  profissão, idade, nome profession,
  age and name
profundidade f depth
profundo(a) deep
proibido(a) forbidden
  proibida a entrada no entry

proibido estacionar no parking
proibido fumar no smoking
proibida a paragem no stopping
proibida a passagem no access
proibido pisar a relva do not walk
on the grass
proibido tomar banho no bathing
promoção f special offer ; promotion
(at work)
pronto(a) ready
propriedade f estate (property)
proprietário(a) m/f owner
prospecto m pamphlet
prótese dentária f dental fittings
provar to taste ; to try on
provisório(a) temporary
próximo(a) near ; next
público m audience ; public
pudim m pudding
pulmão m lung
pulseira f bracelet ; wrist strap
pulso m wrist
pura lã f pure wool
purificador do ar m air freshener
puxar to pull
  puxe pull (sign)

Q

quadro m picture ; painting
qual which
qualidade f quality
quando when
quantidade f quantity
quanto(a) how much
  quantos(as)? how many?
  quanto tempo? how long? (time)
quarta-feira f Wednesday
quarto m room ; bedroom
  quarto de banho bathroom
  quarto com duas camas twin-bedded
  room
  quarto de casal double room
  quarto individual single room
quarto fourth ; quarter
  um quarto de hora a quarter of
  an hour
que what
  o que é? what is it?
quebra-mar m pier
quebrar to break
queda f fall
queijada f cheesecake

queijo m cheese
queimadura f burn
  queimadura do sol sunburn (painful)
queixa f complaint
  quero apresentar uma queixa
  I want to make a complaint
quem who
quente adj hot
querer to want ; to wish
quilo(grama) (kg.) m kilo
quilómetro m kilometre
quinta f farm
quinta-feira f Thursday
quiosque m kiosk ; newsstand
quotidiano(a) daily

R
R. see rua
rã f frog
rabanete m radish
rádio m radio
radiografia f X-ray
raia f skate (fish)
raiva f rabies
raíz f root
rapariga f girl
rapaz m boy
rápido m express (train)
rápido(a) fast
raposa f fox
raqueta f racquet ; bat (for table tennis)
rasgar to tear
ratazana f rat
rato m mouse
R/C see rés-do-chão
real real ; royal
reboques mpl breakdown service
rebuçado m boiled sweet
recado m message
  dar um recado to give a message
receber to receive
receita f recipe
  receita médica prescription
recepção f reception
recibo m receipt
reclamação f protest ; official complaint
recolher to collect
  recolha de bagagem baggage reclaim
recomendar to recommend
recompensa f reward
reconhecer to recognize

recordação f souvenir
recordar-se to remember
rede f net
redução f reduction ; discount
reembolsar to reimburse
refeição f meal
reformado(a) m/f senior citizen ; retired
região f area (region)
  região demarcada official wine-
  producing region
registar to register
regulamentos mpl regulations
Reino Unido m United Kingdom
relógio m watch ; clock
relva f grass
  não pisar a relva keep off grass
remédio m medicine ; remedy
remetente m sender
renda f lace ; rent
  rendas de bilros hand-woven
  lacework
reparação f repair
reparar to fix ; to repair
repartição f state department
repetir to repeat
rés-do-chão (R/C) m ground floor
reserva de lugar seat reservation
reservado(a) reserved
reservar to book ; to reserve
residência f boarding house ; residence
residir to live
respirar to breathe
responder to answer ; to reply
resposta f answer
restaurante m restaurant
retalho m oddment
retrosaria f haberdashery
reunião f meeting
revelar to develop (photos) ;
  to reveal
revisor(a) m/f ticket collector
revista f magazine
ribeiro m stream
rins mpl kidneys
rio m river
rissol m rissole
rochas fpl rocks
roda f wheel
rodovia f highway
rolha f cork
rolo m cartridge (for camera) ; roll
rosé adj rosé (wine)

rosto *m* face
roteiro *m* guidebook
roubar to steal ; to rob
roupa *f* clothes
  roupa de cama bedding
  roupa interior underwear
roxo(a) purple
rua (R.) *f* street
rubéola *f* German measles
ruído *m* noise
ruptura *f* break

S

S. *see* São
sábado *m* Saturday
sabão *m* soap
  sabão em flocos soapflakes
  sabão em pó soap powder
saber to know *(fact)*
sabonete *m* toilet soap
sabor *m* flavour ; taste
saca-rolhas *m* corkscrew
saco *m* bag ; handbag
  saco cama sleeping bag
  saco do lixo bin bag
safio *m* sea eel
saia *f* skirt
saída *f* exit ; way out
  saídas departures
sair to go out ; to come out
sal *m* salt
sala *f* room
  sala de chá tea room ; café
  sala de embarque airport lounge
  sala de espera waiting room
  sala de estar living room ; lounge
  sala de jantar dining room
salada *f* salad
salão *m* hall *(for concerts, etc)*
salário *m* wage ; salary
saldo *m* sale
salmão *m* salmon
  salmão fumado smoked salmon
salmonete *m* red mullet
salpicão *m* spicy sausage
salsa *f* parsley
salsicha *f* sausage
salsicharia *f* delicatessen

salteado(a) sautéed
salvar to rescue ; to save *(rescue)*
sandálias *fpl* sandals
sandes *f* sandwich
  sandes de fiambre ham sandwich
sanduíche *m* sandwich
sangue *m* blood
sanitários *mpl* toilets
Santo(a) (Sto./Sta.) *m/f* saint
santo(a) holy
santola *f* spider crab
São (S.) *m* Saint
sapataria *f* shoe shop
sapateira *f* type of crab
sapateiro *m* shoemaker ; cobbler
sapato *m* shoe
saquinhos de chá *mpl* tea bags
sarampo *m* measles
sardinha *f* sardine
satisfeito(a) happy ; satisfied
saudação *f* greeting
saudável healthy
saúde *f* health
  saúde! cheers!
se if ; whether
  se faz favor (SFF) please
sé *f* cathedral
secador *m* dryer
secar to dry ; to drain *(tank)*
secção *f* department
seco(a) dry
secretária *f* desk
secretário(a) *m/f* secretary
século *m* century
seda *f* silk
sede *f* thirst
  ter sede to be thirsty
segredo *m* secret
seguinte following
seguir to follow
  seguir pela direita keep to your right
  seguir pela esquerda keep to
  your left
segunda-feira *f* Monday
segundo *m* second *(time)*
segundo(a) second
  segundo andar second floor
  de segunda classe second-class
  em segunda mão second-hand

segurança f safety
segurar to hold
seguro m insurance
  seguro contra terceiros third party insurance
  seguro contra todos os riscos comprehensive insurance
seguro de viagem travel insurance
seguro(a) safe ; reliable
seio m breast
selecção f selection
selo m stamp
selvagem wild
sem without
semáforos mpl traffic lights
semana f week
  para a semana next week
  na semana passada last week
  por semana weekly (rate, etc)
semanal weekly
sempre always
senhor m sir ; gentleman ; you
  Senhor Mr
senhora f lady ; madam ; you
  Senhora Mrs, Ms
  a casa de banho das Senhoras ladies' toilet
senhorio(a) m/f landlord/lady
sentar-se to sit (down)
sentido m sense ; meaning
  sentido único one-way street
sentir to feel
ser to be
serviço m service ; cover charge
  serviço de quartos room service
  serviço (não) incluído service (not) included
  serviço permanente 24-hour service
servir to serve
  pode servir? can you serve?
sessão f session ; performance
Setembro m September
seu (sua) his ; her ; your
sexta-feira f Friday
SFF see se faz favor
significar to mean
sim yes
simpático(a) nice ; friendly
sinal m signal ; deposit (part payment)
  sinal de impedido engaged tone

  sinal de marcação dialling tone
  sinal de trânsito road sign
sino m bell
sítio m place ; spot
situado(a) situated
só only ; alone
sobre over ; on top of
  sobre o mar overlooking the sea
sobrecarga f excess load ; surcharge
sobremesa f dessert
sobressalente spare
  a roda sobressalente spare wheel
sobretudo m overcoat (man's)
sócio m member ; partner
socorro m help ; assistance
  socorro 115 emergency service 999
  socorros e sinistrados accidents and emergencies
sogro(a) m/f father-in-law/mother-in-law
sol m sun
solteiro(a) single (not married)
solúvel soluble
som m sound
soma f amount (sum)
sombra f shadow (in sun)
sono m sleep
sopa f soup
  sopa à alentejana garlic, coriander and bread soup topped with poached egg
sorte f luck ; fortune
  boa sorte good luck
sorvete m water ice ; sorbet
sótão m attic
soutien m bra
sua see seu
subida f rise ; ascent
subir to go up
sudeste m south east
sudoeste m south west
suficiente enough
sujo(a) dirty
sul m south
sumo m juice
suor m sweat
supermercado m supermarket
supositório m suppository
surdo(a) deaf
surf m surfing

T

tabacaria f tobacconist's ; newsagent
tabaco m tobacco
tabela f list ; table
taberna f wine bar
tabuleiro m tray
taça f cup
tacão m heel
talão m voucher
talco m talc
talheres mpl cutlery
talho m butcher's
talvez perhaps
tamanho m size
também also ; too
tamboril m monkfish
tampa f lid ; cover ; top ; cap
tampões mpl tampons
tanto(a) so much
tão so
  isto é tão bonito this is
  so beautiful
tapete m carpet ; rug
  tapetes e carpetes rugs
  and carpets
tarde f afternoon
  boa tarde good afternoon
tarde adverb late (in the day)
tarifa f charge ; rate
  tarifas de portagem toll charges
tarte f tart
  tarte de amêndoa almond tart
tasca f tavern ; wine bar ; restaurant
taxa f fee ; rate
  taxa de juro interest rate
  taxa normal peak-time rate
  taxa reduzida off-peak rate
teatro m theatre
tecido m fabric ; tissue ; cloth
telecomandado(a) remote-controlled
teleférico m cable car
telefone m telephone
telefonista f operator
televisão f television
televisor m television set
telhado m roof
temperatura f temperature
tempero m dressing (for salad) ;
seasoning

tempestade f storm
tempo m weather ; time (duration)
  tempo inteiro full-time
  tempo parcial part-time
temporada f season
temporário(a) temporary
tenda f tent
ténis m tennis
tenro(a) tender (meat)
tensão f tension
  tensão arterial alta/baixa high/low
  blood pressure
tentar to try
ter to have
terça-feira f Tuesday
terceiro(a) third
  terceiro andar third floor
  para a terceira idade for the elderly
termas fpl spa
termo m (vacuum) flask
termómetro m thermometer
terra f earth ; ground
terraço m veranda ; balcony
terramoto m earthquake
terreno m ground ; land
tesoura f scissors
tesouro m treasure
testemunha f witness
tímido(a) shy
tingir to dye
tinta f ink ; paint
tinturaria f dry-cleaner's
tio(a) m/f uncle/aunt
tipo m sort ; kind
tira-nódoas m stain remover
tirar to remove ; to take out
tiro m shot
toalha f towel
toalhete de rosto m face cloth ; flannel
(for washing)
toalhetes refrescantes mpl baby wipes
tocar to touch ; to ring ; to play
  tocar piano to play the piano
todo(a) all ; the whole
  toda a gente everyone
  todas as coisas everything
  em toda a parte everywhere
toldo f sunshade (on beach)
tomada f socket ; power point

tomar to take
  tomar banho to bathe ; to have a bath
  tomar antes de se deitar take before going to bed
  tomar em jejum take on an empty stomach
  tomar... vezes ao dia take... times a day
tomate m tomato
tonelada f ton
toranja f grapefruit
torcer to twist ; to turn
torneio m tournament
torneira f tap
tornozelo m ankle
torrada f toast
torre f tower
torto(a) twisted
tosse f cough
tosta f toasted sandwich
  tosta de queijo toasted cheese sandwich
totobola m football pools
totoloto m lottery
toucinho m bacon
tourada f bullfight
touro m bull
tóxico(a) poisonous ; toxic
trabalhar to work (person)
trabalho m work
  trabalhos na estrada roadworks
tradução f translation
traduzir to translate
tráfego m traffic
tranquilo(a) calm ; quiet
transferir to transfer
trânsito m traffic
  trânsito condicionado restricted traffic
  trânsito proibido no entry
transpiração f perspiration ; sweat
transportar to transport ; to carry
transtorno m upset ; inconvenience
trás: para trás backwards
  no banco de trás on the back seat (car)
  a parte de trás the back
tratamento m treatment
tratar de to treat ; to deal with
travar to brake

travessa f lane (in town) ; serving dish
travessia f crossing (voyage)
travões mpl brakes
trazer to bring ; to carry
triângulo m warning triangle
tribunal m court
trigo m wheat
triste sad
trocar to exchange ; to change
troco m change (money)
  trocos small change
trovoada f thunderstorm
truta f trout
tu you (informal)
tubo m exhaust pipe ; tube ; hose
tudo everything ; all
turista m/f tourist

U

úlcera f ulcer
ultimamente lately ; recently
último(a) last ; latest
ultrapassar to overtake ; to pass
um(a) a ; an ; one
unha f nail (on finger, toe)
único(a) single ; unique
unidade f unit (hi-fi, etc) ; unity
unir to join
universidade f university ; college
urgência f urgency
urtiga f nettle
urze f heather
urso(a) m/f bear
usado(a) used (car, etc)
usar to use ; to wear
uso m use
  uso externo for external use
útil useful
utilização f use
utilizar to use
uva f grape

V

vaca f cow
vacina f vaccination
vagão m railway carriage ; coach
vagão-restaurante m buffet car

vagar to be vacant
vagas *fpl* vacancies
vale *m* valley
valer to be worth
validação: validação de bilhetes validate tickets
válido(a) valid
  válido(a) até... valid until...
valor *m* value
válvula *f* valve ; tap
vapor *m* steam
varanda *f* veranda ; balcony
variado(a) varied
varicela *f* chickenpox
vários(as) several
vazio(a) empty
vegetal *m* vegetable
  vegetais congelados frozen vegetables
vegetariano(a) vegetarian
veículo *m* vehicle
  veículos pesados heavy goods vehicles
vela *f* sail ; sailing
vela *f* spark plug ; candle
velho(a) old
velocidade *f* gear ; speed
  velocidade limitada speed limit in force
velocímetro *m* speedometer
vencimento *m* wage ; expiry date
venda *f* sale *(in general)*
  venda proibida not for public sale
  vendas e reparações sales and repairs
vender to sell
  vende-se for sale
veneno *m* poison
vento *m* wind
ventoinha *f* fan *(electric)*
ver to see ; to look at
verão *m* summer
verdade *f* truth
  não é verdade? isn't it?
verdadeiro(a) true
verde green
vergas *fpl* wicker goods
verificar to check
vermelho(a) red
verniz *m* varnish
vertigem *f* dizziness ; vertigo

vespa *f* wasp
véspera *f* the day before ; the eve
vestiário *m* cloakroom ; changing room
vestido *m* dress
vestir to dress ; to wear
  vestir-se to get dressed
vestuário *m* clothes
veterinário(a) *m/f* vet
vez *f* time ; turn
  às vezes occasionally ; sometimes
  uma vez once
  duas vezes twice
  muitas vezes often
  é a sua vez it's your turn
via *f* lane
via via
  via aérea by air mail
  via nasal to be inhaled
  via oral orally
viaduto *m* viaduct ; flyover
viagem *f* trip ; journey
  viagem de negócios business trip
viajante *m/f* traveller
viajar to travel
vida *f* life
vidros *mpl* glassware
vila *f* small town
vinagre *m* vinegar
vindima *f* harvest *(of grapes)*
vinho *m* wine
  vinho branco white wine
  vinho da casa house wine
  vinho de mesa table wine
  vinho doce sweet wine
  vinho espumante sparkling wine
  vinho rosé rosé wine
  vinho seco dry wine
  vinho tinto red wine
  vinho verde young wine
vir to come
virar to turn
  vire à direita turn right
  vire à esquerda turn left
vírgula *f* comma
visitar to visit
vista *f* view
  com linda vista with a beautiful view
visto *m* visa
vitela *f* veal
viúvo(a) *m/f* widower/widow
vivenda *f* chalet ; villa

viver to live
vivo(a) alive
vizinho(a) *m/f* neighbour
você(s) you
volante *m* steering wheel
volta *f* turn
  à volta (de) about
  em volta (de) around
  dar uma volta to go for a
  short walk/ride
voltagem *f* voltage
voltar to return *(go/come back)*
  volto já I'll be back in a minute
vomitar to vomit
voo *m* flight
  voo fretado charter flight
  voo normal scheduled flight
vos you ; to you
vós you
vosso yours
voz *f* voice
vulcão *m* volcano

W
WC toilet
wind-surf *m* windsurfing

X
xadrez *m* chess
xarope *m* syrup
  xarope para a tosse cough syrup
xerez *m* sherry

Z
zero zero ; nought
zona *f* zone
  zona azul permitted parking zone
  zona de banhos swimming area
  zona interdita no thorough-fare

How Portuguese Works

Nouns

> A **noun** is a word such as **car**, **horse** or **Mary** which is used to refer to a person or thing.

Portuguese nouns are *masculine* or *feminine*, and their gender is shown by the words for **the** (o/a) and **a** (um/uma) used before them (the article):

masculine/plural
o/um castelo the/a castle
os castelos the castles
(uns) castelos (some) castles

feminine/plural
a/uma mesa the/a table
as mesas the tables
(umas) mesas (some) tables

It is usually possible to tell whether a noun is *masculine* or *feminine* by its ending: nouns ending in **-o** or **-or** are usually *masculine*, while those ending in **-a**, **-agem**, **-dade** and **-tude** tend to be *feminine*. There are exceptions, however, and it's best to learn the noun and the article together.

Plurals

Nouns ending in a vowel form the plural by adding **-s**, while those ending in a consonant usually add **-es**. The exceptions to this are words ending in an **-m** which change to **-ns** in the plural and words ending in **-l** which change to **-is** in the plural: e.g. **hotel – hotéis**.

NOTE: When used after the words **a** (to), **de** (of), **em** (in) and **por** (by), the articles (and many other words) contract:

a + as = às *ash*	to the
de + um = dum *dooñ*	of a
em + uma = numa *noo-muh*	to a
por + os = pelos *pel-oosh*	by the

This, That, These, Those

These depend on the gender and number of the noun they represent:

este rapaz	this boy	**esta rapariga**	this girl
estes rapazes	these boys	**estas raparigas**	these girls
esse rapaz	that boy	**essa rapariga**	that girl
esses rapazes	those boys	**essas raparigas**	those girls
aquele rapaz	that boy *(over there)*	**aquela rapariga**	that girl *(over there)*
aqueles rapazes	those boys *(over there)*	**aquelas raparigas**	those girls *(over there)*

Adjectives

*An **adjective** is a word such as **small**, **pretty** or **practical** that describes a person or thing, or gives extra information about them.*

Adjectives normally follow the nouns they describe in Portuguese, e.g. **a maçã verde** the green apple.

Some exceptions which go before the noun are:

muito much, many	**último** last
pouco little, not much	**bom** good
tanto so much, so many	**nenhum** no, not any
primeiro first	**grande** great, big

Portuguese adjectives have to reflect the gender of the noun they describe. To make an adjective feminine, **-o** endings change to **-a**, and **-or** and **-ês** change to **-ora** and **-esa**. Otherwise they generally have the same form for both genders. Thus:

masculine	*feminine*
o livro vermelho	**a saia vermelha**
the red book	the red skirt
o homem falador	**a mulher faladora**
the talkative man	the talkative woman

To make adjectives plural, follow the general rules given for nouns.

My, Your, His, Her
These words also depend on the gender and number of the following noun and not on the sex of the 'owner'.

	with masculine/feminine	*with plural nouns*
my	**o meu/a minha**	**os meus/as minhas**
his/her/its/your	**o seu/a sua**	**os seus/as suas**
our	**o nosso/a nossa**	**os nossos/as nossas**
their/your	**o seu/a sua**	**os seus/as suas**

NOTE: Since **o seu**, **a sua**, etc can mean his, her, your, etc, Portuguese will often replace them with the words for of him, of her, of you, etc (**dele**, **dela**, **de você**, etc) in order to avoid confusion:

os livros *dela*	her books
os livros *de você*	your books
os livros *deles*	their books

Pronouns

> A **pronoun** is a word that you use to refer to someone or something when you do not need to use a noun, often because the person or thing has been mentioned earlier. Examples are *it*, *she*, *something* and *myself*.

SUBJECT		OBJECT	
I	**eu** *ay-oo*	me	**me** *muh*
you *(informal)*	**tu** *too*	you *(informal)*	**te** *teh*
you	**você** *voh-se*	you	**o/a** *oo/uh*
he	**ele** *ayl*	him	**o** *oo*
she	**ela** *eluh*	her	**a** *uh*
it	**ele/ela** *ayl/eluh*	it	**o/a** *oo/uh*
we	**nós** *nosh*	us	**nos** *noosh*
you	**vós** *vosh*	you	**vos** *voosh*
they *(masc.)*	**eles** *aylush*	them *(masc.)*	**os** *oosh*
they *(fem.)*	**elas** *elush*	them *(fem.)*	**as** *ush*
you *(informal)*	**vocês** *voh-sesh*	you *(informal)*	**os/as** *oosh/ush*

NOTES

1. **YOU** The polite form of addressing someone would be with **o Senhor** or **a Senhora** using the (s)he form or the verb and the object pronoun **o/a**. The semi-formal **you** is **você** and the informal **you** is **tu** (like French and Spanish).

2. Subject pronouns are normally not used except for emphasis or to avoid confusion:

    > *eu* vou para Lisboa e *ele* vai para Coimbra

    > *I'm* going to Lisbon and *he's* going to Coimbra

3. Object pronouns are usually placed after the verb and joined with a hyphen:

    vejo-o   I see *him*

    However, in sentences beginning with a 'question word' or a 'negative word' the pronoun goes in front of the verb:

quando o viu?	when did you see *him*?
não o vi	I did not see *him*

    Also, in sentences beginning with **that** and **who**, etc, ('subordinate clauses') the pronoun precedes the verb:

sei que o viu	I know that you saw *him*
o homem que o viu	the man who saw *him*

4. **Me** also = to me and **nos** = to us, but **lhe** = to him/to her/to it/to you *(formal)*, **te** = to you *(informal)* and **lhes** = to them/to you.

5. When two pronouns are used together they are often shortened. The verb will also change spelling if it ends in **-r**, **-s** or **-z** or a nasal sound:

dá-mo	(= dá + me + o)	he gives me it
dê-lho	(= dê + lhe + o)	give him it
fá-lo	(= faz + o)	he does it
dão-nos	(= dão + os *or* dão + nos)	they give them *or* they give us

6. The pronoun following a preposition has the same form as the subject pronoun, except for **mim** (me), **si** (you – *formal*), **ti** (you – *informal*).

Verbs

> A **verb** is a word such as **sing**, **walk** or **cry** which is used with a subject to say what someone or something does or what happens to them. **Regular verbs** follow the same pattern of endings. **Irregular verbs** do not follow a regular pattern so you need to learn the different endings.

There are three main patterns of endings for verbs in Portuguese – those ending **-ar**, **-er** and **-ir** in the dictionary.

Verbs ending in **-ar**

CANT<u>AR</u>	<u>TO SING</u>
canto	I sing
cantas	you sing
canta	(s)he/it sings/you sing
cantamos	we sing
cantais	you sing
cantam	they/you sing

Verbs ending in **-er**

COM<u>ER</u>	<u>TO EAT</u>
como	I eat
comes	you eat
come	(s)he/it eats/you eat
comemos	we eat
comeis	you eat
comem	they/you eat

Verbs ending in **-ir**

PART<u>IR</u>	<u>TO LEAVE</u>
parto	I leave
partes	you leave
parte	(s)he/it leaves/you leave
partimos	we leave
partis	you leave
partem	they/you leave

Four of the most common verbs are irregular:

<u>SER</u>	<u>TO BE</u>	<u>ESTAR</u>	<u>TO BE</u>
sou	I am	**estou**	I am
és	you are	**estás**	you are
é	(s)he/it is/you are	**está**	(s)he/it is/you are
somos	we are	**estamos**	we are
sois	you are	**estais**	you are
são	they/you are	**estão**	they/you are

<u>TER</u>	<u>TO HAVE</u>	<u>IR</u>	<u>TO GO</u>
tenho	I have	**vou**	I go
tens	you have	**vais**	you go
tem	(s)he/it has/you have	**vai**	(s)he/it goes/you go
temos	we have	**vamos**	we go
tendes	you have	**ides**	you go
têm	they/you have	**vão**	they/you go

NOTE: Ser and **Estar** both mean **to be**.

Ser is used to describe a permanent place or state:

sou inglês	I am English
é uma praia	it is a beach

Estar is used to describe a temporary state or where something is located:

como está?	how are you?
onde está o livro?	where is the book?

Past Tense

Verbs ending in **-ar**

cantei	I sang
cantaste	you sang
cantou	(s)he/it/you sang
cantámos	we sang
cantastes	you sang
cantaram	they/you sang

Verbs ending in **-er**

comi	I ate
comeste	you ate
comeu	(s)he/it/you ate
comemos	we ate
comestes	you ate
comeram	they/you ate

Verbs ending in **-ir**

parti	I left
partiste	you left
partiu	(s)he/it/you left
partimos	we left
partistes	you left
partiram	they/you left